Plato and
The Trial of Socrates

Routledge Philosophy GuideBook to

Plato and
The Trial of Socrates

Thomas C.
Brickhouse

and

Nicholas D.
Smith

Routledge
Taylor & Francis Group

NEW YORK AND LONDON

First published 2004 by Routledge
29 West 35th Street, New York, NY 10001

Simultaneously published in the UK
by Routledge
11 New Fetter Lane, London EC4P 4EE

Routledge is an imprint of the Taylor & Francis Group

Typeset in Aldus and Scala by
Florence Production Ltd, Stoodleigh, Devon
Printed and bound in Great Britain by
TJ International Ltd, Padstow, Cornwall

Library of Congress Cataloging in Publication Data
Brickhouse, Thomas C., 1947–
    Routledge philosophy guidebook to Plato and the trial of Socrates/Thomas
C. Brickhouse and Nicholas D. Smith.
        p. cm. – (Routledge philosophy guidebooks)
Includes bibliographical references and index.
    1. Plato. Apology. 2. Socrates–Trials, litigation, etc. I. Title: Plato and the
trial of Socrates. II. Smith, Nicholas D. III. Title. IV. Series.
    B365.B73 2004
    184–dc22

British Library Cataloguing in Publication Data
A catalogue record for this book is available from
the British Library

                                                            2003022822

ISBN 0–415–15681–5 (hbk)
ISBN 0–415–15682–3 (pbk)

Contents

TEXTS AND TRANSLATIONS

All citations used for Plato's works in this book refer to the Oxford Classical (Greek) texts. Citations are made by Stephanus page number, section letter, and then line number. All translations we provide in this book are our own. Those we give for Plato's *Euthyphro, Apology, Crito,* and *Phaedo* are from our *The Trial and Execution of Socrates: Sources and Controversies* (Oxford: Oxford University Press, 2002).

ACKNOWLEDGMENTS

We would like to thank our respective colleges for various kinds of support in helping us to complete this book: Lynchburg College (TCB), and Lewis and Clark College (NDS). We are also grateful to Sandra Peterson and Mark L. McPherran for making their forthcoming works available to us to study and to cite. Books like this would not be possible, moreover, without colleagues in the field whose own published works and professional presentations have educated and challenged us. We are forever grateful to all of those whose work we cite in this book. In many cases, we have learned the most from those with whom we end up disagreeing. As the great Plato scholar Gregory Vlastos once wrote, "[O]nly those who are strangers to the ethos of scholarly controversy will see anything but high esteem in my critique" (Vlastos 1991, 39 n.2).

LIST OF ABBREVIATIONS

Aristotle

Metaph.	*Metaphysics*
D.L.	Diogenes Laertius, *Lives and Opinions of Eminent Philosophers*

Plato

Ap.	*Apology*
Charm.	*Charmides*
Euthyd.	*Euthydemus*
Euthphr.	*Euthyphro*
Grg.	*Gorgias*
Hip. Ma.	*Hippias Major (Greater Hippias)*
La.	*Laches*
Lys.	*Lysis*
Phd.	*Phaedo*
Phdr.	*Phaedrus*
Rep.	*Republic*

Xenophon

Ap.	*Apology*
Hell.	*Hellenica*
Mem.	*Memorabilia*

INTRODUCTION

Socrates was born in Athens in 469 B.C.E. Although he wrote nothing of any significance and had no students in anything like the ordinary sense of that term, he became one of the most influential philosophers in western civilization. During his own lifetime, his philosophical activities, which were carried on in public settings and private homes, together with his idiosyncratic demeanor, gained him great notoriety and, indeed, must have made him one of Athens' best known figures. To many, however, he must have been more than a mere curiosity, for in 399 B.C.E. Socrates was tried on a charge of impiety, convicted, and executed after a period of imprisonment.

Plato, who was a member of one of Athens' most aristocratic families and who dedicated his life to philosophy because of Socrates' influence, occupies a central place in this debate. The *Euthyphro, Apology of Socrates, Crito,* and the death scene from the *Phaedo,* the four writings to be examined in this book, are Plato's dramatizations of various episodes in Socrates' final days. The *Euthyphro* purports to be a conversation between Socrates and a self-styled religious expert that takes place in front of the office of the king-archon, where Socrates had been ordered to appear to hear the exact nature of the charges against him. The *Apology* provides Plato's version of three speeches Socrates makes before his jurors at the trial: his defense, a counter-penalty proposal following his conviction, and some final words after he has been sentenced to execution. The *Crito* takes place in the final days of Socrates' incarceration as he awaits execution. The selection from the *Phaedo* provides an account of Socrates' final conversation with his friends and associates, and at the end of the dialogue, he drinks the poison required for his execution and dies.

These four works are often published together and legions of students have studied them as a group. The joint publication of these works, however, has by no means been restricted to modern times. Thrasyllus, the first-century C.E. scholar, whose collection of Plato's writings forms the basis of what we now recognize as the Platonic corpus, treated the four writings with which we are concerned as a unit, although he included the entirety of the *Phaedo* in the group. Indeed, Thrasyllus divided all of Plato's dialogues into groups of four, called tetralogies, of which these four works are the first. Although it is doubtful that Plato himself intended his works to be so grouped, the common background against which the four works with which we will be concerned are set makes it only natural to study them together.

If we accept Plato's description of Socrates' activities and the motivation behind them as at all accurate, the decision to put him on trial as a serious threat to Athens must be seen as a bitterly ironic miscarriage of justice. In Plato, Socrates is a heroic figure who spent virtually his entire life exhorting others to put less stock in worldly matters and to make the improvement of their souls their primary concern. Where Plato's Socrates sought to make others question their values in order to understand better how they ought to live, others saw only the promulgation of moral nihilism. The decision to silence Socrates, then, was a tragic misunderstanding of the philosopher's real intent. Certainly, this is the natural conclusion to reach if we look only to the first tetralogy of the Platonic corpus for our understanding of the motives behind Socrates' trial and execution.

Unfortunately, things are not so simple, as Plato was by no means the only person in antiquity to write about Socrates, and what all of the ancient authors say about him and about the reasons the Athenians put him to death by no means forms a coherent picture. One prominent example is Aristophanes, the comic playwright, whose play, *The Clouds*, first produced some 24 years before Socrates' trial,[1] revolves around the antics of a counterfeit intellectual by the name of "Socrates." Because *The Clouds* figures so prominently in Plato's account of the trial, we can postpone a more detailed discussion of it until our discussion of his *Apology of Socrates*. Suffice it to say now that Aristophanes' purpose could only have been to use Socrates as a caricature for a whole, but quite diverse, group of intellectuals Aristophanes sought to lampoon in the play. However, there must have been sufficient similarity between the character in the play and the real Socrates and between the real Socrates and the intellectuals who were Aristophanes' comic target to make the character named "Socrates" work as a caricature. When Socrates says in the *Apology* (19c2–3) that Aristophanes' misrepresentations of him engendered very dangerous prejudices against him, we have to wonder exactly what was misrepresentation and what was not.

Any attempt to see clearly who Socrates was and why the Athenians would have tried and executed him is further complicated by the fact that in the years following Socrates' death a number of authors, many admirers of Socrates, began to write works in which a character named Socrates is prominently featured. What we know of these "*Sokratikoi logoi*" (Socratic arguments), which included all of the works of Plato except the four dialogues in which Socrates does not appear at all, reveal just how little these authors agreed about what Socrates stood for and what philosophy he propounded. This very troubling fact has led many scholars, especially recently, to dismiss entirely the very idea that a "Socratic philosophy" or accurate historical reconstruction of the philosopher himself can be found in any of this complex and contradictory literature, including especially in the dialogues of Plato.

In fact, Plato's own works make the picture even less clear, principally because different groups of Plato's works portray Socrates and his views in very different ways. Scholars who have sought to reconstruct a Socratic philosophy have generally attempted to separate one group of Plato's dialogues out in which Socrates and his philosophy are represented more or less accurately. On the basis of various characterizations of the differences between Socrates' philosophical views and those of Plato in his own philosophical maturity, and also on the basis of techniques of measuring stylistic differences between the dialogues (called stylometry), many scholars have proposed that a group of dialogues that Plato wrote early in his career represent Socrates and his philosophy reasonably accurately. But as the genre of the *Sokratikoi logoi* became more popular and when fidelity to the historical Socrates and his actual views was neither required nor expected by readers of the genre, Plato eventually began to insert his own philosophical views into the mouth of Socrates. This, according to some scholars (known as the developmentalists,[2] because their account involves the idea that Plato's writings show evidence of him developing from a primarily Socratic point of view into a fully independent philosopher in his own right), explains why the Socrates who speaks in some of Plato's dialogues seems committed to very different philosophical positions than those for which he argues in other dialogues.

So, to what extent do Plato's writings about the trial and death of Socrates accurately portray the philosopher's final days? Are these works historically reliable, or are they fictions that use the names of historical persons? Perhaps not surprisingly, these questions continue to be hotly debated. Those inclined to think these works are fictional tend to be most impressed by the existence of the *Sokratikoi logoi* and argue that Plato's writings must be understood as members of this genre – a genre that represents Socrates in so many different ways that historical accuracy could never have been an interest for any of the writers working in the genre. Developmentalists, on the contrary, argue that none of the other writers had the same close relationship to Socrates as Plato had, and while conceding that even Plato eventually moved away from portraying Socrates accurately, the existence of this genre of writings does not prove that Plato's earlier works were written as part of that genre, or showed the same lack of concern for accuracy that others, writing in that genre, did. Those who discount the historical accuracy of any of Plato's works also sometimes argue that their exceptional literary quality makes it very unlikely that they portray actual events or people accurately. But developmentalists will retort that literary excellence is entirely compatible with historical accuracy.

According to most developmentalists, the *Euthyphro*, *Apology*, and *Crito* all belong to the group of Plato's works regarded as early or "Socratic" works, in which Socrates and his views are as true to the original as we will find in any ancient writings. The *Phaedo*, however, is usually dated somewhat later than these other three, and developmentalist studies of the philosophical content of this dialogue contend that the views for which Socrates argues in this work are no longer those of the historical Socrates, but are instead those of Plato himself. The *Phaedo*, in other words, is generally not counted as a reliable source on Socrates or his philosophy, *even by those who regard some of Plato's other works (the early ones) as historically reliable*. This, perhaps, is one reason why many selections of Plato's works – including especially those devoted to the trial and death of Socrates, include only the last scene from the *Phaedo*, in which Socrates drinks the hemlock poison and dies. When we consider this scene in detail, later in the book, we will discuss the debate over whether this scene should be regarded as accurate about the way Socrates actually died. But few scholars regard the rest of the *Phaedo* as likely to provide an accurate portrayal of the historical Socrates and his philosophy.

That having been said, what about the value of the rest of the first tetralogy as historical sources about the last days of Socrates? To what extent, if any, can we regard what Plato wrote in the other three dialogues as historically accurate? We doubt that evidence exists that would settle this dispute between those who affirm and those who deny Plato's role as a faithful recorder of those famous events. Such a conclusion, however, should in no way detract from our study of Plato's writings about the end of Socrates' life. Few who read the *Euthyphro*, *Apology*, *Crito*, and the death scene from the *Phaedo* will deny that they provide a compelling account of a philosopher so dedicated to "living the

examined life" that he preferred death to a life devoid of philosophical inquiry. In our discussions of each of these works, we will
try to identify the specific scholarly controversies that affect the
interpretation of each dialogue; but we also hope never to lose sight
of the wonder and tragedy of the narrative Plato provides in these
dialogues. In the trial and death of Socrates, there continue to be
many lessons for all of us to learn, lessons that can change our lives
and values forever.

NOTES

1   The play was first produced in 423 and later revised (but what was
    changed in the second edition of the play is unknown). The revised ver-
    sion of the play has survived, and is now widely available in several
    English translations. The play itself continues to be produced and per-
    formed occasionally, and modern students who read it are delighted to
    find that ancient comedy can still make us laugh out loud.

2   All developmentalists are committed to the view that there is a group
    of dialogues written early in Plato's career in which Socrates and his
    views are represented in a more or less consistent way that is different
    from the way in which Socrates and his views are depicted in dialogues
    Plato wrote later on. Some developmentalists are also "historicists";
    that is, they claim that the earlier dialogues represent Socrates and his
    views in a way that is faithful to the historical original. Other develop-
    mentalists are agnostic about – or reject – the historicist theory, claim-
    ing only that Plato chose to change the way he represented Socrates
    from the earlier to the later works, but that this change may only
    represent a change in Plato's own views, and that none of Plato's works
    may be regarded as faithful to the historical Socrates. Our own view is
    a developmentalist one, and though we believe the historicist view pro-
    vides the best explanation of why Plato's dialogues show such marked
    shifts between the earlier and later dialogues, we are open to the idea
    that some other explanation of these shifts may end up explaining
    them more persuasively than the historicists do. To that extent, we also
    count ourselves as somewhat agnostic about historicism. For the sake
    of simplicity, in the rest of this discussion, by "developmentalist" we
    will mean "historicist developmentalist."

1

THE *EUTHYPHRO*

1.1   INTRODUCTION TO THE *EUTHYPHRO*

1.1.1   The legal setting

Most legal cases in ancient Athens were initiated and litigated by private citizens.[1] This meant that the first thing a would-be prosecutor had to do was to write out an indictment and then get the one he was prosecuting to appear before the appropriate magistrate (or *archon*). In cases such as the one against Socrates, it would be the king-archon, whose job it was to make sure the charges were clear and legally appropriate, and whose decision it would be whether to forward the case to a trial by jury. In order to get the accused person to appear before the king-archon, a summons had to be issued. The summons was oral, not written, and would be delivered by the prosecutor himself. So, shortly before the scene we find in the *Euthyphro*, we can imagine Meletus going to Socrates, and before the required two witnesses, Meletus would have confronted Socrates and informed the latter that he was summoned to the king-archon's office on such-and-such a date, and stated the offense, probably exactly as it appeared in the official indictment.

Then, both Socrates and Meletus would appear at the king-archon's office, where Meletus would hand over a written copy of the indictment. Meletus may at that time also have been required to pay a fee (whose amount is not now known).

The king-archon would then set a date for a preliminary hearing on the charges, called an *anakrisis*. In the meantime, prior to the *anakrisis*, the king-archon posted a copy of the charge on a notice-board in the marketplace (the *agora*). Then, the *anakrisis* would be held, at which the indictment would be read aloud, and Socrates would be required to enter his plea. Socrates would then have had to submit a formal statement to the effect that he denied the charge against him. Both sides of the legal case would then respond to questions from the king-archon, which would serve to clarify for all concerned what the issues were and what would be required as evidence at the trial. It appears to be the general rule that prosecutions would almost always be sent to trial, as long as the charges themselves were in appropriate legal order. Those who sought to abuse the courts by initiating frivolous or patently inappropriate charges were fined if they did not win at least one-fifth of the jurors' votes. So, even if the king-archon had serious doubts about the merits of some prosecution, he would ordinarily send it to trial on the assumption that prosecutions lacking in merit would be dealt with this other way. At the end of the *anakrisis*, then, a trial date would be set, and the king-archon would determine what size of jury would be required. In Socrates' case, 500 jurors were selected, chosen by lot from a list of volunteers.

The *Euthyphro* is set on the steps of the king-archon's office. From the way the dialogue begins, Socrates has plainly already received the summons. It is not entirely clear, however, whether Socrates has perhaps come to the king-archon's office for the first time – that is, to have a date for the *anakrisis* set – or whether he meets Euthyphro on the day of the scheduled *anakrisis*.[2] Euthyphro begins the dialogue expressing surprise at seeing Socrates at the king-archon's office (see 2a1–b2). If Socrates were there for his *anakrisis*, the charge against him would already have been publicly posted, in which case one might expect Euthyphro to know about it. Socrates seems to know very little about Meletus (2b7–11), and also seems somewhat unclear about what the exact charges are and what Meletus actually means to be claiming in them (2c2–3a5, 3b1–4, 6a7–9). What Socrates does know seems compatible with his having only been summoned by Meletus, and not yet heard anything more about the charge or evidence to be presented against him than he would normally hear in being summoned. Moreover, at *Euthyphro* 5a3–b8 Socrates (no doubt ironically) proposes to become Euthyphro's student, so that Socrates might become defter in his legal defense strategy. At 5a9–b2, he imagines one successful outcome of becoming Euthyphro's student to be that he might persuade Meletus not to bring him to trial. If he was awaiting the *anakrisis* on the day he talks with Euthyphro, however, unless Socrates somehow thinks that all of his lessons might be completed while they wait in line at the king-archon's office, such an outcome would be impossible – on this very day, if it is the day of the *anakrisis*, Socrates' case will be bound over to trial, and it will be too late to persuade Meletus to desist from the prosecution. So Socrates' playful suggestion that he become Euthyphro's student strongly suggests that the legal proceeding for which Socrates has appeared is not the *anakrisis*, but is, rather, the first meeting in response to the summons.

1.1.2   The charge against Socrates (2a1–3e7)

When Euthyphro first asks what charge is being brought against Socrates (2b12–c1), Socrates first replies that he is charged with corrupting the youth (2c2–3a5). Euthyphro then responds by asking what Meletus (presumably, in the indictment) claims that Socrates does to corrupt the youth, and Socrates responds,

> Absurd things at first hearing, my wonderful friend. For he says that I'm a maker of gods, and because I make new gods but don't believe in the old ones, he has indicted me, or so he says.
>
> (3b1–4)

Euthyphro reacts to this by saying that it must be because Socrates claims to have a divine sign (3b5–9; see also Plato, *Ap.* 31c8–d1, 31d2–3, 40a4–6, 40c3–4, 41d6; *Euthyd.* 272e4; *Phdr.* 242b8–9, 242c2; *Rep.* VI.496c4). Socrates does not contradict Euthyphro's hypothesis – although if we are right that Socrates is only just now appearing at the king-archon's office in response to the summons, he may not be all that clear about exactly why he is being charged as he is. By the time he faces Meletus in court, however, which is what we find depicted in Plato's *Apology*, Euthyphro's surmise turns out to be exactly correct (see *Ap.* 31c7–d4), and this link between the charge of religious innovation and Socrates' "sign" or *daimonion* ("divine thing") is also corroborated by other ancient sources (see Xenophon, *Ap.* 12).

Diogenes Laertius (c. 250 C.E.) makes the incredible claim that the actual indictment against Socrates was still publicly posted over six hundred years after the actual trial:

> The plaintiff's oath in the trial was like this. It is still posted even now, so Favorinus says, in the Metroon. "Meletus, the son of Meletus, of the deme of Pitthos, has written down these things against Socrates, the son of Sophroniscus, of the deme of Alopece, and swears to them. Socrates is guilty of not recognizing the gods that the city recognizes, and of introducing other new divinities, and he is guilty of corrupting the youth. The penalty is to be death."
>
> (2.40)

A much earlier source, Xenophon (*Mem.* 1.1.1), a contemporary of Plato's, also provides the same wording as Diogenes Laertius' version, with one word changed.[3] But here in the *Euthyphro*, as we have noted, and also in Plato's *Apology*, both the actual wording of the indictment and also the order of the three specifications of the charge are given differently. In both instances, Plato has Socrates list the corruption of the youth first, followed by the claims that he fails to recognize Athens' gods and introduces new divinities (see *Ap.* 24b8–c1). It is not at all clear what to make of these differences. The substance of the accusation and its three specifications, however, is the same in all of the ancient reports.

1.1.3 Euthyphro's case (3e8–4e3)

Euthyphro's situation at first appears to be very different from Socrates': Euthyphro proposes to be the prosecutor in his case, whereas Socrates is to be the defendant in his. Socrates is charged with impiety; Euthyphro's charge is murder. A younger man is charging Socrates, now an old man; Euthyphro is indicting his own father, whom he describes as "quite old" (4a4). In fact, however, these contrasts almost certainly form part of the dramatic design of the dialogue, in order to situate the two men in the conversation in parallel, but opposite, circumstances. Despite the superficial differences in the charges, in fact both cases involve religious matters – it is plain from Euthyphro's account of his reasons for the prosecution that he is interested in removing what he perceives as a religious pollution that his father's "crime" caused. One of the specifications of the charge against Socrates is that he "corrupted the youth," thereby turning them against their elders (and even, in Aristophanes' comedy, *The Clouds*, against their own fathers) – a situation ironically called to mind by the young Meletus' prosecution of the aged Socrates. At any rate, by this measure, the text seems to support the claim that Euthyphro has already been corrupted in some way, for he seeks to prosecute his own father for murder. After all, Socrates says no one would think of doing what Euthyphro is intent on unless the victim was another relative (4b5–6). Indeed, Plato has Socrates emphasize this point, by playfully proclaiming that Meletus should prosecute Euthyphro for corrupting his elders and father (5b2–6). So, Plato's dialogue turns the accusation against Socrates on its head: how does Socrates interact with youths who are already corrupted – already turned against their elders and fathers?

Euthyphro's case has engendered a certain amount of scholarly controversy, because the case itself seems to be an extraordinary one. The facts, as Euthyphro presents them, are these: Euthyphro's family hired a day-laborer to help with their farm on Naxos, a small island in the Aegean. This laborer got drunk, got in a fight, and killed one of Euthyphro's family's slaves. It is not clear that Euthyphro's father did anything wrong by binding the killer, throwing him in a ditch, and sending a man to the Religious Counselor (called the *exêgêtês*) in Athens who is to inform him as to what should be done.

From the point of view of law, then, it is not at all clear that Euthyphro's father would have any responsibility towards the killer. But from a religious point of view, the fact that the laborer had killed one of Euthyphro's father's household slaves – and the fact that the killing had presumably taken place on property allotted on Naxos by Athens to Euthyphro's family – required some response. Bloodshed involved great risks of *miasma* or religious pollution, and as the one responsible for the two men and the land, Euthyphro's father seemed to realize that some response was called for. His question was: what should he do? So, he sent to the appropriate religious authority to get some direction in the matter, in the meantime making sure the guilty party did not escape, and evade punishment. The length of time necessary to get a response from the Religious Counselor in Athens, however, was too long, and the prisoner in the meantime (who may also have been injured in the fight with the slave) was not sufficiently cared for. As Euthyphro puts it:

> During this time, he [Euthyphro's father] paid little attention to the captive and really didn't care much if he did die because he was a murderer, which is just what happened. He died from hunger and cold and being bound up before the messenger got back from the Religious Counselor.
>
> (4c9–d5)

It is for *this* death – the death of the man who had murdered Euthyphro's family's slave – that Euthyphro proposes to prosecute his own father for murder. It is also plain that some time has elapsed since these unfortunate events took place. Euthyphro says that all of this took place "when we were working our farm on Naxos." Scholars generally agree that this reference shows that Euthyphro's family had been allotted some land on Naxos (called a cleruchy) by the Athenian government. But the Athenians lost their cleruchies when the Peloponnesian War came to an end (in early 404 B.C.E), and so that meant that at least five years or so had elapsed since Euthyphro's father had committed his alleged "crime." Some scholars have found it so implausible that Euthyphro would wait so long to prosecute his father that they have found Euthyphro's entire situation historically implausible.[4] Others, however, have argued that the entire legal situation in Athens during the aftermath of the war would have been so tenuous that any such prosecution may well have not been possible earlier.[5]

And there is yet another puzzle about this case: the Athenian law on homicide seems to have stipulated that a relative of the victim should legally prosecute on such a charge. In Euthyphro's case, however, it is the alleged *murderer* who is the relative of the prosecutor; the victim was only a day-laborer who worked on the farm Euthyphro's family had at the island of Naxos. No doubt this is one of the reasons Plato has Socrates respond as he does when he hears that Euthyphro intends to prosecute his father for murder:

> Surely the one killed by your father is a member of your family. Of course, that's obvious. I suppose you wouldn't prosecute him for the murder of someone outside the family.
>
> (4b4–6)

Some scholars have argued that the law on homicide did not simply state a preference or presumption that the prosecutor be a relative of the victim; instead, they claim, the law was so restrictive that the prosecutor would have *had* to be a relative of the victim.[6] Now, neither Euthyphro nor Socrates seem to react to Euthyphro's legal situation as if the law were restrictive in this way, for if it were, Euthyphro's case could not be made (or, at any rate, could not be made by Euthyphro himself). And since this passage in the *Euthyphro* is one of three ancient texts on which scholars have based their judgments about the degree of restrictiveness of the homicide law,[7] and because, in our view, neither of the other two texts requires the more restrictive understanding of the law,[8] we are inclined to believe that, however unusual Euthyphro's case may be, it is not one that would have been legally impossible.

The first thing Euthyphro would have had to do is to make a proclamation in the Athenian *agora*, requiring the accused to "keep away from the things laid down by law," which was intended to have the effect of minimizing the risk of pollution from the crime to the rest of Athens and its citizens.[9] The prosecutor would then go to the king-archon and enter his charge, whereupon the king-archon would also make a proclamation reiterating that the accused

should "keep away from the things laid down by law." This proclamation would have the effect of a restraining order, preventing the
accused from setting foot in any temple, from taking part in any
public religious ceremony, from going to the *agora* or any of its
buildings (including any court of law other than the one in which and
only when his own case was tried), and any other public buildings. If
the accused were found in any of these places, he would be sum-
marily arrested and thrown in jail until his trial. The net effect, as
MacDowell puts it,[10] was a kind of temporary disfranchisement.

Assuming that the case met minimal legal standards, the king-
archon would then schedule the first of three preliminary hearings,
in this case called *prodikasiai* (unlike the single *anakrisis*) for other
crimes). These hearings would be scheduled – one per month – over
the next three months, with the actual trial to be held in the fourth
month, and because all of the proceedings had to be held under the
same king-archon, whose term was one year and who could not
succeed himself, this meant that murder trials could not be initiated
in the last three months of the year.

Just as Euthyphro seemed wholly unaware of why Socrates
would have shown up at the king-archon's office, so too, when the
two men begin talking, Socrates has no knowledge of Euthyphro's
case. It is, of course, not impossible that Euthyphro's case might
already have gone through one or more of these preliminary stages
and Socrates not have paid any attention to it. But it also seems
plausible to think that Euthyphro, too, has come for the first meeting with the king-archon, having only just summoned his father
thus far.[11] At any rate, the mirroring of the two men's legal circumstances adds yet another reason for thinking that both had appeared
at the king-archon's office at the same stages in their legal cases,
which we take to be the first meeting to respond to the summons.[12]

1.1.4 The opening and closing scenes of the dialogue (4e4–5c8)

The dialogue begins with Euthyphro greeting Socrates before the
king-archon's office. From the way Euthyphro greets Socrates, it
appears that it is Euthyphro – and not Socrates – who has just

appeared on the scene. There are thus two possibilities one can imagine, and which one we choose will make some difference as to how we interpret the entire dialogue. On the one hand, perhaps we are to imagine that Euthyphro has just completed his business with the king-archon, and is coming out of the latter's office, whereupon he sees Socrates waiting outside for a later meeting with the magistrate. If so, we may assume that whatever legal business Euthyphro had come to do that day had already been completed successfully by the time the conversation began. This view of the scene has had a number of adherents, including John Burnet, whose 1924 edition of the Greek texts of the *Euthyphro*, *Apology*, and *Crito* continues to be widely cited for its erudition. According to Burnet, the opening scene of the dialogue is one in which Socrates is

> waiting outside [of the king-archon's office] till his turn comes, when he is accosted by Euthyphro. As Euthyphro too had a case before the 'King', and as, at the end of the dialogue, he suddenly remembers another engagement (15e3), we must suppose that his business here is over for the present, and that he is coming out of the [king-archon's office] when he sees Socrates.[13]

Burnet is plainly right to understand that Euthyphro's entrance and sudden exit are likely to be significant features of Plato's crafting of the dialogue. But is Burnet right about Euthyphro's entrance? One ancient source, at any rate, seems to have understood the situation markedly differently from the way Burnet does. According to Diogenes Laertius (c. 250 C.E.),

> After discussing something about piety with Euthyphro, who had indicted his father for the murder of a stranger, he [Socrates] diverted him [from what he had set out to do].[14]

In other words, Diogenes seems to suppose that Socrates' conversation with Euthyphro is to be understood as taking place *before* Euthyphro had done his business with the king-archon – otherwise, it would already be too late for Socrates to "divert" Euthyphro from his prosecution. In Diogenes' version of the opening scene, we should therefore picture Euthyphro arriving at the king-archon's office and finding Socrates already waiting there.

The difference between these two views of the opening scene has enormous impact on what we are to imagine about Euthyphro's (proposed) prosecution of his father. For if he has already completed his business at the king-archon's office, as Burnet suggests, then Euthyphro's hasty departure at the end of the dialogue shows nothing more than haste to get away from Socrates' questioning. If Diogenes is right, however – whether we imagine Euthyphro simply as having come to present his summons to the king-archon, or even more strongly, if we imagine him as having come for the preliminary hearing for his case – then Euthyphro's sudden exit from the scene means that he is also abandoning his prosecution, at least for the moment.

Plato does not provide clear "stage directions," as it were, or we would not likely have such a difference of opinion about the beginning and end of the dialogue. Because either conception of the opening scene – and therefore, the consequences or lack of such implied by Euthyphro's departure at the end – is logically compatible with what we find in the text, we do not suppose there can ever be a decisive answer to the question of which of the competing views is correct. Our own preference in this case, however, is for Diogenes' understanding of the dialogue, precisely because it seems to us to add to the dramatic effect, and we therefore think it does more credit to Plato's literary and philosophical craftsmanship.

Notice that when Socrates turns the conversation (at 3e8) to Euthyphro's own case, one of the very first things Euthyphro acknowledges is that he is thought to be insane to be undertaking his prosecution (4a1). Socrates reacts with incredulity (4a7) when Euthyphro explains that it is his father he proposes to prosecute (4a6), and then cries out an expletive ("Heracles!") when Euthyphro says that the charge is to be murder (4a11). Socrates goes on immediately to note that

> Surely most people *don't* see how that's right! Indeed, I don't think this would be done correctly by just anyone, but I suppose it takes someone *far* advanced in wisdom.
>
> (4a11–b2)

Euthyphro admits that his decision betokens an unusual degree of wisdom on his part (4b3), and later acknowledges (what no one would have doubted) that his father and other relatives are outraged at Euthyphro's decision (4d5–e1). Socrates continues to remind Euthyphro throughout the dialogue that the religious stakes Euthyphro faces are very high, indeed: by acting as he proposes to do, Euthyphro actually risks committing an egregious offense against piety, rather than – as he claims – demonstrating an unusual commitment to and understanding of this most important religious virtue (see 4b4–6, 4e4–8, 5c8–d1, 6d2–4, 9a1–b4). Indeed, the very last thing Socrates says to Euthyphro before the younger man suddenly hurries off makes the point vividly:

> If you didn't know clearly what the pious and the impious are, you couldn't possibly be trying to prosecute your elderly father for murder on behalf of a servant, and you'd fear that you'd be at risk with respect to the gods that you would be wrong in doing this and would be held in contempt by men.
>
> (15d4–8)

Euthyphro's relatives are outraged at his reckless plan to prosecute his own father; but plainly nothing they have managed to say or to do has persuaded him to desist from the prosecution. Socrates, however, though obviously shocked at Euthyphro's presumption, never directly attempts to dissuade the younger man from his plan. Instead, Socrates gets him to see and agree that no one would dare risk such an adventure unless he knew clearly and confidently what piety required. But in order to make difficult decisions about piety – in order to make expert judgments about whether some very controversial and highly unusual plan of action is or is not pious – one would surely have to have an expert's knowledge of what piety is. On this point, at any rate, Socrates and Euthyphro agree entirely (see 4a11–b3, 4e9–5a2). If Socrates can show Euthyphro that the latter does *not* have such expert knowledge of piety, then he will also have succeeded in undermining utterly the arrogant confidence that spurred the young man into such dangerous and potentially deadly conflict with his father and other relatives. This, we argue, is precisely what the dialogue shows Socrates doing with Euthyphro – with the result, as Diogenes had it, that Socrates actually succeeds (at least temporarily) in achieving what all of Euthyphro's relatives failed to achieve: Socrates "diverts" Euthyphro from the prosecution. After talking with Socrates for a while, Euthyphro loses his confidence in his religious expertise, and beats a hasty retreat from what he now senses is too risky a course of action, the religious requirements about which have been revealed to be much less clear than he had supposed them to be. Socrates has not *proven* Euthyphro's proposed prosecution to be wrong or impious; he has, instead, only revealed to Euthyphro that the latter is in no position to make the kinds of judgments any such radical action would require.

In Plato's *Apology*, Socrates makes the startling claim that he is no teacher and has never taught anyone anything (*Ap.* 33a5–6, 33b3–6). Instead, he claims only to ask questions and not to promote specific doctrines or beliefs. In the *Euthyphro*, we claim, Plato depicts Socrates in precisely the way in which he has Socrates characterize himself to the jurors – he does not attempt to teach Euthyphro any particular view about Euthyphro's proposed prosecution. But his questions make all the difference, and the difference plays out in most important ways in the moral and legal lives of Euthyphro and his family. Far from being a corrupter of youth, the Socrates of Plato's *Euthyphro* is revealed to be the savior of a young man so badly corrupted that even his family – his own father – could no longer help him. And in saving the young man, Socrates also saves his father and other family members. Precisely because this seems so entirely in keeping with Plato's apparent purposes in his Socratic dialogues, we are strongly inclined to the ancient view of the opening scene, and disinclined to accept Burnet's version – which would have the effect of nullifying all of the above dramatic results.

1.2   DEFINING PIETY

1.2.1   Socrates asks Euthyphro to say what piety is (5c8–6a6)

Euthyphro's name literally means "straight thinker." From the very beginning of the argument, however, Euthyphro's ability to think along straight and logical lines is anything but evident. Having very vividly identified Euthyphro's presumption of wisdom about religious matters, at 5c9, Socrates issues his challenge to the younger man to explain what piety is:

> What sort of thing do you say piety and impiety are as they apply to murder and to other things, or isn't the pious the same thing in every action, and isn't impiety in turn the complete opposite of piety, but in itself the same as itself, and doesn't all that is going to be impious in fact have a certain distinctive feature of impiousness?
>
> (5c9–d5)

Many of Plato's Socratic dialogues are centered around what is known as the "What is F-ness?" question, where F is some significant virtue or other ethical term. In this case, the question of the dialogue will be, "What is piety?" Having established that Euthyphro's present course of action is based on his presumption of extraordinary and sophisticated expertise in this area, Euthyphro eagerly answers Socrates' question. Piety, he proclaims, is doing the sort of thing he now proposes to do: prosecuting wrongdoers no matter what their relation to you might be (5d8–e5). He then compares his own conflict with his father with the myth about Zeus imprisoning his own father, Cronus, and Cronus' earlier castration of his father, Ouranus. Nonetheless, Euthyphro exclaims, people think Zeus is "the best and most just of the gods," but then turn around and get angry with him for prosecuting his father for wrongdoing.

Euthyphro's comparison of his own case to the myths about Zeus and Zeus' father and grandfather is shocking. Greek popular myths about the gods often portrayed them behaving in ways that would be abhorred among human beings. Indeed, many of the stories about the gods characterize them as engaging in activities that would actually be illegal – even to the point of meriting capital punishment – among human beings. The logic of Euthyphro's argument, then, is elusive at best: is he proposing that his family members would not or should not be angry with him if he imprisoned or castrated his father? Or is it, rather, that if they deplore what Euthyphro intends, so, too, should they deplore the actions of gods?

It has sometimes been popular among scholars to think of Euthyphro as a kind of stiff-necked traditionalist about religion.[15] But Euthyphro's incredible arrogance, in comparing his own actions with those of the gods, is enough in itself to prove decisively otherwise.[16] But Socrates already knew as much about Euthyphro, precisely because the young man was ready to take such serious action against his own father, thus plainly violating his duty of filial piety,[17] as he suggested at 4e7–8, and to which he points again at 9a1–b4 and at 15d4–8.

So Socrates does not directly react to this new outrage by Euthyphro, but rather subtly points out the flaw in Euthyphro's own position. Euthyphro has criticized his relatives for what he regards as the contradiction in their views about the gods and Euthyphro's actions. Socrates, in response, notes that the myths to which Euthyphro compares his own situation in effect accuse the gods of evil and shameful acts (6a7–10). If Euthyphro agrees that the actions of Ouranus, Cronus, and Zeus are not the sort that we should associate with moral gods, then Euthyphro cannot simply point to such gods and their actions as moral models for his own behavior. On the other hand, if Euthyphro is really prepared to claim that such myths about the gods are consistent with the gods being fully and flawlessly moral (which, we will soon find, he is not at all clear about in his own mind), then he cannot explain what injustices Ouranus and Cronus did – that is, what wrongs were done by allegedly morally flawless divinities – that would merit such cruel treatment in response by their sons. Briefly, if the gods really do terrible and evil things to one another, on what basis can we mortals judge some of their actions good, and some bad? In order to answer this question, Socrates realizes, Euthyphro would have to be able to be a better judge of morality than the gods themselves appear to be.

1.2.2   Socrates and the myths (6a7–c7)

Now, the way that Socrates expresses this challenge to Euthyphro has sometimes been taken to make a specific and historically

significant claim about what Socrates takes to be the source of the
charge Meletus is making against him.[18] In some translations,
indeed, what Socrates says here is actually given as a direct statement of why he is being charged with impiety.[19] But that is not at
all what the text provides. Rather, Socrates asks a question, and
offers a speculation, and these are worth careful attention as to
what they do and do not claim about Socrates' actual trial:

> Is *this*, Euthyphro, why I'm being indicted — because whenever some-
> one says such things about the gods, I have trouble accepting it for
> some reason? Surely it's for this reason that some, it seems, will say
> that I've committed a crime.
>
> (6a7–10)

In fact, Socrates makes no claim here as to why Meletus actually
charged him with impiety. Recall, as we argued earlier, that all
Socrates is portrayed as knowing so far about his case is what the
indictment states, and this makes it likely that he is being portrayed as waiting at the king-archon's office to answer the summons Meletus made against him. So, in reaction to Euthyphro's
stupidly uncritical use of myths of divine evil-doing and retribu-
tion to justify his own outrageous and offensive plan of action,
Socrates wonders aloud if his own doubts about such myths might
be the reason he has been indicted, and he imagines that some
might even count this as a ground for thinking he committed a
crime. Later on in this dialogue, Socrates will show that he thinks
the gods are responsible for everything good that comes to human
beings (15a1–2), and so it is plain enough why Socrates finds stories of divine evils and shames difficult to believe. But is this the
reason why Socrates was brought to trial and/or convicted, and
should we understand Plato as telling us that in this passage?

There are, in fact, very good reasons for thinking that this
passage tells us no such thing. First, when Socrates first tells
Euthyphro about the charge against him, Euthyphro offers a very
different explanation of the charge against Socrates: it is because
Socrates claims to have a "divine sign" that comes to him (3b5–9), not
because he is some other sort of religious or theological innovator.

As we noted earlier, Euthyphro's surmise turns out to be exactly correct according to all of the other ancient accounts of the trial – the specification of the charge of impiety that has to do with "introducing new divinities" is directed at Socrates' "divine sign" (see Plato, *Ap.* 31c7–d4; Xenophon, *Ap.* 12).[20]

But what about the claim that Socrates does not "recognize" or "believe in" the gods of Athens? Might it not be that *this* part of the indictment points to Socrates' doubts about myths that portray the gods behaving badly? Scholars have debated this point at great length and from several points of view. In one version, Socrates' disbelief in such myths made him guilty of the charge against him:

> What would be left of her [Hera] and the other Olympians if they were required to observe the stringent norms of Socratic virtue which require every moral agent, human or divine, to act only to cause good to others, never evil, regardless of provocation? Required to meet these austere standards, the city's gods would have become unrecognizable. Their ethical transformation would be tantamount to the destruction of the old gods, the creation of new ones – which is precisely what Socrates takes to be the sum and substance of the accusation at his trial.[21]

A similar view is expressed by Mark McPherran, who doubts that Socrates was actually prosecuted for such beliefs, but who detects in Socrates' tendency to moralize the gods a threat to Greek religious cult – that is, to the ritual practices the state required in honoring the gods, which sought to persuade the gods to provide divine assistance of various kinds to Athens.

> It should be clear, then, that Socrates had in essence proposed important reformations of a linchpin of traditional religion: take away the conflicts of the deities and the expectations of particular *material* rewards and physical protection in cult, and you disconnect the religion of everyday life from its practical roots. [...] He [Socrates] thus represented a profound challenge to a fundamental aspect of traditional

Athenian life, and constituted a dangerous threat to those unprepared to understand or change.[22]

In our own day, the figure of a courageous and intellectually subtle philosopher put on trial and executed for disbelief in religious superstitions is a very attractive one, which makes Socrates both a hero of reason and also a martyr for it. But very important reasons to doubt the accuracy of this somewhat romantic view of Socrates come from what Plato has the two main litigants say about the charges and their motives and meanings at the trial itself. From 20c4 to 24b2 in Plato's *Apology*, we find Socrates explaining to his jurors why it is that he finds himself in such trouble. He responds by telling the story about Chaerephon's mission to the oracle at Delphi, which said that no one was wiser than Socrates. Socrates explains that the effect learning of this oracle had on him was that he lived his life questioning people who acted as if they were wise when they were not wise. The charges he now faces, according to Socrates, derive directly from the embarrassments his interrogations of such people have caused to them:

And when anyone asks them what I do and what I teach, they have nothing to say and draw a blank, but so they don't appear to be confused, they say what's commonly said against all philosophers — "what's in the heavens and below the earth," "doesn't believe in gods," and "makes the weaker argument the stronger." But I think they wouldn't want to say what's true, that they're plainly pretending to know, and they don't know anything. Insofar, then, as they are, I think, concerned about their honor, and are zealous, and numerous, and speak earnestly and persuasively about me, they've filled your ears for a long time by vehemently slandering me. It was on this account that Meletus, Anytus, and Lycon came after me: Meletus angry on behalf of the poets, Anytus on behalf of the craftsmen and politicians, and Lycon on behalf of the orators. The result is that, as I was saying when I began, I'd be amazed if I were able to refute in such a little time this slander you accept and that has gotten out of hand. There you have the truth, men of Athens, and in what I'm saying I'm neither hiding nor even shading anything large or small.

(*Ap.* 23d2–24b2)

According to what Plato has Socrates say at the trial, then, doubts about myths that portray the gods quarreling and doing bad things had nothing to do with why he ended up in court – unless, of course, Plato also has Socrates lying when he proclaims that his explanation of the origin of the charges against him involves no "hiding nor even shading anything large or small."

And when Socrates later cross-examines Meletus, we find the prosecutor put in a perfect position to expose Socrates' supposedly "dangerous" religious innovations. Socrates asks Meletus to explain what the indictment means when it claims that Socrates does not "recognize" or "believe in" the gods of the state:

In the name of these very gods that we're arguing about, Meletus, tell me and these men here still more clearly. I'm not able to understand whether you're saying that I teach people not to believe that some gods exist – and therefore that I myself believe gods exist and am not a complete atheist, nor am not a wrongdoer in that way – and yet I do not believe in the ones that the city believes in, but others, and this is what you're accusing me of, because I believe in the others? Or are you saying that I don't believe in gods at all and that I teach others such things?

(*Ap.* 26b8–c7)

Meletus unhesitatingly replies:

I'm saying that you don't believe in the gods at all.

(*Ap.* 26c8)

If Meletus were charging Socrates with believing in some "dangerously" modified version of gods, he would not reply the way he does. So, at least according to Plato's version of the trial and the actual meaning of the charge against Socrates, the sorts of doubts Socrates expresses about myths at *Euthyphro* 6a7–10 had nothing to do with either the prosecution against Socrates, or the prejudices that led to that prosecution. Our view, then, is that we should understand Socrates' expression of skepticism in the *Euthyphro* about the alleged immoralities of the gods as perhaps simply the result of Socrates' not yet being in a position to know why he is being charged, and even more likely, as a way to show Euthyphro one of many flaws in the younger man's thinking.

1.2.3   Clarifying the question (6c8–e9)

We might expect, especially given Euthyphro's own obvious commitment to such myths, that Socrates' expression of skepticism about them might provoke a shocked reaction. But Euthyphro does not seem to find such skepticism all that surprising or "dangerous." Instead, he responds by telling Socrates that there are "still more marvelous things than these, Socrates, which most people don't know about" (6b5–6). And when Socrates expresses more such doubts, Euthyphro eagerly offers to "describe many other things about divine matters for you, if you wish, which I'm certain will amaze you when you hear them" (6c5–7).

Socrates, however, demurs. Instead, he wants Euthyphro to return to the original question: what is piety? Euthyphro, Socrates contends, has not adequately answered this question yet.

> For now, try to say more clearly what I asked you just now. For in the first thing you said, you didn't instruct me well enough when I asked what piety is, but you were telling me that piety happens to be what you're doing now – prosecuting your father for murder.
>
> (6c9–d4)

Socrates then gets Euthyphro to admit that there are many other examples of piety, in addition to this (very controversial) one, and insists that a proper answer to the question must explain what it is about all such examples that makes them examples of piety.

When a philosopher asks what something is, a list of items supposed to be that sort of thing will never qualify as an adequate answer. Consider, for example, the very important religious and philosophical question, "What is (a) God?" One who wants an answer to this question will not be satisfied by an answer that lists some – or even all – of the gods human beings have ever worshiped. The philosopher or theologian who asks such a question does not want a list of examples, but an explanation of the concept of divinity – an explanation of what it is that makes something or some being a god (or the God). According to Hindus, Ganesh is a god; according to Muslims, Ganesh is not a god – only Allah is (a) God. In virtue of what quality or qualities would such a controversy be adjudicated? The answer to "What is (a) God?" must provide an account of what this quality or these qualities might be.

Moreover, if we recall the dramatic scene of the dialogue, a proper answer to Socrates' question about piety will be critical for each of the disputes in which the two discussants are involved – and the legal cases to which these disputes led. In Socrates' case, a clear explanation of what piety is might be applied to his life and activities in such a way as to prove his innocence (or guilt!) decisively; in Euthyphro's case, a clear explanation of what piety is could be applied to his decision to prosecute his father, in such a way as to resolve the dispute between Euthyphro, who claims that his action is pious, and his father and other relatives (and Socrates, as well, judging from his reaction to Euthyphro's plan), who claim that his action is impious. Notice that the way Euthyphro first attempts to answer Socrates' question simply asserts that his action is pious – but, of course, that assertion is exactly the matter under dispute between Euthyphro and others. Euthyphro insists that it is; his relatives insist that it is not. Their dispute, in such terms, is certain to go nowhere, while their hostilities increase exponentially.

1.2.4 Piety as pleasing gods who disagree (6e10–8b6)

What, then, does Euthyphro think it is that makes *all* examples of piety pious? Once he has understood better the nature of Socrates' question, he replies this way:

> What's pleasing to the gods is pious, then, and what isn't pleasing to the gods is impious.
>
> (6e10–7a1)

As we will see, Euthyphro's very murky and ill-conceived conception of piety is somehow centered on the idea that we must please the gods, which is not at all an unusual religious view in ancient or even modern times. But this very common notion does not fit well with the very feature of Euthyphro's own religious belief about which Socrates confessed skepticism earlier: the idea that there are bitter enmities and wars among the gods. Socrates points out that most differences of opinion do not lead to such terrible fights between those who differ:

> If you and I were to disagree about which number is greater, would the disagreement make us enemies and make us angry at each other, or would we quickly get rid of disagreement by resorting to calculation about these sorts of things?
>
> (7b7–c1)

The same kind of reasoning applies, as Socrates shows, to disagreements about size (7c3–5) and weight (7c7–8). Socrates' point, taken generally, is that differences of opinion do not lead to bitter enmities in cases in which there are agreed to be clear objective standards by which to determine the truth of the matter under dispute. So, Socrates asks, what sorts of differences of opinion *do* lead to hostilities between those with opposing views?

> But then about what sort of thing are we enemies and become angry at each other when we've differed and haven't been able to find an answer? Perhaps it is not at the tip of your tongue, but consider what I'm saying – that it's the just and the unjust, noble and disgraceful, and good and bad. Isn't it when we disagree and aren't able to come to a sufficient answer that we become enemies to each other, whenever we do, I and you and everyone else?
>
> (7c10–d6)

Euthyphro agrees that these are the sorts of issues that tend to lead disputing parties to become angry and hostile – and he also agrees that these same issues are what lead the gods to the wars Euthyphro believes they sometimes have (7d7–10). But if the gods do contend and go to war with each other, it must be that different gods suppose that "different things are just, noble and disgraceful, and good and bad" (7e1–3). Each one loves what he or she believes is noble, good, or just, and hates what he or she believes is disgraceful, bad, or unjust (7e6–8). But because they disagree about what is noble, good, and just, the same thing will be loved by some gods and hated by others (8a4–5). If piety is whatever is pleasing to the gods, as Euthyphro claimed at 6e11–7a1, then the very same thing will turn out to be both pious and impious in such cases – assuming, of course, that what the gods love pleases them and what the gods hate displeases them (8a7–8). But this outcome only shows how hopelessly far Euthyphro is from answering the question Socrates had originally put to him: "What is 'piety'?" In asking it, Socrates is looking for what will enable him to resolve disputes, and Euthyphro's answer does nothing to help him out.

Notice that an essential aspect of Socrates' criticism here is an implicit critique of Euthyphro's concept of gods who fight and go to war against one another. To understand this point, let us go back to the distinction Socrates makes between disagreements that can be resolved by appeals to clear and accepted objective standards, and disputes that cannot be so resolved. Let us consider a simple example to understand better just how this works.

> Two shoe salesmen (A and B) get into a dispute about pay. The shoe-store owner has agreed to pay each salesman $5.00 for each pair of shoes they sell. But A claims that B is unfairly receiving more money than A. B denies that he is unfairly receiving more money than A.

How should we resolve this dispute? Notice that there may be a number of possible sources of the dispute, and we will need to be careful to get clear about which of them is (or are) behind the dispute. A good way to do this will be to find out exactly what the two parties to the dispute agree on. Do they agree that B is receiving more money than A? Perhaps A perceives that B is receiving more money, but B claims to be making no more – or even less – than A makes. If the dispute is founded upon different perceptions of how much money B is actually making, then it seems as if a simple solution to resolve the dispute is available – review the records of B's paychecks to determine the exact truth of how much money B has been receiving. The same kind of resolution would be available if the dispute were based upon differences in perceptions of whether B has actually sold more shoes than A. Again, a review of sales records, which will specify who sold each pair of shoes, should resolve the dispute.

But such easy and decisive resolutions would only be possible if an appeal to an accepted, clear, and objective standard could be made to determine the truth of the matter under dispute. If the parties to the dispute cannot agree that there is such a standard, we will find the dispute much more difficult, if not impossible, to resolve. What if we suppose that the dispute is based upon A's perception that B is being paid more money than A, whereas B claims to be making an amount equal to or less than what A is being paid? We propose to review B's paychecks to establish what the truth of the matter is – but A rejects our solution, saying, "What difference does that make? Those records are not accurate or 'objective,' as you claim they are." Or, perhaps in the extreme case, A is confused about the nature of money and even denies that it provides an objective way of deciding who has received what amount. In that case, A is simply confused about what it means to talk about more money and less money – A is confused about judging relative amounts of money; A is ignorant about money.

Suppose we apply this to Euthyphro's gods, however. Perhaps they disagree about what is noble and shameful, good and bad, just and unjust, because they believe that *there are no objective standards of such things*. Many of us suppose this about aesthetic and/or moral values: we sometimes hear people claim that there simply are no objective standards by which to judge such things. If there are no such standards, then it shouldn't surprise us that even gods would not recognize such standards. If this is true, however, then *any* attempt to provide an answer to Socrates' question about piety is doomed from the start, for there *is no answer to the question*. Socrates wants to know what piety is, so that he and Euthyphro can use this answer to judge whether any given action is or is not pious (6e4–7). But if there is no such standard, then *no* such judgment can ever be objective, and there will be no way to resolve disputes about different judgments in this area.

But *if there is no such standard*, then it will also be true that *there can never be an expert* in such matters. Plainly, this is not a result that Euthyphro can be happy with; after all, Euthyphro realizes that his decision to prosecute his father is terribly controversial, but he is confident in making his decision nonetheless precisely because he is convinced that he has a level of expertise in making these kinds of judgments that is considerably greater than what is had by those who oppose his decision (4a11–b3, 4e4–5a2, 15d4–8).

Perhaps, instead, we should understand Euthyphro's gods to be more like the shoe salesman (A) in our example, above. Perhaps they argue and fight about the noble and shameful, the good and bad, the just and unjust, even though there is a clear objective standard to which they could in principle appeal to adjudicate their disputes; but like A and money, they are simply confused or ignorant about what this standard might be. But this now puts Euthyphro in an even more awkward position, for now he will be revealed as thinking that *he* is a wonderful and accomplished expert about whether it is noble or shameful, good or bad, just or unjust, for him to be prosecuting his own father – but the *gods* themselves lack the very expertise that Euthyphro so boldly claims to have, or they wouldn't dispute and go to war over such matters! Euthyphro's gods, in this scenario, turn out to be remarkably stupid and ignorant about the things that matter the most – and yet, as we have seen, Euthyphro's own reasoning suggests that he regards them as appropriate moral role models (recall 5e5–6a6).

In focusing on Euthyphro's idea that the gods fight against one another, accordingly, Socrates raises a very important point about what this implies about moral evaluation, and the gods' supposed authority in such matters. If there are objective standards for such evaluations, then the gods' disagreements prove they are ignorant of these objective standards. If there are no objective standards for such evaluation, then whatever *anyone* (divine or human) does or thinks about morality is irrelevant, and neither gods nor self-proclaimed moral "experts" (such as Euthyphro) have any better grasp of the truth about morality than does the lowest fool – for there is no truth to grasp either well or poorly. In such a case, it is not just that "It is a matter of opinion only"; it is, rather, that every opinion about what is right and wrong or good and bad is as faulty and useless as any other one.

1.2.5 Why Euthyphro thinks that all the gods agree with him (8b7–9d1)

Euthyphro's response to Socrates' argument shows that he misses just how serious a problem resides in his idea that the gods fight and go to war with one another. He dimly perceives only that he cannot define piety as what pleases the gods as long as different things will please different gods, and the same things can be both pleasing to some gods and displeasing to others. But rather than abandoning his view that the gods do fight and go to war with one another, Euthyphro claims only that "about this matter none of the gods differ with each other, namely, that the one who has killed someone unjustly needn't pay the penalty for it" (8b7–9).

This "clarification" of Euthyphro's position entirely fails to sidestep the mess the idea of warring gods puts him in. Socrates immediately recognizes this point, of course, and begins to explicate it to Euthyphro. The problem is that no one disagrees with the claim that those who have committed some injustice should pay the penalty (8b10–c2). Of course, as Euthyphro says, there are no end of disputes about wrongdoing in general (8c3–6), but the disputes are never about whether wrongdoers should be punished, but are, as Socrates notes, always instead about whether some wrong has been done (8d1) or, if all agree that some wrong has been done, they disagree about "who the wrongdoer is, what he did, and when" (8d6). So even if we concede Euthyphro's claim that the gods all agree that one who has killed someone unjustly must pay the penalty for it, the fact that they disagree and go to war shows that they disagree about what specific things are or are not noble or shameful, good or bad, just or unjust, which means that any action that is likely to be morally controversial among human beings (because of the lack of an objective standard of morality, or our ignorance of that standard) is equally likely to be controversial among gods, who must also lack that standard or be ignorant of it. But this means that Euthyphro has not yet in any way shown that his proposed prosecution of his father will not be a matter of moral controversy among the gods, which – according to his account of what piety is – will have the result that his action is both pleasing and displeasing to (different) gods, and thus both pious and impious, which is senseless (9a1–b4; compare with 5d1–5).

Euthyphro is confident that he can prove that his prosecution of his father would not be a matter of moral controversy among the gods (9b5–6, 9b10–11), and we will return shortly to just how much even general agreement of the gods might show about piety. But the main criticism Socrates has made about Euthyphro's warring gods is unaffected even if there are *some* moral issues on which they happen all to agree. If we suppose that the gods nonetheless disagree about many other moral issues, then all of the unfortunate consequences we identified above continue to follow – their disagreements about any moral matter reveal either that there is no objective standard by which to make a judgment in that matter, or else there is such a standard applicable to that matter, but the gods are ignorant of it. In the former case, the whole idea of moral expertise (divine or mortal) is inappropriate; in the latter, the gods are shown not to have such expertise. In either case, we are given no reason to believe that any moral judgment based upon divine positions or pleasures has any greater authority than some judgment that lacks such a basis. Unless Euthyphro can establish the moral expertise and reliability of the gods whose behaviors and moral positions he takes to be adequate models for human behavior, he will be exposed as having no moral expertise himself and no reliable basis for his proposed prosecution.

The problem goes back to the reason why Euthyphro and Socrates agree that some disputes become intractable and lead to hostility, whereas others do not. Euthyphro does not now suggest that the gods are so irrational as to become angry and go to war over matters that do have objective standards of judgment, which they both recognize and agree upon. Nor does Euthyphro seem to suppose that their wars and controversies have to do with judgments other than those about right and wrong, good and bad. So even if they do agree about *some* specific moral judgments, nothing follows about their moral expertise or reliability of their moral judgments in controversial matters.

Moreover, even if their agreement about some specific moral issue *is* the result of their recognition of a reliable and objective standard of judgment, it is that reliable and objective standard – and not the gods' agreement on the issue – that would give moral justification to one who shared the gods' view of the matter. To see this, let us imagine a family of human beings; let us call them the Doxa (after the Greek word for belief) family. (The Olympian gods – at least as they are depicted in Homer and Hesiod, on whose general depiction Euthyphro seems to be relying – are sometimes said to behave like a large human family.) The members of the Doxa family disagree about lots of things, and occasionally surprisingly nasty fights break out among them. Where they recognize objective standards of judgment (for example, in simple matters of counting, or measuring, or weighing things), they are able to resolve differences of opinion quite easily and without hostility. But on many significant moral matters, they find themselves in persistent, intractable, and often disturbingly violent disputes. Now, the Doxas' next-door neighbors, the Pistis family, find themselves caught up in a very heated dispute over whether it is ever morally permissible for a woman to have an abortion in the first trimester of pregnancy. On this topic, however, the Doxas are pleased to find they all agree: it is *never* morally permissible, they all agree, for a woman to have an abortion in the first trimester of her pregnancy. Of course, if the same woman seeks to have an abortion in the *second* trimester of her pregnancy, the Doxas find themselves unable to agree about what is right – now some say it is morally permissible, others say that it is morally impermissible, and still others say that it is morally obligatory for her to have the abortion.

So what are we to make of the fact that the Doxas all agree about one moral issue? Why, absolutely nothing! Precisely because they prove themselves not to be moral experts generally, their agreement about a single moral issue proves nothing at all about that issue. If there is no objective standard of judgment on this issue, their agreement is no more relevant to what is right than is the disagreement suffered among the members of the Pistis family. If, however, there is some standard of objective judgment about that issue, there is no particular reason to suppose the Doxas have discovered it, for they have proven themselves to have a very poor track-record in general of finding such standards.

The only way one could argue that the unanimity of the Doxas was significant, then, would be either to show that they were moral experts – but their disagreements on other matters rules this out – or to show that on this particular issue, they have discovered the relevant and correct objective standard of judgment. But how could one demonstrate this fact, especially given their obvious lack of expertise in related areas? Well, one might produce the relevant standard itself, and then show that the Doxas relied on in it achieving their unanimity. Notice that in this case, what would warrant one's own view – assuming one shared the Doxas' view of the matter – would be the very same objective standard of judgment used by the Doxas themselves. Given that standard, the fact that the Doxas also relied on the standard would be completely irrelevant as a defense of one's position. Consider it this way: given an accurate thermometer, one's own view that the temperature is 70 degrees Fahrenheit is warranted simply by the use of the thermometer. The fact that dozens of other people (or for that matter, the entire Doxa family) have relied on that thermometer and reached the same conclusion matters not at all. If the thermometer is reliable and accurate, it matters not at all to the truth of the temperature measurement it provides whether anyone else has used it, or what results they suppose they achieved in its use. So again, there is simply nothing at all significant in the fact that some group of moral non-experts agrees about some specific moral issue. Even if they are indeed right about this issue, and even if there are right for the right reasons, their agreement is itself logically irrelevant.

Euthyphro's warring and fighting gods reveal themselves not to be moral experts, and so even if we grant that they all agreed with Euthyphro's position about prosecuting his father, their agreement is not in itself any reason to think that Euthyphro is doing the right thing. If these gods – who are so often clueless in other moral matters, as their fights and warring show – happen to be right about this issue, then it will only be because they have gotten lucky this time, or because on this single issue, they have happened upon the correct and reliable standard of judgment. If so, what is it? Euthyphro has not managed yet to say what the answer might be, but unless he can produce that standard or in some other way show that the gods who agree with him are relying on a reliable standard, Euthyphro's case would not be advanced at all even if he could show that the sorts of gods he imagines all agreed with him.

1.2.6   What if the gods don't disagree? (9d1–9e9)

Perhaps the most important argument in the *Euthyphro*, at least from the point of view of the history of philosophy, is the one that comes next in the dialogue. Having been shown that disagreements among the gods creates a difficulty for his attempt to explain what piety is, Euthyphro seems relieved and encouraged when Socrates suggests (at 9d1–5) that perhaps the way to correct the problems Euthyphro's first attempts have landed him in is simply to specify that impiety is whatever all the gods hate, and piety is what all the gods love – and if some of them love and others hate something, it will be "neither or both" (9d4–5).

This formulation might look a lot like Euthyphro's last attempt to explain what piety is, by relying on the idea that piety is what the gods can all agree upon. But in a subtle – and very important – way this new attempt is actually importantly different from the others Euthyphro has made. In his earlier attempts, notice, Socrates was able to use the fact that the gods actually *did* disagree and fight about things to defeat Euthyphro's attempted account. This new formulation, however, does not require one to suppose that the gods ever actually do disagree and fight about anything – it only says that *if* they do disagree and fight about something, it will either be neither pious nor impious or both pious and impious. Now, Euthyphro seems to suppose that the gods really do disagree and fight about some things; but recall that Socrates expressed doubts about this very matter from the start of their conversation (see 6a7–9). Because the new proposed definition does not require one to suppose that the gods actually do quarrel amongst themselves, it might be shown to be a workable account of piety no matter what one believes about the possibility or frequency of divine disagreements.

One aspect of the proposed account, however, might on its face seem to be nonsensical. According to this new account, if the gods did disagree about something, it would be either neither pious nor impious, or both pious and impious. It is not especially odd to suppose that something could be *neither* pious nor impious – after all, it may be that some things are simply irrelevant to the issue of piety and impiety. Is a speck of dust pious? Is a section of bark on a tree impious? It seems reasonable to suppose that many things will turn out to be simply irrelevant to judgments of piety – even if we suppose (as both Euthyphro and Socrates seem to suppose) that at least *some* things are pious and *some* are impious. What might be more puzzling, however, is Socrates' suggestion that perhaps some things might be both pious and impious. That would seem to be a contradiction, in which case it seems unfair for Socrates to foist such a view onto Euthyphro, whose powers of reasoning seem to be already stretched beyond their limits.

In fact, however, the idea that the same thing might in some way be said to have or display both of a pair of opposite qualities later becomes a mainstay of Platonic philosophy. According to Plato's conception of reality (which he develops later in his career), virtually everything we come into contact with through our senses is an example of this kind of conflicting duality. Let us take an example from Plato's dialogue, the *Phaedo* (74b7–9). Suppose we try to find some sticks or stones that are equal in size. We might find two such things that were *very nearly* equal – more nearly equal than any other pair of sticks or stones we could find. So, we might even say of such a pair, "These are the most equal sticks (or stones) I could find," as if things could be more or less equal. But then, if we think more strictly about it, we might find ourselves thinking, "No. That's not right. Equality is not some 'more-or-less' thing – something is either equal or it is not." In thinking this way, we would have to concede that our pair of sticks or stones was, in fact, not equal. But even if we think in this very strict way, we still have to agree that these sticks or stones are more nearly equal than any other pair we could find. So, in this way, it makes a kind of sense to say that they are *kind of equal* and also *kind of not equal*. They display both qualities, in a sense. Plato uses this idea to postulate another very different sort of thing – the Form of Equal, or Equality Itself, as Plato calls it, which is purely, completely, and absolutely Equal, and which works as a kind of standard for all the more or less equal things we experience through the senses, which we can thereby judge as more or less equal in virtue of their degree of approximation to this standard.

Earlier in the dialogue with Euthyphro, Socrates explicitly told Euthyphro the explanation required would have to be of the *Form* of piety, which could thereby be used as a standard against which all examples of piety could be judged (see 5d4, 6d10–11). Scholars have divided over whether or not we should imagine that the way Socrates formulates his requirement is an anticipation – or even a direct expression – of Plato's "theory of Forms." Most scholars these days, however, think that Socrates' request does not, in fact, require us to suppose he has invoked such a metaphysical theory in the *Euthyphro*. It is true that the so-called "theory of Forms" that Plato later provides (in various versions) seems to be intended to explain the metaphysical basis of judgments of various qualities – piety, justice, goodness, equality, and so on. But several features of the "theory of Forms" are not found here in the *Euthyphro* – most importantly, the idea that the Forms exist in some distinct timeless and changeless reality or "place," which can be contacted only by the intellect and not at all through ordinary perception. Socrates' request for Euthyphro to explain the "single form" of piety can, of course, be understood in such a way. But it does not *have* to be understood in this way. Socrates' point only requires that there is *some* single, objective standard of piety such that all correct judgments of piety will have to be made in terms of this standard – and Socrates asks Euthyphro to express this standard and explain it. The standard *could* turn out to refer to some supra-sensible reality of some sort – and Plato's later work will make clear that he thinks it does refer to such a reality. But what Socrates may be thinking about this issue is never made clear in the *Euthyphro*, and so it seems most reasonable not to presuppose any specific theory about this issue in understanding Socrates' line of questioning in this dialogue. On the other hand, precisely because Socrates seems to allow that some things might be *both* pious and impious – but the standard (the Form he seeks) of piety could not be both pious and impious – at least some anticipation of Plato's more developed later theory, which distinguishes Forms from approximations of Forms, does seem to be present here in the *Euthyphro*.

The new approach proposed at 9d1–5, as we have said, does not presuppose that the gods actually ever do disagree. Although Socrates leaves this question open in the way he formulates the revised explanation for Euthyphro, it will probably make the way the next argument works clearer if you imagine the actual revision in Euthyphro's position to be even more dramatic – that is, what would happen if we suppose that the gods actually don't ever disagree (or at least don't ever disagree on matters having anything to do with piety)?

The ancient Greeks were, of course, polytheistic, and many of their myths did portray the gods in squabbles and wars against one another. One of the most obvious differences between monotheistic religions and polytheistic religions is that in monotheistic religions there is no chance that there can be a disagreement among divinities.[23] But this problem for polytheisms is removed – and the difference between polytheism and monotheism significantly diminished – if we imagine that all of the gods, in a polytheistic religion, agree about moral issues. In Judaism and Christianity, for example, the Ten Commandments play a major role in the formation of religious morality. The faithful are supposed to follow these Commandments as having been given to us directly from Jehovah/God. But if all of the gods in some polytheism were to agree completely on a list of behaviors they expected or demanded from us, the fact that these were commanded by many gods – instead of just one – would not seem to make much difference as to their authority or reliability. As Euthyphro found out earlier, patterning one's behavior after what the gods want cannot be a reliable moral guide if the gods disagree about how we should behave. If they never do disagree, however, would this not prove the same kind of reliable guide – with the same degree of reliability – as monotheists imagine they have when they act in accordance with what they take to be the commands of their single god?

1.3 PIETY DEFINED AS WHAT IS LOVED BY THE GODS

1.3.1 The divine command theory of ethics introduced

In fact, it is not at all uncommon for monotheistic religious people to think that the very standard which Socrates and Euthyphro seek can be given in a formula philosophers call "the divine command theory of ethics." The precise formulation of this theory can be a matter of serious dispute among those inclined to it, but for our purposes a rather generic one will probably work best:

> *Divine command theory*: Good (or goodness) is whatever is commanded (or recommended, or prescribed) by God.

Notice that this theory would not be significantly changed if we imagined it situated within a polytheism that supposed the gods all and always agreed on what they should command, recommend, or prescribe. But whether or not we situate this idea within such a polytheism or – as we encounter it more familiarly these days – in a monotheism, how does this do as providing just the kind of reliable and objective standard Socrates and Euthyphro are trying to articulate?

In one way, Socrates and Euthyphro implicitly confront one problem with this conception of the ethical standard that most philosophers would notice first. Even if we ignore challenges to the theory from those who doubt the existence of God (or the gods), one obvious problem with the divine command theory of ethics is that we must first determine exactly what the god or gods to which the account refers actually do command, recommend, or prescribe. Contemporary monotheisms include many different sects of Judaism, Christianity, and Islam and there can be very sharp (even deadly) disputes among different sects of each of these general religions. So, even though the faithful among any one sect of any one religion might feel confident that their own is "the one true way," others of us – even if we are generally inclined to be religious – might feel some very real doubt as to which religion and which sect actually understands God's commands, recommendations, or prescriptions in exactly the right way. Now, it might seem as if Socrates and Euthyphro shouldn't have to face this same kind of problem, given that they are situated within the same culture. But as Socrates' reactions to Euthyphro's conceptions of the gods shows, even within the same culture there can be no presumption that the exact same beliefs about the gods and their preferences apply. So at the very least, the divine command theory of ethics must confront a serious problem of discerning what divine preferences or commands really are, or the formula it provides for determining what is good will be entirely useless.

1.3.2 Socrates' argument about piety and being loved by the gods (10a1–11b5)

This is not, however, the problem that Socrates identifies with this theory. Instead, Socrates shows that there is something inherently wrong with the divine command theory of ethics, and his objection against it works whether or not we attempt to situate the theory within a monotheistic or a polytheistic context – which is why this argument has become such a famous one in the history of philosophy. Once Euthyphro has plainly affirmed the new account, that piety is what all the gods love and impiety is what all the gods hate, Socrates asks a very subtle question: "Is the pious loved by the gods because it is pious, or is it pious because it is loved?" (10a2–3).

At first, Euthyphro is puzzled by the question – he certainly does not recognize its importance to his view. But as Socrates eventually shows, the answer one gives to this question makes all the difference in the world. So let's go through Socrates' argument in stages. Socrates first begins to explain his important question by getting Euthyphro to get clear on the relationship between a thing's being loved by the gods and the gods loving it. The way in which Socrates establishes this relationship can seem quite confusing, however, so it will help if we consider an example of one the general sort that Socrates gives. Socrates give the examples of being carried, being led, and being seen (10a5–c5), but let's stick just to an example of carrying and being carried. Suppose we notice Mary carrying a telephone book. When we say that something is what it is, or is the way that it is, because of something else, we give an answer to a "why" question. Suppose we want to explain what it is that makes the telephone book a carried thing. So we might ask the "why" question, "Why is that telephone book a carried thing?" The answer seems straightforward: "That telephone book is a carried thing because Mary is carrying it." But now suppose we wanted to ask the "why" question about Mary carrying the telephone book: "Why is Mary carrying the telephone book?" What would we make of this answer: "Mary is carrying the telephone book because the telephone book is a carried thing"? Plainly, that can't be right. To answer the "why" question about Mary's carrying the telephone book we will need to know something more about Mary: what are her intentions, what is her goal, in carrying that telephone book? But even though the telephone book is certainly a carried thing, its being a carried thing is the *result* of Mary's acting on her intentions or goals – and not the explanation *for* Mary's actions, intentions, or goals. So the explanatory relationship between being a carried thing and carrying something only goes one way – we can explain being a carried thing in virtue of something or someone carrying it, but we cannot explain the carrying that *makes* it a carried thing in virtue of that thing *being* a carried thing. So, just as Socrates puts it to Euthyphro, it is never the case that someone's carrying something will be *because* it is carried by them – that, as it were, gets the explanatory "cart before the horse"; it will, however, always be the case that something is a carried thing *because* something or someone carries that thing.

So, in making this point to Euthyphro, Socrates is trying to allow Euthyphro to get clearer on what it means to say that something is what it is or the way it is *because* of something else. Well, then, in the case of loving and being a loved thing, something is a loved thing because something or someone loves that thing. In this case, what is loved by the gods is a loved-by-the-gods thing because the gods love it. But we cannot explain why the gods love it by saying that it is a loved-by-the-gods thing. Now, here is how Euthyphro stated his most recent explanation of what piety is:

> I'd say that the pious is what all of the gods love, and the opposite of this, what all of the gods hate, is the impious.

> (9e1–3)

It was this formulation of Euthyphro's position that led Socrates to ask whether it is loved because it is pious or pious because it is loved. The way this works with the earlier discussion should now be easier to see. What is pious is loved by the gods; so being pious is a loved thing. What is pious is a loved-by-the-gods thing *because* it is loved by the gods – it is not loved by the gods *because* it is a loved-by-the-gods thing. The question we must ask now is the "why" question: *why* do the gods love what is pious?

Now, it appears that to this question, there are three general possibilities:

1   The gods love what is pious *because* it is pious.
2   The gods love what is pious for no reason at all.
3   The gods love what is pious for some reason other than that it is pious.

When Socrates asks the "why" question (at 10d4), Euthyphro gives the first of the three possible answers: the gods love what is pious because it is pious (10d5). But this answer is ruinous to his earlier explanation of what piety is, because it shows that his earlier explanation gets the explanatory relationship between piety and being loved by the gods wrong. Recall that explanatory relationships are *one-way* relationships: if what explains the gods' loving what is pious is the piety of what is pious, then the gods' loving what is pious cannot be what explains the piety of what is pious. What makes something pious cannot be the fact that the gods love it – for it is the thing's being pious that makes it lovable to the gods in the first place. If it weren't pious, they wouldn't love it. So what makes it pious cannot be their loving it, since their loving it is the *result* – and not the explanation – of its being pious. So, if we think – as Euthyphro does – that the gods love what is pious *because* it is pious, then we cannot explain piety in terms of something's being loved by the gods. This is why Socrates scolds Euthyphro at the end of the argument for not explaining what piety is (11a6–b1).

It might occur to us at this point to wonder what would have happened if Euthyphro had chosen some other answer when Socrates asked him why the gods love what is pious (at 10d4). So let us try out each of the other two possible answers. Suppose Euthyphro gave answer (2): the gods love what is pious for no reason at all. If this were true, then there would be in principle no explanation for why the gods love what it pious. There wouldn't be *anything at all* about what is pious that *made* it lovable to the gods, and the *fact* that it is pious would be irrelevant to their loving it. But this raises an obvious problem: if the fact that what is pious *is* pious is irrelevant to why the gods love what is pious (and the fact that what is impious *is* impious is irrelevant to why the gods hate what is impious), then how could it be that the gods all agree about loving what is pious and hating what is impious? Why would there be such a complete unanimity and convergence among the gods about what they love and hate? Answer (2) insists that there is simply *no reason at all* for this! The gods love and hate things for absolutely no reason – they just do it. Of course, if this were true, their loves and hates would be completely senseless! Obviously, this is not at all what a serious theist who takes divine preferences to be reliable moral guides wants to say.

The third answer raises other problems. If the gods love what is pious for some reason *other* that its being pious, then the piety of the thing is really irrelevant to its being loved by the gods. But if so, then there is something fundamentally misleading even in saying that the gods love what is pious. To see this, imagine that John loves Barbara. On a whim, Barbara decides to dye her hair green. Now, if Barbara asked John about his preferences, let's imagine that John would say that he preferred her hair its natural color. But because he really loves Barbara so much, he also loves her hair no matter what color it is. Now, imagine further that many of Barbara's friends are actually quite vocal in disliking her new hair color, and – feeling somewhat defensive, Barbara tells her critical friends, "Well, John loves my green hair!" What do we say about Barbara's claim?

Even though it is technically true that John loves Barbara's green hair, to anyone interested in the question of whether her green hair is attractive or not, John's reaction, plainly, is entirely irrelevant. Indeed, if anything, John's actual judgment of the greenness of Barbara's hair is (however mildly, given his love for Barbara) actually negative. Anyone who knew this could quite rightly object to Barbara's claim by saying, "Look, Barbara, John loves your green hair only because it is *your* hair. He would love it any color at all, and so his loving it has nothing whatever to do with its being green. So don't try to fool us by saying that he loves it – he doesn't! In fact, he would prefer it if you did what we are telling you to do and put it back to your natural color!"

If the gods love what is pious, but it is not the piety of what is pious that they find lovable in what is pious, then *saying* that the gods love what is pious is just as misleading as Barbara's claim that John loves her green hair. The idea is that the piety of what is pious is completely irrelevant to why the gods love it, and so there is only an accidental connection between something's being pious and its being loved by the gods. To one who thinks that there is any *real* or *significant* connection between piety and something's being loved by the gods, this is an unacceptable consequence.

So when Euthyphro answers that the gods love what is pious *because* it is pious, he actually makes a very good – indeed, the only sensible – choice, given the options. But, again, this very choice shows that the explanation of piety Euthyphro offered – as what is loved by (all) the gods – is a failure. It fails because the actual explanation must go the other way around: the gods love what is pious *because* it is pious; but this means that it cannot be pious *because* the gods love it.

1.3.3 The applicability of Socrates' argument to monotheistic divine command theory

Once we understand how Socrates' argument works against Euthyphro's latest proposed account of piety, we can also see why this argument is so decisive against divine command theory even when it is applied to a conception of moral value in relation to a single god. The divine command theory of ethics, again, holds that the way to understand what moral goodness is, is to explain it in terms of whatever God commands (recommends, prescribes). Of one who might be attracted to such a theory, we can imagine Socrates asking, "Well, then, does God command such things because they are good, or are they good because God commands them?"

Now, the same sorts of options apply in response to this question as those Euthyphro faced:

1 God commands what He does *because* it is good.
2 God commands what He does for no reason at all.
3 God commands what He does for some reason other than that it is good.

If we are inclined to think that option (1) is the correct answer to such a Socratic question, we must admit that the divine command theory is thereby defeated: if whatever God commands is commanded by God because it is good, then its goodness is the explanation of *why* God commands it and that goodness thus cannot be explained *by* God's commanding it. It has to be good *in order* for God to command it – it doesn't *become* good by *being* commanded!

Think of it this way: if you go to the store to buy some bread, then your intention to buy bread explains your going to the store. If someone then asks, "Well, why did you buy the bread?" you can't then answer, "Well, because I went to the store!" This gets the explanation wrong. You didn't buy the bread because you went to the store – as if you went to the store for no reason and then, when there, it occurred to you to buy some bread; you went to that store for that purpose, to buy the bread. So you can't say that you bought the bread because you went to the store – it's the other way around: you went to the store because you wanted to buy some bread. So, similarly, if God commands something because it is good, then its goodness explains the command and not vice versa. But divine command theory holds that the explanation goes the other way around: it is good *because* God commands it.

Now suppose you still find yourself attracted to the divine command theory, but you understand that option (1) defeats your view, so you decide to defend the explanation the other way around: it is good, you claim, because God commands it. So now Socrates asks, "OK, then, why does God command it?" and now you must give one of the other two answers:

2   God commands what He does for no reason at all.
3   God commands what He does for some reason other than that it is good.

It is probably already obvious why these are not going to be satisfactory replies to such a question, but just to be very clear let us look at each one in order. Suppose (2) is your answer. This answer means that God's commands are inherently arbitrary and whimsical. God has no reason whatsoever for doing things one way or another. (Imagine God thinking about what to command, or even whether to command anything, and settling on what to command just by flipping coins.) Moreover, because God is fully in control of what is commanded (they are *God's* commands, after all!), God can decide to change commands from day to day or even minute to minute. Maybe it gets boring where God is, and so changing commands is a way to keep things interesting. "*Thou shalt not kill*! Oh! Wait a minute! It's Friday, isn't it? Oh, well, then, for today, *Thou shalt kill*! On second thought, we did that last Friday. This Friday, let's make it, *Thou shalt commit adultery*." It really doesn't make any difference to *God* what is commanded, after all, since there is no reason for God to make any one command over another: nothing is good or bad, according to this account, except when (and only when, and then because) God commands it. *"Thou shalt burn and torture small children until I change my mind!"* Obviously, this would make God into a very irrational being, and would leave the moral order a matter of simple (albeit divine) whim.

And suppose we now ask, all right, by the divine command theory, things are good *because* God commands them. So, "good" just means "commanded by God." But now let's ask, *why* should we obey these commands? If the answer is that we should obey them because God commands them, we might ask, but what is it about God that deserves our obedience? Theists (or monotheists, at any rate) generally believe that God is a good being, even a perfect being. But consider what it means to call God good if the divine command theory were correct: "God is good" now means just that God commands you to say (or believe) that God is good; that's all. Of course, *any* being powerful enough to enforce its will over mere human beings might make such a command, but why should we accept it? Satan might make some command of this sort, but should we believe it – or if Satan commands us, should we obey, and if so why – or if not, why not? Notice that if we are committed to the divine command theory of ethics, we can't say that we should accept God's command to say (or believe) that God is good, because that's the good thing to do. If we should accept God's commands *because* they are good, we obviously are back to the first option again – the commands aren't good *because* God commands them; God commands them *because* they are good. Similarly, Satan's commands aren't good (or bad) because Satan commands them. We should not obey Satan's commands because *Satan* is bad. But Satan isn't bad simply because someone (or something) *says* Satan is bad – even God! If God says that Satan is bad, it is because Satan *is* bad. So, again, the goodness or badness of things explains why God commands what God commands, and not the other way around.

But we haven't yet considered option (3). Might it not be that God commands what He does for some reason other than that it is good? Now here we have two options: either (A) God commands only good things, or (B) God commands some things that are good and some that are bad. Obviously, if (B) is the case, then the divine command theory cannot be correct – if God commands some bad things, then it can't be that goodness *just is* whatever God commands! What if (A) is the case? Well, if God commands only good things, but God commands them for some reason other than that they are good, then we should suppose that God commands them because this other reason is what makes things good. Suppose, for example, that God commands things because they are conducive to the survival and flourishing of living things. Well, then, *this* is what makes things good – this is *why* things are good – and God knows this, and that's why God makes commands. But that shows that the divine command theory is wrong – after all, in this or any other version of option (3) in which God commands only good things, it is not, after all, God's commanding something that makes that thing good – it is, rather, that God commands it because it is conducive to the survival and flourishing of living things. And if *that* is what makes things good, then notice their goodness *does not depend* upon God's commanding them, but the other way around: God's commanding them depends on what makes things good (namely, the survival or flourishing of living things – or whatever else it might be that makes things good, which God recognizes). One way or another, then, divine command theory is shown to get the explanation of moral value (or any specific moral value, such a piety) exactly backwards: God commands (or loves) things *because* they are good (or pious), or else because of whatever it is that makes them good or pious; they are not good (or pious) just because God commands (or loves) them.

1.4   SOCRATES TAKES THE LEAD

1.4.1   Euthyphro's complaint (11b6–e2)

By the end of the argument we have been discussing, Euthyphro is obviously bewildered and somewhat frustrated:

> But Socrates, I can't tell you what I know. What we propose somehow always moves around us and doesn't want to stay where we set it down.
>
> (11b6–8)

Socrates' response is light-hearted: what Euthyphro is saying about him makes him sound like one of his ancestors, Daedalus. Daedalus was the legendary Greek inventor. Here is what J. E. Zimmerman's *Dictionary of Classical Mythology* has to say about him:

> **Daedalus.** The first aviator. A descendant of Erechtheus, king of Athens, he was the most ingenious artist of the age. He invented the axe, wedge, wimble, level, sails for ships, and many other mechanical instruments. Talos, his nephew, promised to be as ingenious an inventor as his uncle so Daedalus killed him. After this murder Daedalus and his son Icarus fled Athens to Crete; there Daedalus built the famous labyrinth for Minos [where the Minotaur was kept]. When Minos ordered him confined in the labyrinth, Daedalus made wings with feathers and wax for himself and Icarus, but the wax on Icarus' wings melted and he fell into what is now the Icarian Sea. The father landed at Cumae, where he built a temple to Apollo.
>
> (1971, 79)

Socrates' ironical comparison of himself to Daedalus is made more amusing when he goes on to say that unlike his ancestor, who could invent things that could then move about on their own, Socrates is able to make other people's creations move about on their own – and yet, the worst irony for Socrates, as he puts it, is that

> I'm wise unwillingly. For I wanted my arguments to stay put and remain settled more than to have the riches of Tantalus in addition to the wisdom of Daedalus.
>
> (11d6–e1)

Socrates turns Euthyphro's complaint into a joke. But as it turns out, this sort of reaction to Socrates is no laughing matter. In Plato's *Apology*, as we will see, Socrates explains to his jurors why he thinks he has been put on trial, and one of the prejudices he mentions there that is often associated with philosophers is that they "make the weaker argument the stronger" (see *Ap.* 19b5–c1, 23d7); that is, they are trained word-twisters who can confuse and trip people up in debates, and make very implausible or immoral positions seem quite plausible. For people like Euthyphro, who begin their conversations with Socrates puffed up with pride in their knowledge and expertise, Socrates' uncanny ability to expose their ignorance and reveal their terrible confusions no doubt seemed a kind of devious cleverness. But as Socrates protests to Euthyphro, it is not *Socrates'* fault that Euthyphro's positions end up seeming twisted and confused – they are *Euthyphro's* words, after all, and it is what Euthyphro says that is creating the problems. Socrates only reveals the problems inherent in the words. But we can well imagine Euthyphro's discomfort at this point; and it is all too easy to imagine that there were many others who found themselves in a similar position, when they were confronted by Socrates ... and some of these surely held a grudge against the philosopher in the aftermath of their humiliation. In Plato's *Apology*, this very process is the real and whole truth of why he ended up on trial for his life (see *Ap.* 23c2–24b2).

Another example of such a confrontation, which would perhaps explain the animosity that Anytus, one of the prosecution team, had for Socrates, may be found in Plato's *Meno*. There, Socrates invites Anytus to join the discussion about how and by whom virtue might be taught. Anytus does not realize it at first, but he is a very vulnerable target for Socrates; for Anytus is a famous and very influential politician. Like Euthyphro, politicians were (and are today!) generally people who supposed they know enough or have such wisdom or expertise that they can make important decisions that affect not only themselves, but also all of the other citizens in a place. On the basis of his "examinations" of others, which he describes and explains in the *Apology* (20e8–24b2), Socrates has reason to believe that the kind of arrogant confidence politicians rely upon in taking such roles in the city is wholly without foundation. Socrates describes one such encounter this way:

> After thoroughly examining him – I needn't mention his name, Athenians, but he was one of the politicians that I had this sort of experience with. After conversing with him, I thought that this guy

seems to be wise to many other people and most of all to himself, yet he isn't. And then I tried to show him that he thought he is wise but he isn't. And so, as a result, I became hated by him and by many of those who were there.

(*Ap.* 21c2–d2)

The episode Socrates describes in this passage in the *Apology* could easily be the same one that Plato recounts in the *Meno,* for just as Euthyphro discovers, Anytus finds that it is easier to pretend to have some special wisdom when Socrates isn't there to expose the ignorance that underlies such pretense. Here are Anytus's final words, as he makes a hasty retreat from his own discussion with Socrates:

I think, Socrates, that you too easily say bad things about people. I would advise you, if you're willing to be persuaded by me, to be careful. It may be the same even in other cities that it is easier to do harm to someone than to do good for them, but it most certainly is true here. I think you realize this yourself.

(*Meno* 94e3–95a1)

There can be no mistaking the menace inherent in Anytus's words here, and no doubt Plato has included this exchange in the *Meno* partly to explain the politician's participation in the trial of Socrates. So when we find Euthyphro accusing Socrates, in effect, of "making the weaker argument the stronger," we should surely recognize his discomfort and his response to it as one example of how Socrates ended up in so much trouble. Under the circumstances, moreover, we should also see this interlude as part of Plato's *defense* of Socrates: although people certainly did become confused and angry when they talked with Socrates, what they might say about the episodes that led them to feel these ways may not at all be well explained by them. The true explanation of these reactions, in Plato's writings, is given by Socrates – those who became angry with Socrates were only the victims of their own arrogance and ignorance.

1.4.2   Socrates' own proposal (11e2–5)

Despite Euthyphro's obvious frustration, he is still at this point will-ing to continue the discussion. He is, however, at a loss here as to what he should say next. In most of Plato's early or Socratic dia-logues, once an interlocutor reaches this point (called "*aporia*" – being at a loss), the conversation ends. In Plato's *Apology* (23b4–7), Socrates claims to spend his life searching out people who seem (or claim) to be wise, and if he finds that they are not wise, he shows them that they are not. Usually, he seems to think he has adequately achieved this goal with someone when he reveals to them – as he has now done with Euthyphro – that by expressing their supposed "wisdom" they can be shown to be terribly confused and at a loss.

Here in the *Euthyphro*, however, Socrates make the unusual and very interesting move of taking the lead in the discussion. Exactly what we are to make of his maneuver is controversial. On the one hand, there is at least some reason to suppose that Euthyphro has not yet had his ignorance and *lack* of wisdom adequately revealed to him, for his complaint reveals that he thinks his problems are the result of something that *Socrates* has done, when really they are the result of his own confused and thoughtless views. So, perhaps Socrates continues here – even though Euthyphro seems to have nothing more to contribute – because he notices that Euthyphro still needs more "work," as it were, to make his ignorance evident to him.

On the other hand, it is quite obvious from the way Euthyphro responds with such sluggishness and uncertainty to the way Socrates presses on that what follows for the rest of the dialogue cannot be supposed to be coming entirely from Euthyphro. It is now *Socrates* who is proposing views for consideration, and though he requires Euthyphro to make several decisions and to make sev-eral commitments along the way, there is no reason to suppose that any of what emerges would have been forthcoming without Socrates' own contributions of ideas for Euthyphro to respond to.

Now, some scholars argue that we must conclude that the views Socrates begins to introduce here are his own views, which he may or may not have worked out completely, but which he thinks are better than any other views he has encountered. (They could hardly be worse or more confused than those he has heard from Euthyphro!) Other scholars have argued, on the contrary, that the views Socrates expresses in the rest of the dialogue are simply more "bait" with which to hook Euthyphro into continuing the conversation and having his ignorance and ineptitude even more plainly revealed. There can probably be no decisive argument for either of these positions, but we are inclined to think that the views Socrates expresses at this point are his own. There seem to us to be two reasons for thinking this. First, we find the views that Socrates works to get Euthyphro to understand and respond to entirely consistent with everything else we can learn about Socrates in Plato's early dialogues. If we think of Socrates as actually holding some incompletely formed version of the views he begins to articulate in the rest of this dialogue, it can help us to explain and understand other things he says and does elsewhere. Second, Euthyphro quite obviously does not at all understand the views that Socrates begins to introduce, at least at first, and if all that Socrates is trying to do at this point is to run Euthyphro around in more circles to expose his ignorance even more clearly, we can't think of any good reason why he would choose to do this by introducing ideas that Euthyphro can obviously only barely follow. It just seems to us that the most effective way to reveal someone's pretense of wisdom as a sham is to show them that *even when they think they know what they're talking about,* they are confused. But showing someone that they are confused about views and issues they never supposed they understood all that well anyway seems like a waste of time and not a very effective way to undermine their pretense of wisdom about matters they think they *do* understand. If this is right, Socrates' comments between 11b4, where he takes the lead in developing a new definition, and 14b8, where he signals that he can no longer agree with Euthyphro, are likely to express a number of substantive claims that Socrates actually believes about piety. As we shall soon see, our view that Socrates is beginning to express something of his own conception of piety here gains significant support from what he says in other dialogues about the nature of the various moral virtues.

1.4.3   Piety as a part of justice (11e4–12e5)

At 11e4–5, Socrates asks Euthyphro if he thinks "all of the pious is just." Euthyphro readily agrees to this, but when Socrates turns the question around, and asks whether all of the just is pious, or if their relationship is such that all of the pious is just, but some of the just is, and some is not pious, Euthyphro replies, "I'm not following what you're saying" (12a3).

Socrates responds with obvious irony about Euthyphro's combination of youth and wisdom, relative to Socrates, and then offers to clarify his question by making an analogous case in the relationship between reverence and fear. Socrates explains his view of their relationship, with Euthyphro's agreement, in such a way as to say that wherever there is reverence there is also fear, "since hasn't whoever revered and felt ashamed about something at the same time both feared and worried about a bad reputation?" (12b9–c1). But it is not the case that wherever there is fear there is also reverence, because many people fear several sorts of things without also feeling any reverence for what they fear. From this asymmetry, Socrates draws the following conclusion:

> Then it isn't right to say that "where there is fear there is reverence," but where there is reverence there is fear; however, it's not the case that everywhere there's fear, there's reverence. For I think that fear's more extensive than reverence, for reverence is a part of fear – just as odd is a part of number, so that it's not that wherever there's number, there's odd number, but wherever there's odd number there's number.
>
> (12c3–8)

Having in this way made clear what he means by one thing being "a part of" another, Socrates presses his initial question to Euthyphro in these terms: is piety "a part of justice," where justice is "more extensive" than piety (12c10–d3)? Euthyphro's response doesn't exactly ring with confidence, but he agrees that it seems to be that piety is "a part of" justice, in the way that odd number is "a part of" number. Throughout the rest of the conversation between

Socrates and Euthyphro, this way of conceiving of the relationship between piety and justice is accepted.

The most controversial feature of this particular agreement between Socrates and Euthyphro is that it seems to commit Socrates – assuming, again, that in this passage he is expressing his own views – to a very different sort of relationship among these two virtues (piety and justice) than he seems to express elsewhere. The *Euthyphro* is not the only place in which Socrates seems to introduce the idea that some virtues can be proper parts of others, or that some virtues are proper parts of virtue conceived as a whole. In Plato's *Laches*, for example, it is Socrates who introduces into the discussion the idea that courage is a proper part of virtue (190c6–d5; repeated at 198a1–b2). Nothing in the context of his claim in that dialogue suggests that he is expressing any view but his own about this. Similarly, in Plato's *Meno*, it is again Socrates who introduces the notion that each of the virtues is a *part* of the whole of virtue (78d7–e1), when his interlocutor has given him no reason to talk about virtue – or any of the several virtues – in such a way. So the idea that there are part–whole relationships among the virtues, or between the virtues and virtue as a whole, is one that appears often enough in our texts, always introduced by Socrates himself, that we can safely suppose that Socrates believes that such relationships exist among the virtues and within virtue itself.

But in Plato's *Protagoras*, Socrates seems to be arguing for what looks like a very different view of the relationships between all of the virtues, including justice and piety, which has come to be called "the unity of the virtues." At one point in the *Protagoras*, Socrates seems to be ready to affirm that all of the virtues are "one and the same" (333b4–6). But it would seem this can't possibly be the case if some virtues are proper parts of other virtues, or of virtue as a whole – since if all of the virtues are "one and the same," each one will also be exactly identical to each other one, and will also be identical to the whole of virtue.

There have been roughly three general strategies for resolving this problem, which collectively appear to cover all of the available logical ground. Some scholars[24] have argued that there can be no reconciliation of the two positions. Others[25] have argued that the account Socrates gives in the *Protagoras* is the one we should attribute to him, and have then gone on to try to explain the apparently inconsistent versions given in other texts in an appropriate way. But most scholars[26] have tried to come up with accounts that have attempted to explain Socrates' comments in the *Protagoras* in a way that makes them compatible with his talk of part and whole relationships in other dialogues. Although this is hardly the place to examine every one of the variety of views scholars have offered, it may be worthwhile to consider a few of the most influential ones to see how well they explain Socrates' comments here in the *Euthyphro*.

Perhaps the first and most controversial account of the relationships between the virtues was the one given in 1973 by Terry Penner, which has come to be known as the "identity thesis." Penner argues that Socrates literally means what he claims in the *Protagoras*: each of the different names of the virtues refers to the exact same psychological state. Accordingly, each of the virtues truly is "one and the same" as all of the others. They are all the same psychological state, because, as we discover later in the *Protagoras*, they all turn out to be nothing other than *knowledge* of good and evil (361a3–b7). Over the years, there have been many criticisms of Penner's view, but in our view the most effective of these is that this account cannot be squared with Socrates' talk about virtue – or certain individual virtues – having parts, as he does in several other dialogues, including here in the *Euthyphro*.

We said earlier that some scholars have claimed that we should not understand Socrates as introducing his own views here in the last part of the *Euthyphro*. This, indeed, is what Penner and his supporters have had to say about *all* of the passages in which Socrates talks about parts and wholes among the virtues. Instead, Socrates proposes this idea to trip up his interlocutors, and perhaps if they are clever enough, they may be able to figure out later that they were tripped up by supposing that virtue has parts (or some individual virtue, such as justice, has parts). Such a reading, if plausible, would indeed allow Socrates' views about the virtues to be consistent (and best understood in accordance with the identity thesis) – but the question is, is this reading of what Socrates says about parts and wholes really plausible?

We have already given several reasons for why we think it makes much better sense to understand this section of the *Euthyphro* in such a way as to suppose that Socrates is, in fact, introducing his own views. In this passage – and indeed, every other one in which part–whole relationships among the virtues (or within virtue itself) are introduced – it is always Socrates who introduces this idea. Those who wish to defend the identity thesis by claiming that when Socrates introduces the idea of parts and wholes, he realizes that the premise is faulty must explain why Socrates would do that in each case – what does Socrates or his interlocutor gain by considering such a faulty premise? Does this advance Socrates' interest in revealing his interlocutor's ignorance? How so? If the interlocutor is shown to be confused on the basis of a premise that he or she never accepted anyway, this only shows that they cannot defend *that* premise – but that premise wasn't anything they believed in the first place! Or should we simply suppose that at a certain point in his conversations, Socrates simply abandons his main goal to reveal the interlocutor's ignorance, and simply toys with his opponents, running them around in circles simply for sport?

In Euthyphro's case, the implausibility of the identity thesis is most evident. As we noted earlier, the idea of part–whole relationships is so far from anything Euthyphro himself believed that Socrates has to explain it very patiently to the younger man – and even then, the discussion only continues when Euthyphro seems to go along with what Socrates says without any obvious conviction in his agreement. And if the whole point of introducing the part–whole idea is to trip Euthyphro up again, it is not at all clear what value Socrates could suppose he would thereby achieve. Euthyphro is already completely confused and at a loss when Socrates introduces this idea, and there is no reason to believe at the end of the dialogue that Euthyphro's conceit of wisdom has been any further deflated than it was when he found himself at a loss earlier. He does, of course, leave the conversation in some haste, and as we said earlier (when we discussed the beginning and the end of the dialogue) there is good reason to count this as a Socratic victory of sorts. But it is not clear that the same victory couldn't have been achieved by Socrates simply by forcing

Euthyphro to face up to what his being at a loss earlier in the dialogue shows about his "wisdom." At least this much is clear – there is absolutely no reason at all to think that Euthyphro is left in a position to think that his error, in this later discussion, was in agreeing with the premise (one, again, that would never have occurred to him in the first place without Socrates proposing it) that piety is a part of justice. Euthyphro's failure later in the conversation, as we'll see, actually suggests a very different view about the relationships between the virtues than the one proposed by the identity thesis.

Interestingly enough, however, the idea of part–whole relationships among the virtues also creates problems for what has generally been regarded as the main rival to Penner's account, the "equivalence thesis," which was first and most famously argued by Gregory Vlastos. According to the equivalence thesis, each of the virtues refers to a distinct piece of moral knowledge, but because Socrates is convinced that no one can have any of the virtues without being wise – and because if one is wise, then one will have *all* of the other virtues – it turns out that anyone who has any of the virtues will also have every other one of them. But it is not clear how this view is any better at explaining how there can be part–whole relationships among the virtues than the identity thesis was. After all, if the equivalence thesis is correct, there would be no cases of someone being just that was not also a case of someone being pious – since, according to the equivalence thesis, everyone who was just would also be pious and vice versa. But when Socrates gets Euthyphro to agree that piety is a *part* of justice in a way that is similar to the odd being a part of number, it follows that there will be no examples of piety that are not examples of justice, but there *will be* examples of justice that are *not* examples of piety. So it looks like the equivalence thesis does no better at explaining how there can be part–whole relationships among the virtues than the identity thesis does.

1.4.4 *The virtues as* powers *in the* Protagoras

One of the most striking features of the discussion of the virtues in the *Protagoras* is that it actually introduces two different sorts of part–whole relationships: the different virtues might all be parts of virtue in the way that the mouth, nose, eyes, and ears are parts of one's face, or the different virtues might all be parts of virtue in the way that different pieces of gold will all be "parts" of gold, where there is no difference between the parts themselves, or the parts and the whole, other than size (*Protagoras* 329d3–8). The way these two sorts of part–whole relationships differ, according to Socrates, is that the different parts of the face all have different *powers* (*dunameis*), whereas the parts of gold would all have the same power (*Protagoras* 330a4–b3, 349a8–c5). In the entire discussion of the *Protagoras*, in fact, it is plain all along that virtue (and the virtues) would be counted as *one thing* if it were shown to consist in a single power; and it would be counted as several things (or the several virtues would be counted as distinct entities) if they were shown to consist in distinct powers. So the question in the *Protagoras* is this: in virtue, and in the several virtues, is there a single power in all, or are there several different powers involved? The answer to this question in the *Protagoras*, as we have seen, is that there seems to be a single power at work in all of the virtues, and this is what it means when Socrates suggests that all of the virtues are "one and the same" thing (333b4–6). Later on, we find Socrates characterizing the kind of power that is shared by all of the virtues as a kind of *knowledge* (*epistêmê* – 361a6–b2).

1.4.5 How the virtues have different aims or goals (12e6–13e13)

Once Euthyphro has agreed that piety is a part of justice, Socrates challenges him to explain *what* part of justice it is. Euthyphro obliges by explaining that

> The part of justice that seems to me to be both holy and pious is what concerns service to the gods, and the remaining part of justice is what concerns service to men.
>
> (12e6–9)

Socrates' first response is uncharacteristically favorable and encouraging, but he then goes on to ask for a bit more explanation of what Euthyphro means by "service to the gods." One kind of service, he explains, is the kind in which one improves what is served. But he and Euthyphro quickly agree that this can't be the kind of service that is rendered to the gods in the case of piety, on the obvious ground that it is not "within human capacity" to improve the gods (12e10–13c10). So Euthyphro suggests that it is a different kind of service that is rendered to the gods in piety – more like the kind of service that is given by slaves to their masters, that is, a kind of "assistance" (13d6–7). And then Socrates asks Euthyphro what our assistance is supposed to accomplish for the gods (13e6–9). Those who assist physicians aim at health – for that is the goal or aim (*ergon*) of medicine (13d10–12). Those who assist shipbuilders aim at producing a ship, since that is the goal or aim of shipbuilding (13e1–2). Those who assist house-builders aim at producing a house, since that is the goal or aim of house-building (13e4). So, Socrates asks, what is the "all glorious" goal or aim the gods accomplish with our service (13e6–7)?

The idea that justice and piety are both examples of service opens up Socrates' question: service to what end? It is plain in this context, then, that the difference between piety and justice is to be understood in terms of some difference in their goals or aims. Notice, too, that the analogies Socrates provides are all to certain sorts of distinct, specialized skills (medicine, shipbuilding, house-building), generally called "arts" or "crafts." The artisans or crafts-people have certain kinds of knowledge or ability, and they use this knowledge or ability to achieve certain sorts of goals or aims. So, too, according to Socrates' craft-analogy, piety and justice (and in other dialogues, all of the other virtues, too) are craft-like in the sense that they consist in knowledge that achieves certain sorts of aims or produces certain sorts of goals. The question Euthyphro must answer, then, is what is the distinguishing aim or goal of piety?

Now, it will soon become apparent that Euthyphro is unable to specify what the "all glorious" goal or aim of piety is, and the dialogue will end when, confused and frustrated once again, he hurries off. We are now in a position, however, to see how Socrates can be understood as maintaining a consistent picture of the relationships among the virtues. In the *Protagoras*, recall, we found him arguing for a kind of "unity" of the virtues, where that unity was to be conceived in terms of some *power* (*dunamis*) they share, where this power is to be understood as some sort of knowledge. But in the *Euthyphro* and in other dialogues, we find Socrates distinguishing the virtues into parts and wholes in virtue of different aims or goals (*erga*) they achieve. So, another way to put the questions we confronted about the different things Socrates says about the relationships between the virtues is: can the same *power* or *knowledge* be applied to distinct *aims* or *goals*, such that the different applications might reasonably be distinguished in the same sort of way as different crafts are distinguished? If so, can some of these applications be characterized as "parts" of other, more generic applications?

Consider the specialized skill – the "craft" – of riding a motorcycle.[27] Generally speaking, the accelerator on a motorcycle is in the right twist-grip on the handlebars. The clutch is a lever (much like the rear brake on a bicycle with hand-brakes) on the left handlebar, and the left foot operates the gearshift. The right foot operates the rear brake, and the front brake is a lever on the right handlebar. To one who has not ridden a motorcycle before, it can take some time to get used to these controls – to gain the skill necessary to ride the motorcycle. Now consider the skill of riding a snowmobile – we find a somewhat simplified version of the same control configurations on a snowmobile as those we find on a motorcycle – so much so that one trained on a motorcycle will be able to use the controls on a snowmobile immediately, without any further training, whereas one who has never ridden either kind of machine will have to go through some training to learn to use the controls on either one of them. The operation of the shared controls on either machine might be characterized as the *same set of skills* – the same *power* or *knowledge*. And yet we wouldn't say that there was *no* difference between motorcycling and snowmobiling, since in each of these two activities, one practices the relevant skills in order to control very different machines in very different sorts of settings. So, this is an example of different applications of the same set of skills, yielding different "arts" or "crafts": the art of motorcycling, and the art of snowmobiling.

But can the same skill or set of skills be applied in different ways, such that one way might be counted as a *part* of some other more generic art or craft? To see how this might work, let's consider a different sort of example.[28] Many forms of navigation (especially the different versions of coastal navigation, such as sea-coast navigation, harbor navigation, and river navigation) employ the geometrical technique of triangulation. The same technique is employed, as well, in surveying. Although each uses the same basic skill, the sorts of problems each craft (navigation and surveying) is intended to solve are so different that we distinguish the two activities as different crafts or skills. Similarly, we might call harbor or river navigation "parts" of the more generic activity of coastal navigation – we distinguish each one by its special aims or goals (navigating harbors or rivers), but do not suppose, in making such a distinction, that the basic skill involved is different in either case. So, we might say that the most generic skill in all of these cases is triangulation. Surveying and coastal navigation are specific applications of this skill (such that wherever we find surveying, we find triangulation, but not vice versa – just as we find in Socrates' example of odd number and number), and within coastal navigation, we find even more specific applications in sea-coast navigation, harbor navigation, and river navigation.

In the *Euthyphro* and in several others of Plato's early dialogues, we find Socrates characterizing his own view of the virtues in such a way as to compare them to the arts or crafts. In the *Protagoras*, we find him arguing that each and every virtue consists in the same *power* or *knowledge*. In the *Euthyphro* and other dialogues, he distinguishes the virtues in terms of different *aims* or *goals*, and on the basis of these differences, he says that each virtue is a *part* of virtue as a whole, and that some virtues are parts of other virtues. When we consider if the same sort of "unity" can apply to different arts or crafts, which are distinguishable in terms of different aims or goals, we find that each of the apparently conflicting claims Socrates makes about the virtues can, in fact, fit into a consistent and coherent general conception of virtue and the several virtues.

1.4.6   The end of the discussion (13e11–16a4)

When Socrates asks Euthyphro to specify the aim or goal that distinguishes piety as a part of justice, Euthyphro's first attempt to do so is impossibly vague.

SOCRATES: So say, by Zeus, what is this all-glorious result that the gods accomplish by using our assistance?

EUTHYPHRO: Many wonderful things.

(13e11–14)

Plainly, this won't distinguish piety from any other sort of activity whose aims or goals we value, and Socrates is quick to point this out: generals produce victories in wars, and farmers produce food, but plainly neither of these is the same as piety. Euthyphro needs to be much more specific. But his attempt to do so lands him back in trouble again. He says that praying and sacrificing in such a way as to please the gods are what piety consists in. Socrates immediately scolds Euthyphro for the inadequacy of his answer, since it plainly does not specify the special aim or goal that distinguishes piety from (the rest of) justice. Instead, now Euthyphro claims that piety is pleasing the gods through prayer and sacrifice. Euthyphro seems to have a kind of exchange relationship in mind: prayer is a kind of asking for things from the gods, whereas sacrifice is a kind of giving to the gods (14c8–10). What is interesting about this conception of prayer and sacrifice is how very limited in focus it is: not all forms of prayer are petitionary, of course. Some prayers simply offer recognition or gratitude to (the) god(s). But Euthyphro plainly ignores such other forms of prayer, focusing instead only on the benefits of prayer and sacrifice: "These things preserve private households and the common good of cities" (14b4–5). Socrates has no trouble seeing the inadequacy of this account: it turns religious activity into a kind of crass business arrangement between human beings and divinities (14e6–8). But business arrangements are based upon traded goods or services, and this raises a very serious problem for Euthyphro's "business arrangement" account of prayer and sacrifice. Socrates presses the point:

> But tell me, what benefit do the gods happen to get from the gifts they receive from us? What they give is clear to everyone. For we have nothing good that they don't provide us. But how are they benefited by what they get from us? Or do we get so much more from them from this business, that we get all good things from them but they get nothing good from us.
>
> (14e10–15a5)

Some business deal Euthyphro has in mind! We get everything, and the gods get nothing! Even stupid Euthyphro realizes that something has gone awry in this account, so he insists that the gods do get *something* back from us in this "deal": they are pleased and gratified by the honor and respect they get from us. And this is valuable to them, because it is what they love best (15b1–3). So, Euthyphro's final attempt to explain what piety is has returned to the defective account he gave earlier: piety is what is loved by the gods (15b4–6).

In returning to this inadequate explanation, Euthyphro's "wisdom" about piety is revealed yet again as a complete sham, and Socrates is quick to point out that it is not *Socrates* who is at fault for the persistent wheel-spinning and confusion in this conversation (15b7–c10). So, Socrates says, they have to start over again:

> For if you didn't know clearly what the pious and the impious are, you couldn't possibly be trying to prosecute your elderly father for murder on behalf of a servant, and you'd fear that you'd be at risk with respect to the gods that you would be wrong in doing this and would be held in contempt by men. But now I'm quite confident that you think you know what the pious and the impious are. So tell me, good Euthyphro, and don't hide what you believe it is.
>
> (15d4–e2)

Of course, Euthyphro has no such wisdom to share with Socrates and never did. The great expert on piety has been shown to be a complete phony – one whose pretense of wisdom has managed to persuade him to embark on the reckless and impious course of prosecuting his own father for the most dubious of reasons. Euthyphro does not concede all of this, of course, and Socrates still says of him, "You think you know what the pious and impious are." But Euthyphro's confidence has plainly been shaken, and he is not ready to try again. Instead, he hastily departs, claiming some errand he has forgotten until right now. Right, Euthyphro – we all can see what is really going on!

We said at the beginning of our commentary on the *Euthyphro* that the way the dialogue ends should be seen as Socrates having achieved at least temporarily what Euthyphro's family had failed to achieve – at least for this day, Euthyphro will desist from his proposed prosecution of his father. As satisfying as this result might be, we should also realize that it is a very fragile and perhaps only very temporary victory. Euthyphro may well go away and think about the conversation and decide again – as he had earlier in the discussion – that all of the dead ends of the discussion had been Socrates' fault and not his own. Perhaps he might go away and think of some answer to Socrates' questions that seem to him to be more adequate than the ones he actually gave, and which would again restore his confidence that prosecuting his father was the right thing to do. So despite his hasty retreat on this day, Euthyphro might again proceed to prosecute his father. That we hear of no further prosecution from later sources is not reassuring – too much of the history of the ancient Greeks (including any relevant history involving Euthyphro) is lost to us.

In Plato's *Apology*, as we will see, Socrates makes no claim that anyone who speaks with him is ever significantly taught anything of great value or improved by doing so. The only hope he holds out for improving ourselves is if we lead what he calls "the examined life" (38a5–6), by which he means not one or an occasional philosophical conversation in which we examine the principles by which we live and on the basis of which we act, but a dedicated and frequent (if not daily) confrontation with ourselves, through which we consider and reconsider our whole lives and purposes. Socrates is the one whom the oracle identifies as the "wisest of men," on the basis of his recognition of his own profound ignorance (*Ap.* 23a5–b4), and he proclaims his innocence of the charge of impiety on this ground: everything he has done has been a service to the god (*Ap.* 23c1, 30a7) on the basis of this oracle and his understanding of its meaning. If we are to come up with an answer to the question that Euthyphro so badly answered in the *Euthyphro* – what sort of service to the god(s), and with what aim or goal, does piety consist in? – we may best look to the sort of service performed by Socrates himself.

NOTES

1   Essentially all of the details of the legal setting provided in this section are derived directly from the account given in MacDowell 1978, 237–242.

2   Some scholars seem simply to assume that Socrates is there for the *anakrisis* – see, e.g. McPherran 1996, 31 – but for the reasons we give below, we think this is unlikely.

3   Xenophon's version gives a different word for "introducing."

4   See Tulin 1996, 68–71 and the sources he cites.

5   See Burnet 1924, 105.

6   See, e.g. Tulin 1996, McPherran 1996, 32 n.11. The opposite view is argued by MacDowell 1963; Panagiotou 1974; Gargarin 1979, 302–313; Sealey 1983.

7   The other two texts are Drako's Code (IG i³ 104) and pseudo-Demosthenes 47.68–73 (*Against Euergos and Mnesiboulos*). All three texts are discussed at length in Tulin 1996, who reaches a conclusion about the restrictiveness of the law that is opposite to ours. These are also the three texts cited in MacDowell 1963 and 1978 (111), whose position we follow. We find it highly implausible that murder would be in principle beyond the reach of Athenian law if anyone did not have family members (no more distant than cousins, according to the law) to instigate a murder trial – as if it might be a kind of murderous "open season" on anyone without such family ties in Athens. This, however, is what the more restrictive interpretation of the law would entail.

8   For arguments, see the works cited in note 6, above.

9   See MacDowell 1978, 111–122, from which our own account derives.

10   Ibid., 111.

11   See Tulin 1996, 72 n. 175.

12   Ibid., 98–100, and McPherran 1996, 32–33 also notice the mirroring of the two cases, but should be far more troubled by the fact that this mirroring would be significantly disrupted if, as they claim and we deny, Euthyphro's case were actually legally impossible. Meletus' case against Socrates, after all, turned out to be all too possible. On the other hand, even if Tulin and McPherran were right about the legal impossibility of Euthyphro's case, Tulin's own conclusion – that the *Euthyphro* should be regarded as a kind of historical fiction – is only warranted if we also make the additional claim that the dialogue must be read in such a way as to understand that Euthyphro's case has passed one or more rounds of legal scrutiny. If, as we claim, the dialogue is best understood in such a way as to have Euthyphro's conversation with Socrates take place on the day he intended first to undertake his prosecution (about which, see also section 1.1.1, above), even if his case were not legally possible, Euthyphro might well not have known or understood this yet. Accordingly, nothing follows about the *Euthyphro*'s historical accuracy on any point from the putative impossibility of Euthyphro's case, since nothing in the dialogue requires that the case be legally valid.

13   Burnet 1924, 82. See also Tulin 1996, 74–76.

14   D.L. 2.29. An interesting question is whether Diogenes supposes that the conversation in the *Euthyphro* actually took place, for Diogenes often writes about Socrates and the other subjects of his biographical sketches as if he were recording events that actually took place. Our comment about how Diogenes understands the conversation, however, is meant to imply nothing whatever about whether *Plato* intended for us to understand the conversation in the *Euthyphro* as based on an actual interchange that took place between Socrates and an Athenian named Euthyphro. Unless otherwise noted, subsequent references to Diogenes should be understood in the same way.

15   See, e.g., R. E. Allen 1970, 9; Cornford 1952, 311; Grote 1865, Vol. 1, 322; Guardini 1948, 9, 26; Heidel 1900, 165; Jowett 1953 vol. 3, 61; Versenyi 1982, 36.

16   Others who share our view in this matter include: Burnet 1924, 85–87; Furley 1985; Hoerber 1958, 95–98; Hoopes 1970; Klonoski 1984; McPherran 1996, 34–35; Rosen 1968, 105–109; A. E. Taylor 1952, 147.

17   About which, see Aristophanes' *The Clouds* 1303–1453; Plato, *Crito* 50e2–51a2, *Laws* 717b–718a, 869a–b, 931a.

18   See, e.g., Beckman, 1979, 41; McPherran 1996, 37, 70 n. 113, cF. 147; Nilsson 1964, 275; Tate 1933A, 1933B, 1936; Vlastos 1991, 165–167.

19   See, e.g., G. M. A. Grube's translation in Cooper 1997 (also in Grube 2000, after revision by J. Cooper); Lane Cooper's 1941 translation in Hamilton and Cairns 1961.

20   A contrasting view, however, is given in Gocer 2000, 125.

21   Vlastos 1991, 166. As textual support for "what Socrates takes to be the sum and substance of the accusation at his trial," Vlastos quotes the passage at *Euthyphro* 3b1–4 (misidentified in his book as *Euthyphro* 2B).

22   McPherran 2000, 102; see also McPherran 1996, 139–167. A more radical version of this approach may be found in Garland 1992, 142–144. A sharply critical response to McPherran's and Vlastos's views is offered in Gocer 2000.

23   In fact, it is not actually quite as simple as this – Judaism and Christianity are both counted as monotheistic religions, yet there are textual grounds for saying that both recognize more divinities than just one. The Book of Job in the Old Testament (which is sometimes also called the "Hebrew Bible"), for example, tells of a disagreement or wager between God and Satan. The exact status of Satan among different sects of Jews and Christians is a matter of controversy, but Satan's presence in the Bible (as well as other divinities, such as angels and archangels) appears to make these supposedly monotheistic religions at least appear more complicated. Perhaps the most important thing about these religions, however, in contrast to polytheisms, is that they leave no doubt as to which of the existing divinities one should worship and obey (even to the exclusion of the others). Disagreements between divinities, therefore, would not be grounds for uncertainty about which divinity to follow in any given case.

24   See Devereux 1992.

25   See Irwin 1977; Penner 1973 and 1992.

26   See Ferejohn 1982 and 1983–1984; Kraut 1984; Vlastos 1981, 221–269 and 418–423; Woodruff 1976. Our own interpretation follows Ferejohn's version of this sort of view.

27   We get this example from Ferejohn 1982.

28   The following example is the one we proposed in Brickhouse and Smith 1994, 70–71.

2

THE *APOLOGY OF SOCRATES*

2.1 INTRODUCTION TO THE *APOLOGY OF SOCRATES*

2.1.1 *"Apologies of Socrates"*

In spite of Socrates' notoriety and the great attention his trial must have attracted, there are relatively few things about his trial and surrounding circumstances about which we can be confident. We can be quite sure that it took place in the spring of 399 B.C.E. and that the legal charges Socrates was required to answer were made by an Athenian named Meletus. The law Socrates was accused of having violated was one forbidding impiety. The ensuing trial resulted in Socrates' conviction, and the jury accepted Meletus' proposal that he be put to death. Officials of the city of Athens subsequently carried out the sentence. To one degree or another, anything else is speculative.

Our uncertainty about the details of the trial is not due to a failure on the part of Socrates' contemporaries to write about it. In fact, just the opposite is the case. We have good reason to think that "the case of Socrates" continued to be the subject of ongoing debate for many years after he was executed, although whether the controversy centered around a single aspect of the philosopher's life or several, we cannot know. However, we have good reason to think that a number of "apologies"[1] of Socrates were written. Of these our knowledge of some, while intriguing, is quite fragmentary. To our great fortune, Plato and Xenophon, both of whom counted themselves among Socrates' friends, wrote lengthy "apologies of Socrates" that have come down to us intact. What is problematical about this material is its historical reliability, an issue we will take up in more detail below.

Setting aside the question of historical accuracy, of the two "apologies" we have, Plato's and Xenophon's, the former is almost universally regarded as the more compelling piece of forensic oratory. In Xenophon's version, far from providing an effective rebuttal to the charge that he did great damage to the city through his philosophizing, Socrates actually alienated the jury with his arrogance, or "big talk," as Xenophon calls it.[2] To explain away the appearance of ineptness on Socrates' part, Xenophon maintains that Socrates wanted the jury to convict him because he believed he would soon suffer "the afflictions of old age" and that the god was actually using the occasion of his trial as a way of ending Socrates' life "in the easiest way" (6–7). So it was, then, according to Xenophon, that Socrates bragged about his great value to Athens, knowing that the jury would become incensed and order his execution. In short, Xenophon's *Apology* is not really a defense at all. It is an explanation of why Socrates failed to be acquitted. What it leaves utterly unexplained, however, is why Socrates' conduct before the jury would remain a subject of intense debate for years after the trial. To put it simply, there is little about the Socrates of Xenophon's *Apology* that would incline anyone to keep the memory of his speech alive after he was executed.

The Socrates of Plato's *Apology* stands in sharp contrast to the Socrates of Xenophon's. Even though scholars differ profoundly on how to understand particular sections of Plato's *Apology* and, indeed, what effect Plato intended to have on his audience, few who read Plato's version would disagree that Plato paints a captivating portrait of unwavering devotion to the value of the philosophical life. Unlike our reaction to Xenophon's, when we finish reading

Plato's *Apology* we readily understand why Socrates lived as he did and why others of great intellect were attracted to him. This is not to say that Xenophon's version should be dismissed. It should not, for it provides a variety of fascinating points of comparison with Plato's version. Although Xenophon's *Apology* repays careful study and should be read in addition to Plato's version by anyone with a serious interest in Socrates, it is Plato's version with which we will be concerned. When we refer to the *Apology* in what follows, unless we indicate otherwise, we will be referring to Plato's work.

2.1.2 The date of the composition of the Apology

Most commentators consider the *Apology* to be among the earliest of Plato's writings. One reason to think so is the commonsensical idea that Plato would have wanted to write about the controversial trial of his friend and mentor while the events were still relatively fresh in his mind. Perhaps even more significant is the fact that the Socrates of the *Apology* more closely resembles the character we find by that name in the other early dialogues of Plato, including the *Euthyphro* and *Crito*, with which it forms a trilogy, than he does the Socrates of the middle dialogues. For one thing, the Socrates of the *Apology* seems to have the markedly narrow philosophical focus that is characteristic of the Socrates of the early dialogues. He tells the jury that he does philosophy by questioning people who claim to be "wise" and showing them through their own answers to his questions that they are not. Nowhere does the Socrates of the *Apology* suggest that he has deep and sophisticated metaphysical theories that Plato himself developed and put into the mouth of the character named "Socrates" in his middle-period works.

Scholars who are unconvinced by these considerations can point out that the stylistic and thematic evidence is hardly decisive. There is, after all, evidence that interest in Socrates' trial remained strong for many years, certainly well into the time when Plato began to publish the sophisticated metaphysical and epistemological doctrines we associate with high Platonism. Moreover, in the *Apology*, Socrates defends his philosophical activity with a polished effectiveness that only an accomplished writer could achieve.[3] Those who are skeptical about assigning an early date to the *Apology* can argue that such rhetorical effect could only have been maintained by someone who labored over the composition for many years. Few scholars would deny that Plato, who became an absolute master of Greek prose, could have written a speech that is itself devoid of the elements of Platonism, at a time when the author himself was well along in the development of the views so closely associated with Platonic philosophy. Although this is a decidedly minority view, there is simply not sufficient evidence to refute it. Nonetheless, we think the balance of considerations still favors an earlier date of composition, probably within several years of the trial itself.

2.1.3   The basic structure of the Apology

The *Apology* is written *as if* these are the words Socrates actually uttered at his trial. The work itself is divided into three major parts, of unequal length. The longest part of the *Apology* is the first speech. It, too, can be divided into several major sections. In the first, Socrates defends himself against the widespread and longstanding prejudice that he is a troublemaker. He then interrogates his prosecutor regarding the actual legal charges that have been brought against him. He concludes the first major speech with a stirring defense of philosophy itself. The first major speech closes as the jury votes on his guilt or innocence. The second speech begins after the jury has voted to convict Socrates. There we hear Socrates' explanation of the penalty he proposes to pay as his punishment. The third speech, which is not to be understood as part of the formal proceedings, consists of two sets of remarks: one directed at those jurors who voted to condemn him and the other at those who had found him innocent. But before we turn to our analysis of the speeches themselves, it will be helpful to examine some of features of Athenian legal procedure that Plato could assume that his audience was familiar.

2.1.4   The type of trial – Graphê and Agôn Timêtos

In Athens, legal cases fell into one of two basic categories: the *graphê* and the *dikê*. The distinction is not to be confused with the modern distinction between criminal and civil cases. Rather, it turns on who may press a legal accusation before a court. In a *graphê, any* citizen could bring a specific charge of wrongdoing. In a *dikê,* on the other hand, only the victim of an alleged crime (or the nearest male relative) could charge another with having illegally caused the harm.[4] Socrates' case is a *graphê.* Indeed, in the *Euthyphro* he claims that he has never even met the man bringing the accusation against him (2b7–9).

As we just noted, the second speech that makes up the *Apology* concerns Socrates' offer to the jury of what punishment he is willing to pay. The explanation of why Socrates would have been given this opportunity after his conviction lies in the fact that some *graphai* carried penalties fixed by law and others did not. An *agôn timêtos* was one in which the penalty was not stipulated in the law. In a case of this sort, the law required that the jury decide what the defendant "deserved to suffer or to pay" by choosing between the penalty the prosecutor requested, stated at the end of the indictment, and a "counterpenalty," or *antitimêsis,* which would be proposed by the defendant after conviction. As we will later see, it is significant that the jury was required to choose between the two proposals and was not allowed to impose another penalty of its own devising. After a vote to convict was taken and announced to the court, the defendant was apparently given a relatively brief time to explain why he was proposing the particular penalty he was. Because Socrates was charged with impiety, a charge calling for an *agôn timêtos,* the jury was required to choose between the penalty sought by Meletus, which was indicated at the end of the official specification of the charges against Socrates, and the counterpenalty Socrates proposed following his conviction. As we will also see, how we understand Socrates' *antitimêsis* is of crucial importance to how we understand what Socrates hoped to accomplish with his speech, at least according to Plato.

2.1.5 *The court*

As we noted in the last chapter, Socrates' trial was preceded by an *anakrisis,* or preliminary hearing, conducted by the king-archon, the purpose of which was to decide whether the charges warranted a trial. Of course we do not know what actually transpired other than that the official must have thought that Meletus' accusations had sufficient merit to be decided by a jury. As a result, the accusation that Socrates was guilty of violating the law against impiety was forwarded to one the jury-courts, which were called the *Êliaia*, or Heliastic Courts. Although we cannot be certain, it appears likely that the court was located in a large, covered public building at the extreme southeastern side of the Athenian *agora*, below the acropolis.[5] Although some juries consisted of as few as two hundred members, those judging the most important cases could be as large as several thousand.[6]

The buildings that housed the courts had to be large enough to accommodate sizable juries.[7] In front of the seating for jurors there must have been a platform on which the speakers stood. The speakers included not only the principals, but also any witnesses and "supporters," or *sunêgoroi*, whose use by both accusers and defendants was not at all uncommon. Their legal role was apparently not limited to giving speeches. Those who spoke against defendants in *graphai* were doubtless responsible for helping to prepare the prosecutor's case. Moreover, if fewer than one-fifth of the jurors ended up voting for conviction, the co-accusers shared liability with the prosecutor to pay the very substantial fine of 1,000 drachmas for what amounted to abuse of the legal process.[8] We have no reason to think that anyone spoke on Socrates' behalf either as a "supporter" or as a witness (despite one very implausible story in a much later source[9]). Advocates or lawyers were not allowed to speak for either of the parties. Instead, each party was required to present his own case to the jury, although we know that it was not uncommon for an individual to hire a professional writer familiar with the law to prepare a speech for him. The prepared speech was then committed to memory and delivered in court. In fact, Diogenes Laertius, a third-century C.E. biographer, claims that the great orator Lysias actually wrote a defense for Socrates, but that Socrates declined to use it.[10] Plato's Socrates, however, strongly implies that he is not giving a speech that was prepared in advance (17c4–5).

Because the prosecutor was asking that Socrates be executed if convicted, Athenian law required that the case be completed in one day, a fact to which Socrates himself alludes (37a7–b1). The accuser and anyone else called upon to support the accusation were given the morning in which to make their speeches. The defendant and those called to speak on his behalf were given the afternoon. In addition to the principals and their supporters, if any, there was a presiding officer whose legal duties consisted in nothing more than initiating the proceedings, assigning someone to attend to the "water-clock" that measured the time allotted to the speakers, and conducting the voting. As there were few procedural and evidentiary rules to be considered, the presiding magistrate did not serve the function of a judge in modern, Western law. The public was allowed to gather around the court to hear the proceedings, and given Socrates' notoriety it is quite likely that a very large crowd encircled the court to hear what was said. In the absence of rules requiring decorum during the proceedings, unpopular comments were frequently interrupted by outbursts either from those in the audience or from jury members themselves. We see several examples of this sort of unruliness in Plato's *Apology* (20e4, 31a5, 27b1–5, 30c2). We should not infer that Socrates' jury was unusual in this regard.

2.1.6 The jury

Athenian juries could range in size from 200 to 2,500. A trial such as Socrates' would probably require 500 jurors. In older scholarship on the trial, one often finds the number of the jurors sitting in judgment at Socrates' trial given as 501, where the odd number was supposed to ensure against a deadlocked jury. Although the Athenians did go over to such a system only a few years later, at the time of Socrates' trial, the juries were apparently even-numbered, where tie votes would be counted as victories for the defendant.[11] Some scholars are nonetheless inclined to disagree with this conclusion, because of the very confused report of the votes given six centuries or more later by the mid-third-century C.E. biographer, Diogenes Laertius, whose *Lives and Opinions of Eminent Philosophers* can be a very important source of information about earlier antiquity. In this case, however, there is no reason at all to prefer what Diogenes tells us to what we find in Plato's version.

According to Diogenes, Socrates was convicted by "two hundred and eighty-one votes more than those for acquittal" (2.41). This, of course, is mathematically impossible given an even-numbered jury, and would also make the original vote against Socrates a very lop-sided victory for the prosecution (391 to 110, given a jury of 501). We know of no scholars who prefer Diogenes' account of this first vote to what is given by Plato. Indeed, Diogenes' account of the 281-vote difference simply looks like a confusion of the 280 votes in favor of conviction that Plato's account implies.

To hear a public case, a juror had to be at least thirty years old and a male citizen in good standing. Jury duty was strictly volun-tary. From those who volunteered, 6,000 were chosen at random, and of these, groups were assigned, again at random, to the various courts. Every juror at the time of Socrates' trial received three obols (one half of a drachma) a day for his service. Although the practice of paying jurors was probably instituted to encourage members of Athens' poorer classes to serve and thereby to make Athenian juries more democratic, it may be that the pay was not sufficient to attract large numbers of able-bodied workers, who could earn twice as much through regular employment. Aristophanes, the comic poet, jokes that Athenian juries were com-posed of impoverished old men who served on juries to support themselves.[12] While this is doubtless an exaggeration, it is likely that Athenian juries were composed largely of the less sophisti-cated members of Athenian society.[13] Socrates certainly assumes that the members of the jury hearing his case know about him – not because they were at all familiar with his philosophical views, but only because they had heard the gossip that had been circulated about him for many years (18b2).

2.1.7   Socrates' accusers

It would be understandable if one who is coming to the *Apology* for the first time has a hard time figuring out just who actually brought the charges against Socrates. The *Euthyphro* makes it clear that Socrates' prosecutor is a man named Meletus. Yet in the open-ing line of the *Apology*, Socrates refers to his "accusers" (17a2), and a few lines later he seems to identify those accusers as "Anytus and those with him" (18b3). Still later Socrates refers to the attacks against him launched by Meletus, Anytus, and Lycon (23e3–4). Towards the end of the *Apology*, he attributes his conviction, in part, to the fact that Anytus and Lycon joined Meletus in presenting the case against him (36a8–9). The explanation for all of these references is that Meletus was officially the prosecutor and that Anytus and Lycon served Meletus as "supporters" (*sunêgoroi*). Despite Meletus's official position as prosecutor, *Apology* 18b3 makes it clear that Socrates regarded Anytus as the driving force behind the prosecution. Had Anytus not chosen to have Socrates brought to trial, it is doubtful, at least in Socrates' eyes, that either Meletus or Lycon would have taken the initiative.

So who was Meletus? The perhaps surprising answer is that, except for his role in having Socrates condemned to death, little or nothing is known about the man. In the *Apology*, Socrates says that Meletus was angry with him "on behalf of the poets" (23e4–5), but we have no independent reason to think that Meletus was himself ever a poet or even related to poets.[14] Some scholars have wondered whether Socrates' accuser is the same man who brought a charge of impiety against Andocides in the same year as Socrates' trial.[15] If so, we would have some reason, independent of Plato's *Apology*, for thinking that Socrates' official accuser had a special interest in freeing the city from irreligion. It is quite unlikely the accusers in the two cases are really the same man, however. For one thing, the Meletus who prosecuted Andocides also participated in the notoriously unjust arrest of one Leon years several earlier.[16] Were he the same man who formally accused Socrates of impiety, Socrates could hardly say, as he does in the *Euthyphro*, that Meletus is unknown to him. Moreover, it is unlikely that Anytus, who had been exiled from Athens by the same men who ordered Leon's arrest, and who testified on Andocides' behalf, would have joined forces with someone who had been on the opposite side in both of these other instances. Finally, as we will see, Socrates himself refers to the arrest of Leon during his defense (*Ap.* 32c3–e1 – see section 2.33, below). It is difficult to believe that he would have failed to remind the jury that his own prosecutor had participated in an injustice in which he himself had bravely refused to engage. It seems more likely, then, that Meletus was, as Socrates suggests, simply a friend of Anytus, whom Anytus persuaded to bring the formal charges against Socrates.

We can say scarcely more about Lycon than we can about Meletus. Socrates tells the jury that Lycon was supporting the action against him on behalf of the orators (24a1), but there is no independent evidence linking him to that group. As we have already noted, Socrates says that Meletus would not have even received one-fifth of the votes had not Anytus *and* Lycon spoke against him. This may suggest that Lycon was a known and respected public figure, though just what he had done to earn his reputation remains a mystery.[17] It certainly not impossible that Lycon agreed to support the action against Socrates because he wanted to curry favor with Anytus, who wielded considerable political influence in Athens at the time.

Socrates says that in speaking against him, Anytus is representing both the craftsmen and politicians (23e6). There is some logic to this (which perhaps also shows that Meletus and Lycon were in some way really connected to the groups with whom Socrates associates them), for Anytus had been a tanner before his rise to prominence in the public eye and at the time of the trial he certainly qualifies as a well-known politician. Immediately after Athens' capitulation to Sparta, which marked the end of the Peloponnesian War, the democracy was suspended in Athens and a pro-Spartan group of thirty commissioners (the 'Thirty') was appointed to recodify the laws. We will discuss their despotic reign and Socrates' relationship with the leading members of the Thirty in some detail below. Here we need only point out that Anytus was one of the leaders of the faction that restored the democracy after a period of brief but intense military conflict with forces loyal to the Thirty. Not only did Anytus risk his own life in this conflict, he apparently continued to play a leading role in the rebuilding of a moderate democracy in the difficult years between the fall of the Thirty and the trial of Socrates. Anytus' respectability, therefore, must have given significant weight to the prosecution.

As we will see, in his third speech, after he has been convicted and sentenced to death, Socrates suggests that his fate will be better than that of those who spoke again him. What evidence there is that Meletus, Lycon, and Anytus did indeed meet an unhappy end we will postpone considering until our discussion of Socrates' final remarks to the jury.

2.1.8 The charges against Socrates

The Athenians, like other Greeks, believed that people could offend the gods in various ways, and that when they did, the gods might well condemn the entire city to terrible evils. To discourage what might anger the gods, the city passed a law forbidding impiety, and it was this law that Meletus charged Socrates with violating. The law itself was vague, leaving it to the prosecutor to specify in just what way the accused had been illegally impious. Although the specific ways in which the defendant was alleged to be impious were stated in the indictment that Meletus swore before the king-archon, the specifications were not really treated as separate charges. Moreover, there is no reason to think that prosecutors had to adduce specific evidence regarding any or all of the specific ways the defendant was charged with impiety.

Socrates says that Meletus charged him with being impious in three ways: Socrates does not believe in the gods of the city, he introduced new divinities, and he corrupted the youth (24b8–c1). Although Socrates never claims to be stating the specifications of the charge against him precisely, what he says is almost identical to the version given by Xenophon[18] and later by Diogenes Laertius, who claims that Favorinus actually saw the charges against Socrates because they had been preserved in the Athenian law archives.[19] As we will see, although an allegation of impiety was a serious charge whose gravity was only increased by Meletus' three specifications, the formal complaints were actually based on other, informal allegations of wrongdoing made apparently by many Athenians about Socrates for many years before the trial.

2.1.9   *The historical accuracy of Plato's* Apology

Before we turn to the content of the speech itself, we would do well to take up the question of the extent to which Plato's words provide us with a historically accurate account of what Socrates actually said to the jury. While no scholar has seriously argued that Plato's version is a close, word-for-word record of what Socrates said, some have argued that Plato's *Apology* probably captures the substance of Socrates' defense and the tone in which it was delivered. In trying to assess this theory, we might think it is helpful to turn to Xenophon's version of the speech, the only other complete version that has come down to us. Now although Xenophon, by his own admission, was not actually present at the trial, he claims to have heard about the speech in great detail from a certain Hermogenes, who was present. It is clear that Xenophon is attempting to explain both *why* Socrates gave the kind of talk that he did and *what he said*. We might accordingly suppose that Plato, too, was attempting to "capture" what Socrates said at his trial and how he said it.

Unfortunately, we cannot infer from Xenophon's claim to have a particular goal in mind that Plato had the same goal, even though the subject matter of both works is the same. Moreover, on a number of significant points the speeches differ markedly. Some points that Plato emphasizes Xenophon omits altogether, and vice versa. Finally, even when both Plato and Xenophon agree that Socrates mentioned something, they usually differ about the point Socrates was making.

The great Scottish Hellenist John Burnet offered a different sort of argument in favor of this view that Plato's *Apology* provides us with an understanding of the way Socrates conducted himself in court.[20] First, Burnet reminds us that twice in the *Apology* (34a2, 38b7) Plato mentions that he was present at the trial. Nowhere in his other works does he actually claim to have heard anything Socrates said. Second, since Plato's goal in writing the *Apology* was "to defend the memory of Socrates by setting forth his character and activity in their true light," he would have defeated his own purpose were he to have strayed too far from what Socrates actually said to the jurors. After all, Burnet reminds us, in addition to the sizable jury there were doubtless many spectators who crowded around the court to hear what the notorious Socrates would say in his defense, and many of them would still have been alive at the time the *Apology* was written. Were Plato to have misrepresented what was actually said, there would have been many who had been present that day who were in a position to recognize the distortion.

Other scholars have vigorously contested the notion that the *Apology* serves as an important historical document about Socrates' conduct in court, however. First, the assumption from which Burnet argues, that Plato's intent was to "put forth [Socrates'] character and activity in their true light" is simply question-begging.[21] Whether, indeed, that was Plato's goal is the very thing that must be shown. Even if there are some things in Plato's version that the historical Socrates almost certainly said, we cannot be sure that they were said in the same way that Plato presents them. Perhaps Plato used what is actually said by Socrates to make an entirely different point. One scholar sums up his skepticism as follows: "I would dare assert that there is, on the one hand, no single sentence in the Platonic *Apology* that Socrates could not actually have pronounced, and, on the other, that the published work contains no passage so specifically un-Platonic that it cannot be Plato's work."[22]

Some scholars go beyond mere skepticism about the historical accuracy of the *Apology* to claim that the *Apology* simply displays too much evidence of being a carefully crafted literary composition and that it is best understood as a piece of Platonic fiction, doubtless intended to be a stirring defense not of the life of the historical Socrates, but of the life dedicated to philosophical reflection and examination.[23] Plato's *Apology*, far from trying to set down for posterity the words uttered by the historical Socrates, is actually an exhortation to the speech's audience to engage in philosophy. Those who advance this interpretation are apt to point out that there existed in the first half the fourth century B.C.E. a genre known as "exhibition speeches" or "display speeches" in which the author made no pretense of capturing some historical event, but rather sought to demonstrate his, the author's, own persuasive powers.[24] In this view, Plato's, as well as the other "apologies" written in the years following Socrates' death, simply belonged to this genre in which a character named "Socrates" was used to advance an author's own position, or figured only in a fiction designed to display the author's skill as a writer.[25] Plainly, if this hypothesis is correct, we learn little or nothing about what the historical Socrates actually said from Plato's *Apology*. Those who take this line can bolster their claim by pointing out that the speech Plato wrote appears to be the product of reflection and careful polishing. The idea is that such careful tailoring could not have been done impromptu by Socrates himself, but must have been accomplished by Plato as he labored over the composition before revealing it to the public.

What makes both the historical accuracy thesis and the thesis that the *Apology* is purely Plato's invention difficult to disprove is the inherent vagueness of both theses. As we noted, the most that is claimed for the historical accuracy thesis is that the speech is reliable in substance and tone. Its defenders are fully prepared to concede that the *Apology* shows signs of what may well be Plato's literary craftsmanship. Indeed, they can even allow that no single passage can be identified as something Socrates *must* have said. Thus, adherents to this position can allow that Plato's version may well emphasize some of Socrates' comments, omit others altogether, and perhaps fabricate still others, for their interpretation is driven by a view of what Plato's goals must have been in writing the speech and the idea that achieving those goals required that those who heard the speech could say, "Yes, that is essentially what he talked about and how he said it."

Those who take the *Apology* to be fiction, on the other hand, have to concede that, at most, it is *basically* fiction, for no sensible person would hold that nothing at all in the *entire* speech could be anything but the product of Plato's imagination. When defenders of this interpretation have finished enumerating all the things they believe Socrates did not actually say, it is not clear that they will have pointed out anything defenders of the quasi-historical accuracy interpretation would dispute. It could still be true that Plato's version of the speech is in many other important ways really quite like the one Socrates gave.

Any serious attempt to sort out these issues will take us too far from the central task, the examination of what Plato says in his

Apology. Therefore, we will here adopt an essentially neutral stance about the question of historical accuracy. When we speak of "Socrates" in what follows, unless we indicate otherwise, we are referring to the character delivering the three speeches and who, mid-way through the first speech, interrogates Meletus. This is not to say that we will avoid drawing inferences about what Plato probably intended in certain passages or what the *speaker* is trying to accomplish by saying what he does. We will, and in so doing we will develop the elements of an interpretation of the entire speech. The emerging interpretation, we will argue, is more coherent and provides a better fit with Plato's text than does its principal rivals.

2.2 SOCRATES' INTRODUCTORY REMARKS TO THE JURORS

2.2.1 The introduction to the first speech (17a1–18a6)

When we turn to the *Apology* itself, we are immediately struck by the fact that Socrates does not begin right away to construct a defense or even to characterize the charges he faces. Instead, he makes a number of introductory remarks intended to prepare the jury for what it will hear from him. Socrates begins by informing the jury that although his accusers warned them not to be taken in by his clever way of speaking, in fact, they, his accusers, are the masters of deception.

> I don't know what effect my accusers had on you, Athenians, but they were speaking so persuasively that I almost forgot who I am. And yet they said virtually nothing that is true. Of their many lies about me, one surprised me most of all: when they said you needed to be on your guard against getting tricked by me, because I'm a clever speaker.
>
> (17a1–b1)

Socrates goes on to say that he will immediately refute them by demonstrating that he "is not a clever speaker at all ... unless they mean by 'clever' one who tells only the truth" (17b1–5). He is going to speak "at random" and in the language he is used to using "at the merchants' tables" in the marketplace where he is so often seen. He simply is not used to the stylized language of the law-courts, since this is the first time he has ever appeared in court, and, in any case, it would not be fitting for him, at his age, he says, to "come before you like a boy planning out what it is going to say" (17c5–6). He is not about to abandon his customary way of expressing himself in favor of what would be for him a wholly artificial way of speaking. Having implored them not to be put off with his manner of speech, he closes his introductory remarks with a reminder that they must meet their obligation as judges, and so must he as a speaker before the court: He says, "pay attention and concentrate on this one thing: if what I say is just or not. This is the virtue of a judge, and that of a speaker is to tell the truth" (18a3–6).

2.2.2   Socrates and conventional forensic oratory

Commentators have often observed that virtually everything Socrates says in his initial remarks can also be found in the intro-ductions prepared by professional orators for speeches that given by their clients in law-courts.[26] How can we think Socrates is being anything but disingenuous when he says that he is not familiar with the way people talk in court and that he is not a clever speaker and then goes on to demonstrate that he is familiar with what is said?

Now Socrates cannot very well be telling the truth if he means that he has *no* familiarity with anything litigants typically said and did. His introductory remarks are enough to show that he is. Moreover, at the end of the first speech he makes it clear that he is perfectly familiar with the practice of defendants bringing in their wives and children to try to win sympathy from jurors (34b7–d10). It seems more likely that Socrates means that, since he has never spoken before a court, he is not used to saying what the jury is used to hearing. Surely one can be quite familiar with the elements characteristic of, say, elegiac poetry but not be able to write an even passably good elegiac poem. If Socrates is only denying that he is *practiced* in the ways of the courts, he is only saying what is true in his introduction, namely that if he is to assist the jury in its task of deciding whether what he says is right, it is better that he use the language he employs "in the marketplace at the merchants' tables," the language he is used to using. If this is right, the fact that his opening remarks consist of comments of the sort one finds in speeches prepared by professional writers gives us no reason to think that Socrates is being dishonest right at the outset.

2.3 THE "FIRST ACCUSATIONS" AGAINST SOCRATES

2.3.1 The "first accusations" (18a7–19d7)

Although the jury must decide whether Socrates is guilty of the specific legal charges Meletus has brought against him, Socrates begins his defense by saying that it is "right" for him first to take up what he calls "false first accusations made against him and the first accusers." Indeed, he says that he fears these first accusers more than he fears his actual accusers, although he considers them to be dangerous too (18b3–4). He fears the first accusers so much because there are so many of them and they have been engaging in slanderous talk about him for such a long time. He is well aware, then, that he has been viewed with suspicion long before Meletus actually brought the charges he must answer in court. He also understands that if he is to have any hope of convincing the jury that he is innocent of the legal charges, he must first convince them that there is nothing to the "first accusations" that have for so long swirled around him.

Socrates also understands that it will not be easy to rebut the first accusations effectively. What makes the task so difficult, Socrates says at one point, is that "it is not possible to bring any of [the first accusers] here, and it is absolutely necessary in making my defense to shadow-box as it were, and to ask questions when no one answers" (18d4–7). It is not surprising, then, that he thinks it is unlikely he can remove a longstanding prejudice in the short time that he has to speak.

So just what are these slanders, the "first accusations," as Socrates calls them. He actually offers two versions. First, he tells the jury, "They said that there's a certain Socrates, a wise man, who thinks about what's in the heavens and who has investigated all the things below the earth and who makes the weaker argument appear to be the stronger" (18b7–c1). Later, at 19b4–c2, he gives a virtually identical version of the "first accusations" as if he were reading from an actual affidavit:

> Socrates does wrong and is too concerned with inquiring about what's in the heavens and below the earth and to make the weaker argument appear to be the stronger and to teach these same things to others.

Socrates has not been able to answer these accusations, not because he did not know about them but because the disastrous rumors are mostly spread about privately and anonymously. About those who slander him in this way, as he says, "it is impossible to know and say their names, except one who happens to be a certain writer of comedies" (18c9–d2). A few lines later Socrates names that "certain writer of comedies": Aristophanes, the most accomplished of all the ancient Greek comic playwrights. Socrates assumes that many of the jurors saw the play in which a character named Socrates is "carried around, saying that he is walking on air and all kinds of other nonsense, which I don't understand at all" (19c3–5). Now the play to which Socrates is referring is *The Clouds*, which was first produced in 423 B.C.E., some twenty-four years before the trial. And indeed the plot of that play concerns a pseudo-intellectual by the name of Socrates, who operates a *phrontisterion*, a think-shop, and a bumpkin by the name of Strepsiades, who goes to the shop to learn from Socrates how to argue in slick ways in order to cheat his many creditors. As the farcical plot unfolds, Aristophanes' Socrates reveals himself to be an atheist and an utter immoralist. At one point this Socrates explains that the clouds and various natural forces have replaced Zeus and that those who recognize the clouds as the new deities will have bestowed on them ability to trick people and win every debate. As Aristophanes has the chorus of clouds proclaim, natural forces are the gods and Socrates is their minister.

Scholars generally agree that Aristophanes was simply using his character "Socrates" to serve as a caricature, drawn in bold strokes, for an entire but really quite diverse group of intellectuals, who, considered as a group, threatened to replace the old intellectual order with radically different ways of thinking about the universe and morality. Some of these intellectual "revolutionaries" were really proto-scientists, "philosophers of nature." Our knowledge of them is only fragmentary, but what we know indicates that, to generalize, they were interested in explaining occurrences in nature in terms of naturalistic causes or principles. To be sure, the explanations they proposed were quite crude by modern scientific standards, but the importance of their attempts to explain the workings of nature in terms of naturalistic principles rather than in terms of divine wish is obvious: scientific explanations eliminate the role traditionally assigned to the gods in the explanation of why things in nature happen as they do. When Socrates says that one of the old accusations maintains that he is "concerned with inquiring into what is in the heavens and below the earth," he is referring to the fact that he has been identified in the popular mind as one who investigates natural phenomena and what happens at death in an attempt to debunk the stories about these matters promoted by traditional Greek religious myths. Those who inquire "into what is in the heavens and below the earth," in other words, seek to replace religion with science. As he tells the jury, "People who hear such things believe that people who inquire about such topics don't believe in the gods" (18c3–4). One of the slanders, then, for which Aristophanes bears at least some of the responsibility, is that Socrates is an atheist.

The other major intellectual revolutionaries were teachers, or "sophists," as they were usually called. Of these, some of the most famous and financially successful claimed to be able to make their students excellent human beings and citizens by teaching them what *aretê* (virtue or excellence) is and how to obtain it. Citing the examples of Gorgias, Prodicus, and Hippias, Socrates tells the jury just how convincing these sophists could be. "Each of them is able to go into any city and persuade the young – who can associate for free with any of their own citizens they want to – to abandon their associations with the local people and to associate with them instead and pay them and thank them on top of it all" (19e4–20a2).

In *The Clouds*, Aristophanes seems particularly interested in lampooning those sophists who claimed to know the art of rhetoric and claimed that they could make their students persuasive. This skill was especially prized in Athens for at least two reasons. First, its unique form of government, which allowed every citizen to speak in the Assembly, saw those citizens rise to the pinnacle of prestige and power who could win a majority of citizens over to their way of thinking. Then, doubtless because Athens had become a vibrant commercial center, law-suits, heard before juries of ordinary men, were commonplace, and since, as we have seen, citizens had to plead their own cases in court, it behooved all who might become entangled in the law to know how to win over a jury. Of course, the object of the teachings of these sophists was success in one's endeavors, whether it was getting elected to some post or winning one's case in court. But teaching one how to be successful, as most Athenians clearly realized, did not necessarily mean teaching them to be just, or to know or tell the truth. How to win one's point, even if one had to be dishonest to do it, was what these "professors" taught. Not surprisingly, many Athenians saw them as little more than purveyors of dishonesty. So, when Socrates says one of the "first accusations" against him is that he makes "the worse appear the better argument and that he teaches these things to others," he is referring to the fact that many people had been going around saying that he was a sophist who corrupted the youth by teaching them how to be successful through dishonesty.

There can be little doubt that Aristophanes played an important role in spreading Socrates' reputation as one of the new breed of intellectuals who were out to overthrow the values most Athenians held dear. Thousands of persons would have seen *The Clouds* when it was put on and there must have been thousands of others who heard second-hand about how it made vicious fun of Socrates.

The first thing we can say is that Socrates must have already been an instantly recognizable public figure at the time the play was produced. Moreover, he must have already been identified in the minds of the audience as one of the intellectual revolutionaries; otherwise, Aristophanes could not count on his use of a central character named Socrates who runs a "think-shop" being amusing. So, it has to be the case that, prior to the trial, Socrates had been doing things that at least resembled, in the eyes of the ordinary Athenian, what Aristophanes was making fun of.

So, what did Socrates do that made him seem like these other intellectuals? As Socrates himself makes clear later in the *Apology*, he talked to people about how they ought to live and the crucial importance of making themselves as good as possible (29e1–2). In this respect, then, he was concerned with one of the very things the most famous and successful of the sophists made the focal point of their lectures. Second, if we can rely on Plato's other so-called "Socratic writings," Socrates' opponents in arguments sometimes believed that they had been tricked and that Socrates did not always say what he himself believed.[27] Finally, Socrates mentions in the *Apology* that he had followers. Not only were these the sons of the rich who had the leisure time to be with him, but also they enjoyed imitating the way he argued with others about how to become excellent. In fact, Socrates attributes part of the anger that has been directed at him to the fact that people think he has corrupted those who imitate him (23c2–8). Add to all this the fact that Socrates engaged others in discussion in public – "in the market-place," he says, "at the merchants' tables" (17c8–10) – so that over the years he would have been observed, surrounded by wealthy young men, by countless Athenians as they went about their daily routine in Athens' commercial district. It is not difficult to imagine that the typical Athenian viewed with deep mistrust the spectacle of Socrates arguing about excellence, surrounded by young men of the wealthy class. Aristophanes no doubt chose Socrates for his caricature precisely because so many people already believed he was up to no good. Perhaps he did not hold his lectures in rented halls, as did the other sophists, but he was corrupting his young associates nonetheless with all his talk about how to live. Although not at all engaged in the same sorts of "teaching" as the sophists, to many ordinary Athenians, he appeared to be one. Socrates was, in other words, the victim of a kind of mistaken identity.

2.3.2   The defense against the "first accusations" (19d8–20c3)

Socrates' response to the claim that he engages in scientific inquiry of some sort is surprisingly brief. Without addressing the question of whether those who engage in scientific explanation are likely to be atheists, he simply denies that he has any such wisdom (19c4–5). His witnesses that he is telling the truth, he says, must be the members of the jury themselves, and so he challenges anyone to speak up and "tell each other if you have ever heard me discussing such things in any way at all" (19d5–6). Having dissociated himself from those who investigate nature, however, Socrates does not actually deny the legitimacy of some sort of scientific inquiry; nor does he deny the possibility that it might yield knowledge. Instead, he tells the jury, "I don't mean to disparage knowledge of this sort, if anyone is wise about such things – may I not have to answer such charges from Meletus as that" (19c6–7). Whether anyone actually possesses wisdom of this sort, Socrates does not presume to say.

What about the second slander, that he "makes the weaker argument appear the stronger"? Perhaps surprisingly, Socrates fails to address the charge directly. Of course, he has already stated in his introductory remarks that his speech will demonstrate that his accusers could not have been right when they called him "clever" and that he will act as a true speaker ought by saying only what is true (17b1–d1). These promises, of course, are consistent with his being a master of making bad arguments look good and good arguments look bad. His response to the second charge is simply to deny it, and as proof to ask, once again, that the members of the jury speak up if any have heard him engaging in form of sophistry the second charge alleges. "From this you'll know that the other things people say about me are no different [from the false claim that I practice scientific inquiry]" (19d6–7).

The way Socrates states his denial that he has ever been a teacher or that he has received pay for his teaching suggests that he regards the third charge as the most widely believed of the three. As we have seen, he understands why people would be envious of people like Gorgias, Prodicus, and Hippias. It would be a mistake to think that Socrates is dismissing the seriousness of what the sophists claim they do. His report of a recent encounter with Callias, a man of considerable wealth, is intended to underscore the importance of what the sophists claim they do. Callias, we learn, has turned his two sons over to the sophist Evenus of Paros, who, for five minas, has promised to improve them as "men and as citizens" (20b4–8). Now five minas was a very considerable sum of money in the eyes of most of the jurors, worth more than many of them could expect to realize as income in over a year.[28] Although we can be sure that Socrates never for a moment believes that Evenus actually had the knowledge of how to improve Callias' sons, he says that he would count Evenus "blessed" if he really did possess it and for providing the greatest of all gifts for such a "moderate fee." Since teaching one how to become good as a human being and as a citizen would be the most important information one could ever convey, no fee would be too great. So perhaps unlike many of the jurors, Socrates does not condemn charging a fee for the teaching of virtue. In fact, he says that he himself would be very proud to possess the knowledge Evenus claims to have, but he emphatically denies that he does (20c2–3).

2.3.3 Are the "first accusations" the only charges made against Socrates?

Some commentators have doubted that the three "first accusations" were the only, or even the most serious, charges that had been made against Socrates. One possible charge is decidedly political in nature: the notion that Socrates' political sympathies were an important issue to many jurors is not wholly without foundation. Aristophanes made Socrates the butt of many jokes, and sometimes he suggested that Socrates was sympathetic to Sparta, Athens' enemy during the Peloponnesian War.[29] In a famous passage in

Memorabilia (1.2.9), Xenophon suggests that after Socrates' death he had been accused of making his companions contemptuous of the quintessential democratic practice of assigning certain public officials by lot. Even Plato's Socrates criticizes democratic practices and leading democratic politicians. Consider this passage from Plato's *Protagoras* (319b5–d7) in which Socrates takes a shot at how the democratic Assembly conducts its business:[30]

> [Socrates speaking] I say that whenever we gather in the Assembly and must take some actions concerning construction in the city, the builders are sent for to deliberate about the construction, and when it concerns ship-building the shipwrights are sent for, and other matters that they think can be understood and taught are pursued in this way. But if someone else tries to advise them, whom they do not regard to a craftsman, even if he is handsome and wealthy and well born, they don't receive him well but instead shout him down and laugh at him until the guy who is trying to speak either steps down, or the archers drag him away or throw him out by order of the Board. They proceed in this way in matters that they think concern a craft. But whenever it is a question of deliberating about the management of the city, anyone can stand up and counsel them like the craftsmen – copper worker, shoemaker, merchant, ship-captain, rich, poor, well born, lowly born, and no one gives them a hard time as they do the others on the ground that they don't know what they are talking about or that he hasn't been instructed by a teacher, when he is trying to offer advice. The reason is that they don't think that this sort of thing is teachable.

Here Socrates is explaining his doubts about whether the sophist Protagoras really can provide the instruction he claims, namely how to make the citizens of Athens good. It is also clear, however, that Socrates thinks that, w*ere* there a craft of improving the city itself, it would be irrational to let just anyone speak to the Assembly. The Assembly should always defer to the expert, just as it does when it comes to public building projects. Plato's Socrates, then, seems to agree with Xenophon's at least to this extent: political *principle* does not require that every citizen be free to speak his mind about how the city should be governed. If someone really possesses a real craft of politics, democracy should be abolished.

Other commentators, relying on evidence from later writers,[31] believe that the real concern about Socrates involved his well-known association with three men in particular, Alcibiades, Critias, and Charmides, who, in different ways, did enormous damage to Athens. Alcibiades, who was the most closely associated with Socrates, later became an Athenian general who actually betrayed Athens at a crucial time during the Peloponnesian War rather than answer charges that he had been involved in revealing certain religious rites to the uninitiated. Critias and Charmides were among the thirty Spartan sympathizers who were appointed as commissioners to rewrite the laws at the end of the war. As we noted in section 2.1.7, the "Thirty Tyrants," as they were called, quickly seized control of the city and began a reign of terror. Although hundreds fled the city rather than live under the despotic regime of the Thirty, Socrates was not among them. The reign of the Thirty ended only when the exiles, of which Anytus was one of the leaders, retook the city by force. If Socrates really had directly aided the Thirty, or had been in some way responsible for their having turned on their native city, it would be entirely understandable that the Athenians would have wanted Socrates to answer for his crimes against the state.

The picture is further complicated by a general amnesty passed in 403/2, four years before Socrates was placed on trial, that among other things called for a revision of the laws and forbade prosecutions of alleged violations of decrees passed by the Assembly prior to the amnesty. As John Burnet points out, the conditions of the amnesty in effect ruled out any prosecution of Socrates for alleged political crimes that preceded 403/2. Some scholars have also understood the amnesty as making it illegal even so much as to mention such alleged crimes in court. So, for example, Burnet writes, "It could not be brought up against him that he had been [among those who remained in the city], nor could anything be said about his relationship with Critias and Alcibiades, though these things doubtless weighed with Anytus."[32] In this view, even if the jury had been entirely willing to punish Socrates for his past association with such well-known enemies of the city, the prosecutors would have scrupulously avoided any allusion to them. Whatever his animus towards Socrates, according to this argument, Anytus was sincerely interested in seeing stability returned to Athens and a violation of the amnesty, whose purpose was to help restore that very stability, would have undermined Anytus's ultimate goal.

Were there, then, "hidden charges" that Anytus could not explicitly raise but of which he knew the jury was aware and for which they would punish Socrates? We are very skeptical of this view. Let us turn first to the political charge, that Socrates was an opponent of democracy. The first thing to be said is that we cannot be certain about the status of the "accusation" quoted by Xenophon. Scholars generally agree that Xenophon's discussion of this topic in the *Memorabilia* is a response to a pamphlet by Polycrates circulated several years after the trial.[33] But there is no reason at all to suppose that the issues Polycrates wrote about in his pamphlet had anything at all to do with the actual trial or how it was conducted – and the historical reliability of Polycrates' work was doubted even in antiquity.[34] Second, whatever his criticisms of specific democratic institutions may have been, we have no evidence that Socrates actually favored oligarchy, rule by a (wealthy) minority, the faction that had traditionally been democracy's principal rival for control of the city. His criticism of democracy, it appears, is that it allows the incompetent to rule. But Socrates also applied this criticism equally to oligarchy. He pointedly reminds the jury later in the speech that he always made justice his first concern and thus he refused the bidding of the oligarchic regime of the Thirty even though it would have cost him his life had their reign not ended when it did (32c2–e1). Third, although it is difficult to say to what extent he regarded his own views about how a city might best be governed to be a serious concern to the jury, he does remind them that Chaerephon, his life-long and devoted friend, did fight with the democratic faction in the civil war as a result of which the city was returned to democracy after the rule of the Thirty (20e8–21a2). If Socrates was a dangerous oligarch, it is hard to understand why such a good democrat remained so loyal to him. Fourth, he reminds the jury of his distinguished military service on behalf of the city (28e1–3), service that is hardly characteristic of someone working to bring about the overthrow of the democracy then in power. And finally, even if Socrates thinks that rule by someone or some group of people who actually possess knowledge of how to make human beings good would be preferable to democracy, which so often allows the ignorant to promote further ignorance, Socrates has good reason to value democracy. As we will see, Socrates is far from certain that there can be a craft that aims at making good citizens in the way that there is a craft of shipbuilding that aims at building good ships. He believes, instead, that human improvement will come only through open discussion and examination of people's views about how to achieve excellence. One of the essential features of Athenian democracy is *parrêsia*, freedom of speech. As he tells the jury after he has been convicted, when he explains why he will not go into exile (37c4–e2), if the people of Athens will not endure him and his philosophical examinations of others, surely people in other cities will be even less accepting of him. But Socrates has good reason to think that the jury would have understood at the outset of the trial that he favors Athenian democracy over the alternative forms of government existing in other cities at the time. Even if they did not know that he very rarely left the city for any length of time except to go on military campaigns (*Crito* 52b1–8), they could hardly have missed the fact that Socrates was a fixture in Athens, clearly preferring it to any other city. Moreover, it was well known that he had fought heroically on behalf of the city during the war only recently concluded. We believe, then, that when one looks at the entirety of the evidence concerning the alleged role of Socrates' attitude toward democracy, there is no reason to think that *he* believes his political views were at all responsible for his legal troubles. When Socrates introduces the "first accusations," he says he hopes he will be successful (19a2–4). It would make little sense for him to say that he wants to remove the prejudice if, in fact, he is aware that he is not even going to address one of the significant elements constituting that prejudice.

Let us turn now to the second supposed "hidden" accusation, that he had corrupted Alcibiades and/or Critias and Charmides. It is true that the conditions of the amnesty would have prevented the prosecution from charging Socrates with any crimes involving his three most famous former companions. But as a matter of fact (and contrary to Burnet's assumption, quoted above), prosecutors were in no way prevented from citing evidence of crimes committed before the passage of the amnesty in court cases. The amnesty of 403/2 did not include any provisions about admissible evidence; it simply prevented prosecutions for crimes alleged to have been committed prior to its passage. Had his prosecutors wished to link Socrates with any of these notorious figures, or the crimes they committed, nothing prevented their doing so at the trial. Moreover, the amnesty certainly did *not* prevent *Socrates* from mentioning them if he thought his past associations were a matter of special concern. As we will see, later in the first speech he invites anyone who claims to have been corrupted by him to come forward and accuse him. If none is willing to do so, Socrates says, any of their relatives is free to come forward (33c9–d9). None does, however. It would have been extraordinarily inept on Plato's part to have Socrates say that he wants to remove the prejudice against him and then fail even to address what he would have known to be one of the principal elements in that prejudice. Of course, one might say that Alcibiades, Critias, and Charmides were all dead by the time of the trial,[35] and perhaps none of their relatives was present (and willing) that day to talk about the pernicious influence Socrates had on their famous relatives.[36] This objection hardly meets the spirit of Socrates' offer to have people speak against him. Although he only invites his "victims," if there are any, and their family members to come forward, it is clear that he would not deny time to anyone who wishes to testify about any alleged corruption. The fact that *no one* comes forward to say that he must answer for the harm he did to *anyone* strongly suggests that none of his particular associations was especially worrisome among whatever concerns people had about Socrates. This is not to deny that some Athenians may have been convinced that Alcibiades, Critias, and Charmides were worse men because of their friendship with

Socrates and that, to that extent, Socrates was responsible for the disasters that befell Athens. We doubt, however, that Socrates believed that he would have to address his past association with these men directly if his defense were to be successful. To focus on some individuals, even quite evil men, would have run the risk of deflecting the jury's attention from the root cause of the prejudice, that he was a sophist. If so, his defense against the "first accusations" is just what it should have been: Socrates does not deny that he had ever known or even been associated with people who did Athens great harm. What he denies is that he taught anyone anything.

2.4 SOCRATES' WISDOM

2.4.1   Human wisdom (20c4–e3)

As we have just seen, Socrates straightforwardly denies that he possesses the sort of wisdom that would qualify him as one of the intellectuals most Athenians viewed with hostility. But he also realizes that if he is not wise in the way so many people seem to believe, he needs to explain why he has come to have that reputation. His explanation is presented in one of the most perplexing passages in Plato's *Apology*. He begins with the following remark.

> Athenians, I acquired this reputation on account of nothing other than a sort of wisdom. Well, what sort of wisdom is this? It is, surely, just human wisdom. It's likely that I really am wise in that sense. These men, to whom I was referring just now, might perhaps be wise in a way that's greater than human, or else I don't know what to call it. For I'm certainly not wise in that way, and whoever says I am is either lying or saying it to slander me.
>
> (20d6–e3)

Socrates concedes, then, that he does possess wisdom of a sort, what he calls "human wisdom," and although he does not here tell us just what this human wisdom consists in, he contrasts it with a "wisdom greater than human," which is what the sophists he just mentioned possess, if they really are wise at all. The wisdom they claimed to possess consists in the knowledge of how to produce *aretê*, and Socrates does not categorically deny that it is possible for human beings to possess that knowledge. He does deny, however, that he possesses such wisdom himself.

2.4.2 The Delphic oracle and the origin of Socrates' mission (20e3–24b2)

So far we do not have an explanation of why anyone would have thought that Socrates was in any sense a wise man. Socrates next proceeds to recount the story of his friend Chaerephon's visit to Delphi, where, for centuries, Greeks believed that the god Apollo revealed various things – often truths about the future – which were otherwise obscured from human beings. These "revelations" were often in the form of riddling answers given by a priestess (the Pythia) to questions asked by petitioners. Chaerephon, it seems, was a life-long friend of Socrates and, convinced that Socrates was extraordinarily wise, actually went to Delphi to ask the oracle if there existed any man wiser than Socrates. The oracle replied, "No one is wiser."[37]

The story is illuminating in a number of ways. First, it is reasonable to infer that Socrates must have already been engaged in philosophical activity of some sort with a circle of friends before Chaerephon's journey. Otherwise, Chaerephon would never have gotten the idea that Socrates really was extraordinarily wise. For how long before Chaerephon's fateful journey Socrates had been engaged in such activity, we can only speculate. We can be confident that Chaerephon's visit to Delphi must have taken place many years before the trial. Recall that Aristophanes' *The Clouds* was produced in 423 B.C.E. and at that point Socrates must have already had a reputation with the Athenian public as a sophist. Now if Socrates began engaging in the activities from which his reputation with the public derived only after the oracle, we can infer that the oracle must have been prior to the production of *The Clouds*. Moreover, since Socrates must have been well known to the public well before the production of *The Clouds*, the oracle must have been delivered at some point well before 423 B.C.E., though exactly when we cannot say.

Second, when he heard what the oracle said, Socrates' response was emphatically *not* to lecture Chaerephon on the irrationality of belief in the reliability of oracles. Rather, Socrates is perplexed about what the god meant, for he says, "I understand that I am not wise at all," but he is also convinced that "the god does not lie. That is not divinely sanctioned for him" (21b4–7). Plainly, then, Socrates took the oracle with the utmost seriousness, believing that Apollo is conveying something true, though in some obscure way, for which the Delphic god is so famous. When Socrates says that in an attempt to understand the real meaning of the oracle he undertook to refute it (21c1), he means that he was attempting to refute the *apparent* meaning of the oracle in order to get a better idea of what the oracle really meant. It was only with "great reluctance" (21b8), Socrates says, that he first went to one of Athens' politicians who thought he was wise and who also had a reputation for wisdom, only to discover that the man was not wise at all. Two important results followed in the wake of this discovery. First, Socrates concluded that he really was wiser than the politician he had examined, even though neither "knew anything worthwhile." But, Socrates reasoned,

> At least this guy thinks he knows something when he doesn't, whereas I, just as I don't know, don't even think I know. At least, then, I seem to be wiser in this small way than this guy, because I don't even think I know what I don't know.
>
> (21d5–8)

Second, the politician, whose ignorance had been exposed, made known his dislike for Socrates, as did those who witnessed the exposure of the fraud. Socrates came to the same conclusion when he approached a second man, another politician, we must assume, and once again, this man, just like the first one, instead of thanking Socrates for exposing his pretense to wisdom, became angry. Indeed, as he proceeded to examine others, he says that it was with "sorrow and alarm" that he saw the enmity against him growing.

Although Socrates does not actually say so explicitly, it appears that we can date the hostility to him from these first attempts to find someone among the politicians wiser than he.

Socrates gives the impression that he had questioned many politicians. After failing to find any one among them who would refute the apparent meaning of the oracle, he turned to the poets who wrote tragedies and dithyrambic poetry (22a9–b1). This would have been a natural place for Socrates to turn next, since these writers were widely regarded in the Athens of the classical period as being profoundly wise. Socrates does not deny that the poems themselves contain important insights. But he says when he began to question the poets themselves about what their works meant, he found that almost anyone who was merely standing around could have done a better job of interpreting them. He concluded that the poets with whom he spoke were not really wise at all but composed their works through some "innate talent and inspiration" (22c1) and were actually more like seers who utter great truths but understand nothing of what they are saying.

The third group to which Socrates turned were the hand-craftsmen. Importantly, he affirms that they knew "many fine things" (22d2), but, because they could practice their crafts well,

> each one believed he was supremely wise in other things – the most important things – and this very mistake of theirs seemed to me to overshadow that wisdom they did have. So I asked myself on behalf of the oracle whether I would prefer to be simply as I am, neither being wise in their sort of wisdom, nor ignorant in the way they are ignorant, or to be in both ways as they are. Then I answered for myself and the oracle that I'd be better off being simply as I am.

> (22d6–e6)

Here we see that Socrates is not a skeptic about the possibility of any knowledge whatever. Clearly, he thinks that some people have the knowledge that constitutes various crafts and that through the knowledge they possess they are able to produce good works. What, then, is the knowledge that they lack and which they mistakenly think they possess? At this point, Socrates says only that it is wisdom about "the most important things" (22d7); but later in the speech (30b1–2) he tells the jury that the most important thing one can care about is the "best state of the soul."

We are now in a position to see what Socrates thinks his "human wisdom," which he claims to possess and which is more valuable that the wisdom possessed by the hand-craftsmen, amounts to. Socrates possesses the "human wisdom" that he *lacks* the wisdom of the "most important things." Now if we think of good things as things that contribute to happiness – either as constituents of happiness or as instruments that bring about the constituents of happiness, whatever they happen to be – we can see why Socrates thinks that his "human wisdom" is actually preferable to the wisdom that the craftsmen possess, conjoined, as it is, with the false belief that they also possess some wisdom greater than human, which is wisdom about the most important things. Socrates states the conclusion he reached as follows:

> But what's likely, men, is that the god is really wise and that in this ora-cle he means that human wisdom is of little or no value. And he appears to mean that such a person is Socrates and to have used my name, taking me as an example, as if to say, "This one of you, O human beings, is wisest, who – as Socrates does – knows that he's in truth worthless with respect to wisdom." And so even now I go around searching and questioning, in keeping with the god, any citizen or stranger whom I think is wise. And when he doesn't seem to me to be so, I help the god out and show that he isn't wise. It's because of this occupation that I have no leisure time worth mentioning to do anything for the city or for my family, but instead I'm in complete poverty on account of my service to the god.

> (23a5–c1)

If we are right about what Socrates thinks "real" wisdom con-sists in, we can see what he means when he says that it is the god who is really wise. We can also see why he would say that human wisdom is "worth little or nothing" once we consider how Socrates sees the place of happiness in the structure of things we value. Not only does he think that happiness is the most important thing to value, so that if we had a choice between it and something else, say, wealth, we should, if we are rational, choose happiness. It is likely that he also thinks that happiness is the single good that we value only for its own sake. Everything else we value, that is, everything else we count as a good, we value because and only because we believe that it in some way contributes to happiness. If this is right, Socrates thinks that happiness – our own happiness – provides us with the sole reason we have for valuing anything else that we value. We want health, then, not for itself, but because we think that by being healthy we shall thereby be happier. The same can be said of the moral knowledge, which Socrates identifies with moral virtue (30a7–b4), although such knowledge would be of special value since it alone enables one to understand all that happiness requires.[38]

So how valuable, then, would be any knowledge other than the knowledge of "the most important things," which, as we have just seen, includes the knowledge of what happiness is? Plainly any other form of knowledge is less valuable, since we have reason to want that knowledge only if we think that its exercise is going to yield happiness. Someone who is truly ignorant of the most important things, someone who thinks he possesses that knowledge and does not, may well have knowledge of some sort; but the knowledge he possesses is not going to benefit him at all if he is pursuing the wrong idea of what is most important. Such a person's knowledge, as Socrates says, is only a form of mere human knowledge and is worth "little or nothing."

More puzzling still is Socrates' inference that he "helps out the god" whenever he reveals someone's pretense to real wisdom. Once again we must make several assumptions if we are to make sense of Socrates' extraordinary conclusion. As we saw in our discussion of Euthyphro's final attempt to define piety, Socrates seems to assume that the proper definition must at least reflect the fact that any pious person is disposed to serve the gods and that the sort of service such a person renders is not the sort that grooms give horses but rather the sort that servants give masters.[39] That is, just as servants try to aid their masters by carrying out their masters' rational wishes, so pious people try to aid the gods by carrying out the gods' wishes. Since the master wants the servant to produce some good through his or her service, the question is what the good is that the gods want the pious person to produce. In the *Euthyphro*, Socrates cannot get Euthyphro to identify the good that the gods want from us; but as we will see, later in the *Apology* Socrates identifies the "best condition of the soul" with "wisdom and truth" (29e1–2), which he then identifies with *aretê*, virtue or excellence as a human being. Even if Socrates himself lacks that wisdom that is greater than human, he benefits his interlocutors by showing them that they have need of further inquiry into what real wisdom consists in. Socrates, then, does not make his interlocutors wise. But insofar as he shows them through the demonstration of their shameful ignorance that they still need to pursue what is best for them, Socrates makes them better off and, to that extent, "helps out the god."[40]

This allows us to see why Socrates would describe his activities from the time he discovers that no one is wiser than he is as a "mission" he has undertaken on behalf of the god. Once the truly pious are confident that they understand what the gods want and that they can indeed work to accomplish what the gods want, they will put that work before their own personal concerns and desires. In this respect pious people are like good servants, who never ignore or put off doing their masters' work in order to pursue other concerns. Thus, Socrates says, "It's because of this occupation that I have no leisure time worth mentioning to do anything for the city or for my family, but instead I'm in complete poverty on account of my service to the god" (23b7–c1).

Socrates generally performs his "service to the god" – to *seek out* those who think they are wise about the most important things and to show them that they are not – in public settings, although as we know from Plato's early works Socrates will confront those in need of his therapeutic examination in private homes if the opportunity presents itself. It is these interrogations of others that explain why he has a following. Those who are so often seen in his company, he says, are the sons of the rich, who do so "of their own free will and have plenty of leisure time" to follow him around. They do so because, according to Socrates, they take "pleasure in hearing people questioned, often imitating him and questioning others" (23c2–6). Although there must have been some who recognized that freeing people from the pretense of wisdom is the best thing one can do for them, Socrates is careful not to deny that there may also have been some among his followers who were motivated solely by the pleasure they received in catching people in apparent contradictions or in posing questions others could not answer. In any event, the practices of his youthful followers were an important source of the animosity Socrates faced. Those whose ignorance was exposed by Socrates' youthful followers became angry with Socrates himself, believing that he had corrupted these young men. Of course, whenever Socrates' detractors were asked just how he corrupted the young, they could only fall back on the accusations that, Socrates says, are "made against all philosophers" by those who do not understand them: "They inquire about the things in the sky and beneath the earth," "they do not believe in the gods," and "they make the worse appear the stronger argument" (23d6–7). In other words, they just repeat the old accusations that have been made against Socrates for years.

Socrates concludes his discussion of the first accusations as he started, by saying that he is aware how unlikely it is that he can refute the slanders the jury has accepted for so long (24a2–4). He also thinks that he has probably angered many of the jurors by even bringing up the first accusations and their causes (26a6–7). But he insists that he has told them the entire truth about the matter, something they will discover for themselves if they "investigate these things either now or later" (24b1–2).

We may think that the fact that Socrates devotes so much time to the first accusations only shows that he is not seriously trying to convince the jury that he be should be released. It simply makes no sense, we might think, for anyone who wants to be released to dredge up the past, knowing that it will only alienate those who are to pass judgment on him. Indeed, it would make no sense if Socrates could achieve his release without responding to the first accusations. But as we saw in our discussion of Socrates' introductory remarks, he is convinced that the first accusations are the "more dangerous" to him and ultimately the source of the widespread suspicion that he has done great harm to the city. Thus, even if he narrowed the scope of his defense to a tightly worded and effective rebuttal of the "newer accusations" that Meletus wrote up, the jury would nonetheless be disinclined to release him, for they would still be convinced that he was in fact a criminal of the very sort they had heard about for so many years. If he is to have any hope of gaining his release, then, he must address and try to rebut the first accusations even if there is a substantial chance that doing so will only further alienate some members of the jury.

There is a second point to be made here. Socrates has much more to say to the jury before that vote on his conviction or acquittal. He may well think, then, that even if his recounting the accusations made against him for so many years will anger some of the jurors, there is still ample time for their anger to subside as they listen to his account of what his divine mission consists in before the vote is taken. If so, and if he believes that his release requires that he successfully explain why he has faced so much hostility for so long, it makes good sense for him to address the formal charges head on, leaving nothing unsaid, even though the most prejudiced members of the jury will be angry when they are made to recall what they have for so long believed about him.

2.5 SOCRATES' DEFENSE AGAINST THE OFFICIAL INDICTMENT

2.5.1 *Meletus and the formal charges (24b3–c3)*

As we noted at the beginning of the chapter, according to Socrates, the formal charges – that he corrupts the youth, that he does not believe in the gods that the city believes in and that he introduces new divinities – are actually the three specifications of the more general charge that he violated the law against impiety, the law Socrates was charged with breaking.[41] Presumably, it was open to Socrates to argue that one or more of the three specific charges are not actually impious. He declines to take that option, presumably because he thinks that each one, if true, would constitute impiety. Instead, he calls Meletus to the speaker's platform and, by

questioning him, undertakes to "examine" each one of the specifications (24c2–3). The result, Socrates says, will be a demonstration
that, in fact, it is Meletus who is the wrongdoer because "he's playing around in what is serious business, thoughtlessly putting people on trial, while pretending to be serious and troubled about
matters he has never cared about at all" (24c4–8).

One important question we need to try to answer in this section
is just what Socrates is trying to accomplish by showing that
Meletus is "playing around in what is serious business." Is that all
Socrates is attempting to do, or is the interrogation aimed at estab-
lishing Socrates' innocence of the charges Meletus has brought
against him? We should note that the former by itself is compatible with Socrates employing various verbal tricks and clearly falla-
cious arguments to show Meletus' lack of understanding of the
issues at stake. If Meletus had bothered to think carefully about the
accusations, Socrates would not be able to trip him up, at least not
easily. The fact that Socrates so easily shows that Meletus' characterization of Socrates' wrongdoing cannot be right demonstrates
that Meletus has not given the accusations the care that he should
have. Indeed, many commentators have argued that this is precisely what Socrates is up to in his interrogation. They maintain
that Socrates crafts his questions in such a way that Meletus ends
up looking foolish, but the proof that Meletus is "playing around
in what is serious business" establishes nothing about Socrates'
guilt or innocence with respect to the formal accusations.[42] As we
will see in the last part of our discussion, several commentators
have argued that in fact Socrates is guilty of at least one of the
specifications of the charge against him, namely, "not believing in
the gods that the city believes in," and that Socrates does not
address the charge head on because he knows he cannot.

Now we might think that Socrates should not be worried about
whether he can prove his innocence of one of the charges, for if he
can show that Meletus himself, the person who is prosecuting him,
does not really understand them sufficiently well to avoid getting
tangled up in Socrates' arguments, the jury will have no choice
but to declare Socrates' innocence. After all, a demonstration of
Meletus' failure to understand the charges should be enough for a

verdict of innocence. But we need to be careful about assuming that Athenian trials were like American trials. Unlike American criminal cases, where the law places a clear and relatively heavy burden on the prosecution to prove charges "beyond a reasonable doubt," Athenian law placed no such requirement on the person bringing a charge against a defendant. As we have already seen, there were no standards of evidence to guide juries as they made their decisions. An Athenian jury could legally conclude that a prosecutor's case fell far short of proof of guilt but nonetheless convict the defendant anyway because they had heard about the case before the trial and already believed he was guilty. Since Socrates believes that the jury has already made up its mind that he is guilty based on the first accusations it has heard (18e5–19a6), acquittal requires that he not *merely* show that Meletus is a bungler. Socrates must also show that he is, in fact, worthy of acquittal.

But even if Socrates really is trying only to demonstrate Meletus' incompetence and not his own innocence, he must be careful about how he does so. To the extent that he tricks or unfairly traps Meletus into saying what he does not sincerely believe, Socrates runs the risk that jurors will conclude that one of the "first accusations" is right and that Socrates really is a sophist, a man who merely "makes the weaker argument appear the stronger." Now it seems very unlikely that Socrates simply does not care about whether the jury understands who he is and what he has been doing in Athens all of these years. In the first place, his duty to the god to continue his philosophical mission requires that he do everything in his power short of violating any of his moral principles to gain his release. Beyond that, as we will see, before the jury takes its vote on his guilt, Socrates says that it is his duty as a speaker before the court to instruct and persuade them (35c1–2). Socrates would hardly be faithful to his duty to "instruct" the jury if he knowingly creates the impression, by the way he interrogates Meletus, that in fact he cares nothing for the truth and the often-made claim that he is a sophist has been accurate all along. Socrates would have to weigh any gain to be derived from tricking Meletus in some way against the grave harm he would do by reinforcing the notion that he is unfair in the way he argues. The more prudent course for Socrates, we contend, would be the more straightforward one. That way, if Meletus fails to serve his own cause well, it will be clear to all that he has not given the accusations the careful thought the court has every right to expect of prosecutors, and only those who are already beyond persuasion will be able to suppose that Meletus' ineptitude is somehow really Socrates' fault.

2.5.2   The corruption of the youth (24c4–26b7)

We might think that Socrates begins his interrogation with an irrelevancy. Instead of asking why Meletus thinks he corrupts the youth or how he makes them worse, Socrates begins by asking who improves the youth. Meletus, of course, stumbles right out of the gate, answering that the laws improve the youth, which, as Socrates somewhat contemptuously responds, is not what he had asked. *Who*, he repeats, not *what*, improves the youth? (24d9–e2). Meletus, no doubt hoping to curry favor with the jurors, says that it is jury members who improve the youth through education (24e4–5). Moreover, all of them make the youth better, not just some (24e8). Not only that, but all of the members of the Council and the Assembly, too, improve them (25a3–8). The upshot, as Socrates is careful to note, is that "all Athenians make the youth admirable and good except me, and I alone corrupt them" (25a9–10).

Meletus' answer is incredible on its face. But to show just how unlikely it is, Socrates deploys the sort of analogy we saw in the *Euthyphro* (13b9–c1).[43] Is it really reasonable to think that only one person makes the youth worse and that most people improve them when just the opposite is the case with respect to other things for which expertise is required? Horses, for example, are improved only by a few, the horse trainers, whereas most people, when they are around horses, make them worse (25b2–5).

Plainly, if Meletus had given even the slightest thought as to how the youth are improved and made worse, he would not have answered as he did. But has Socrates in some way tricked Meletus?[44] It is hard to see that he has. On the contrary, Socrates' questions could hardly be more straightforward. Moreover, even if the analogy fails to establish that Socrates does not harm the youth, it does show that "most people" (and hence presumably most jurors) are responsible, to some extent, for making the youth of Athens worse. This inference can hardly be supposed to curry unfair favor with the jurors, though we have no way of knowing how many jurors would have drawn that conclusion. Socrates doubtless believes that it is true, however, and he does not back away from using an analogy that implies it.

Socrates now questions Meletus about a different point: is it reasonable to hold Socrates accountable even if he has corrupted the youth? The argument Socrates constructs from Meletus' responses is quite simple. First, Meletus agrees that (a) bad people do evil to those who are around them (25c7–8) and, then, (b) that no one wishes to be harmed (25d1–2). Of course, Meletus also agrees to (c), that Socrates voluntarily corrupts the youth – the wealthy young men he allegedly teaches – and contributes to their becoming bad, for were he to cause harm involuntarily he would not be guilty in the eyes of the law (25d5–7). Since those who are corrupted will harm (do evil to) those around them, but no one wished to be harmed, (a) and (b) imply (d), that no one knowingly corrupts those they associate with. (d), however, is clearly inconsistent with (c), since anything done unknowingly is not done voluntarily. Socrates states the outcome of the argument as a disjunction:

> Either I don't corrupt them, or if I do, I corrupt them involuntarily, so that either way, you're not telling the truth. If I corrupt them involuntarily, however, the law isn't here to bring people to trial for errors of this sort but to take them aside in private and to admonish them. For it's clear that once I understand, I'll stop doing what I am doing involuntarily.
>
> (25e6–26a4)

Once again we need to ask whether Socrates has in some way tricked Meletus. Socrates clearly does not coax Meletus to answer as he does. Nor is it clear which premise or premises skeptical jurors might think Meletus should have been more careful about. (a) certainly seems to be true. Bad people – if they really are bad – are disposed to harm those with whom they associate. But none of

Socrates' accusers can plausibly claim that as soon as Socrates had corrupted the young men with whom he associated, he put sufficient distance between himself and those harmed that he could not be harmed in return. Moreover, (b) is hardly implausible if we take the "harm" Socrates has in mind to be "harm all things considered." Socrates can readily allow that sometimes people knowingly do what is to their disadvantage in the short term because they believe that they will in the long term thereby gain a greater advantage. So, with (b) Meletus is only agreeing to what many jurors probably think is true: no one intentionally does what is contrary to his interest all things considered. Finally, Socrates is not suggesting that involuntariness has a scope that many jurors would find peculiar. He is not suggesting here, as he does elsewhere, the famously paradoxical claim that *all* wrongdoing is involuntary because each instance of wrongdoing actually harms the agent and no one wishes to harm himself.[45] Were he to have relied on that view without giving it some defense, many jurors would have quite understandably assumed he was tricking Meletus into saying something Meletus does not believe. In fact, Socrates is really making a very simple and intuitively plausible point against Meletus. But if he corrupted anyone, it is not reasonable to think that he would *knowingly* cause people to become bad or immoral and then turn around and associate with them. So since he clearly makes a practice of associating with them, it must be the case either that he hasn't really made them immoral or, if he did, that he did it unknowingly. Either way, he claims, he deserves "admonishment in private," not punishment by the court. Even if the result is a surprising one, there is no reason to suppose that Socrates has tricked Meletus in any way here.

Socrates now develops a different line of questioning. In what way does Meletus think that Socrates has corrupted the youth? Meletus' response conforms to Socrates' understanding of the indictment: the corruption charge is tied to the other charges. Meletus is alleging that Socrates makes the youth worse by teaching them not to believe in the gods the city believes in, but instead to believe in the new divinities that Socrates has concocted (26b3–7). We might wonder why Meletus links the corruption charge to the distinctly religious charges in this way. This is puzzling because by so doing Meletus is forgoing the opportunity to exploit the widely believed "first accusation" that Socrates is a sophist and that he teaches those with whom he associates "how to make the weaker argument the stronger." Why would Meletus throw away what surely was one of the best arrows in his quiver?

One answer is that, regardless of how hostile most people were to the sophists,[46] there was no law that proscribed sophistry *per se*, something Socrates would have surely pointed out to the king-archon before the trial even took place. So, if Meletus wants to retain the idea that Socrates makes those with whom he associates worse, the accuser needs to connect the manner in which Socrates allegedly corrupts them to something that is arguably illegal. Thus, Meletus asserts that the law Socrates has violated is the law forbidding impiety, and one of the ways Socrates breaks that law is by teaching his associates to reject the traditionally recognized gods and to accept in their place the "new divinities" he has discovered. Of course, Meletus is well aware that those jurors who are convinced that Socrates *also* corrupted his associates by teaching them how to argue sophistically will use that as a reason to convict him even though it is not formally one of the charges. We must remember that there was no presiding judge or other legal procedure to instruct the jurors to cast their vote *only* on the evidence presented that the accused has violated some law. By linking the corruption charge to the religious charges, then, Meletus can, on the one hand, continue to exploit the well-established notion that Socrates is indeed a corruptor of the youth and argue that the harm he does to his "students" constitutes an illegality, on the other.

2.5.3 Not believing in the gods the city believes in and introducing new divinities (26b8–28a2)

Socrates chooses not to call attention to the fact that Meletus has narrowed the scope of the charge that Socrates corrupts the youth. Instead, he focuses on the peculiar way Meletus has stated one of the religious charges. What, he now asks, does Meletus mean by saying that Socrates does not believe in the "the gods the city believes in"? First, there is reason to believe that Athenian juries did regard atheism as a serious offense[47] and there was no "official" list of deities. Because there was no presiding judge or officer of the court to make a determination as to what any legal charge actually meant, Meletus, the author of the charges, is the only person to whom Socrates can turn for clarification. In effect, the charge means only what Meletus says that it means, and so it is appropriate for Socrates to ask Meletus for the needed clarification. Is Meletus claiming that Socrates believes in some gods, but gods that happen not to be the gods the great majority of Athenians accept, and that he teaches others to believe in those other gods, or is Meletus claiming that Socrates believes in no gods at all, and so is an atheist, and teaches others to be atheists (26b8–c6)?

When Meletus answers that Socrates is a complete atheist (26c7), Socrates makes two responses. First, having elicited Meletus' assertion that Socrates does not even believe that the sun and the moon are gods (26d1–5), Socrates points out how implausible it would be for anyone to want to become his student when the books of Anaxagoras, perhaps the most famous of the atheistic nature philosophers, are available to anyone for such a small amount of money (26d6–10). People would, Socrates says, just laugh at him if he tried to pass himself off as the author of such views, "especially since they are completely unbelievable" (26e2).

Socrates' second response is to show that the claim that he is an atheist is inconsistent with one other part of the indictment, that he introduces "new divinities." To develop this second point, Socrates warns the jury not to interrupt him since he is going "to present my argument in the way I am used to" (27b1–2). His point is easily made by means of the maddeningly simply analogies for which he was apparently notorious: since anyone who believes in what is associated with horses must believe in horses, and since anyone who believes in what is associated with flute players must believe in flute players, so anyone who believes in what is associated with "divine things" (*daimonia*) must believes in divinities (*daimones*, 27b5–c2). But since Meletus swore in the indictment that Socrates believes in divine things of some sort – Meletus himself has affirmed that Socrates believes in divinities. Socrates now only needs to secure Meletus' admission that divinities are either gods themselves (27d4–5) or they are the illegitimate children of gods, "either from nymphs or others from whom it's said that they come" (27d8–9). But if it is the latter, Socrates must believe that gods exist after all, for clearly if one believes that something exists and that it comes from a certain kind of source, one can hardly deny that the source exists (27d4–e3).

How good is this second argument? Some scholars suspect Socrates of being less than sincere when he suggests to Meletus that any sensible person accepts that divinities are either gods or the illegitimate offspring of the gods.[48] But it is not at all clear that Socrates is being dishonest here. It is true that he tells Euthyphro that he does not accept at least some stories about the gods (6a6–8), but Socrates does not say there that he cannot accept the idea that the gods have offspring by mating with mortals or other beings lacking the full status of gods; nor is there any ancient evidence that Socrates rejected this standard view.[49] But wondering whether Socrates accepted every detail of each of the multitude of stories and fables about how the gods and their offspring misses the point Socrates is making. Socrates' point is simply that anyone who believes that there are divinities must believe that these divinities are themselves gods of some sort or that they are, in some way, connected to gods. Put this way, we can see just how powerful Socrates' point is. Meletus could hardly deny that there are divinities. Even Meletus can see that Socrates would immediately point out the irony that it is he who is charged with irreligion when it is, in fact, Meletus who is now openly disavowing one of the basic Athenian religious convictions. Nor can Meletus deny the connection between divinities and gods. Socrates would immediately seize on the implausibility. If divinities have not *in some way* the gods or godliness as part of their nature, Socrates will quite rightly ask, what could their divine nature possibly be? No one would say that there are indeed divinities but they are just another part of the ordinary world of nature. Nor could Meletus very well shift his position and say that it is Socrates who does not believe in "divine things" or in divinities. In the first place, his own indictment asserts that Socrates *does* believe in divine things. It asserts that he believes in "new divine things." To disavow that would surely run the risk of undermining the jury's confidence in the other parts of the indictment. Moreover, many of the jurors, as Meletus must know, are familiar with Socrates' often-made claim that he himself is contacted by a "divine thing," his *daimonion* (31c7–d2).

So, Socrates has shown that Meletus' own construal of the indictment is contradictory. If Meletus is right about the charge that Socrates introduces "new divinities," it cannot be the case that Socrates is an atheist, which, as we have just seen, is what Meletus says he meant when he charged Socrates with "not believing in the gods that the city believes in." But this is not all that Socrates has shown. Socrates can happily concede, as he does when he openly discusses the crucial role his own *daimonion* has played in his life (31c7–e1), that he does believe in divine things, from which it follows, coupled with the rest of the argument he has developed from Meletus' answers, that the atheism charge is simply false.

But by readily admitting that he has a unique relationship with what he calls his *daimonion*, is Socrates not admitting that at least one of the formal accusations is true? Has he not introduced at least one "new divinity" into the city? Of course, in one straightforward sense he has, but this is not the sense that the indictment assumes. The indictment does not treat "not believing in the gods the city believes in" and "believes in other, new divinities" as distinct in the sense that Socrates could be guilty of one and not the other. Instead, it treats "believing in new divinities" as an exclusive alternative to "not believing in the gods the city believes in."[50] By showing that it is false that he is not an atheist, then, Socrates has shown that he is not guilty of the second charge either. Finally, since Meletus himself ties the first charge – that "Socrates corrupts the youth" – to the atheism charge, by showing that he is not an atheist, Socrates has shown that, as Meletus construes his own charges, Socrates is innocent of each one. If this is right, Socrates is not misstating or exaggerating what the interrogation has shown when he says at its conclusion, "Well, anyway, Athenians, that I am not guilty according to Meletus' indictment does not need much of a defense, and what I have said about it is enough" (28a2–4). To be sure, Meletus is deeply confused and Socrates is right to accuse him of "pretending to be serious and troubled about matters which he has never cared about at all" (24c6–8). Meletus' carelessness is not simply in having written up incoherent charges such that if one part is true, the other part is false. Instead, as Socrates says, he is "playing around in serious business" (24c5–6), for he is trying to have a man killed by making charges that are so easily refuted.

2.5.4 Was Socrates actually guilty?

We have been arguing that once Meletus himself construes the charge of "not believing in the gods that the city believes in" as not believing in any gods at all, Socrates is able to show that he is not guilty of the charges. Although Meletus is ensnared, the trap is entirely of his own making. But some scholars have argued that Socrates was actually guilt of impiety because the Athenians would have regarded anyone as impious who does not believe in the gods they recognize and they would not have countenanced Socrates' own conception of perfectly moral gods as the same gods they accept.[51] Moreover, since Meletus believes that the recognition of false gods is impious, and since most Athenians also believed that the gods would surely be angered by any city that tolerated impiety in its midst, he would naturally think he is doing the city a great favor of ridding it of such an affront to the gods. According to some scholars, then, Meletus simply blunders when Socrates asks him what is meant by the expression "Socrates does not believe in the gods the city believes in." Had Meletus said what he really meant, "Of course, you believe in what *you* call gods, Socrates. You just don't believe in any gods that we in this city recognize as gods," Socrates could not have refuted him, for in fact Socrates is guilty of the charge understood in that way.

There are a number of reasons why we are not persuaded by this way of thinking. It is true, of course, that charging Socrates with believing in false gods would have prevented Socrates from refuting Meletus in the precise way he did. But the alternative, that Socrates believes in the wrong gods, would have presented another, perhaps even more intractable problem for Meletus. Had he conceded that Socrates does indeed believe in gods of some sort, Meletus would have lost the connection between the impiety charge and the "first accusations." As Socrates says, Meletus put his faith in the "first accusations" (19a9–b2) when he decided to prosecute Socrates, for he knew that the "first accusations" expressed what Socrates' criminal behavior consisted in. Were Meletus now to say that Socrates really does believe in some gods, just not the gods of the city, Socrates could easily seize on the answer as evidence that Meletus himself thinks that at least one of the "first accusations" is unfair to him and that, contrary to what so many have said about him for so long, even his prosecutor believes Socrates is a religious person after all, just not religious in the way most Athenians are. Given the grip that the picture of Socrates as an atheistic nature-philosopher had on the minds of most of the jurors, Meletus must have realized that it would be exceeding risky to plant the idea that the "first accusations" may not be completely fair to Socrates. Moreover, bear in mind that Meletus has already offered his speech to the jury. If Socrates were not wildly off the mark in suggesting that Meletus was relying on the older, first accusations, then Meletus could offer such a significant amendment to them – saying now that Socrates is not really a complete atheist – only at the cost of significantly undermining whatever persuasive force his own speech had. So, while it is true that Meletus could have avoided making inconsistent assertions about Socrates' belief in the gods, he could not likely have won more votes among the jurors by suddenly denying that Socrates was an atheist.

Moreover, if Meletus really believed at the time he wrote the indictment that he could successfully prosecute Socrates for believing in the wrong gods, why did he not say so when Socrates asks him to interpret what he meant by saying that he "does not believe in the gods that the city believes in"? According to the interpretation we are criticizing, Meletus' blunder in response to Socrates' request for a clarification is simply inexplicable. Meletus may not be the brightest opponent Socrates has ever faced, but it is difficult to believe that he is as inept as the interpretation we are now considering requires.

We should also recall that Euthyphro, who seems quite familiar with Socrates, does not assume that Meletus is troubled by any differences between Socrates' views about the gods and those of the typical Athenian. When he first hears from Socrates that he must answer a charge that he is a maker of new gods and does not believe in the old ones" (3b1–4), Euthyphro does not answer, "Well, of course, Socrates, Meletus is angry because you have utterly transformed the traditional gods into something none of us can recognize." Instead, Euthyphro immediately assumes that the "innovations" Socrates is charged with making concern his *daimonion*, which Socrates characterizes as a divine voice that he hears and which turns him away from evil. This is the way Xenophon, too, apparently understood the charge.[52] Perhaps most telling is the fact that Socrates tells the jury that it is his *daimonion* that Meletus "was making fun of" in his indictment (31c7–d2). We think it is significant that not a single ancient source about the trial of Socrates suggests that his belief in morally perfect deities was of any concern to those who were responsible for bringing Socrates to trial.

Nor does Socrates understand that Meletus is troubled by the sorts of gods he believes in, something he surely would have understood after his appearance before the king-archon had it been the real charge Meletus wished to make against him. Instead, Socrates tells the jury that Meletus was relying on the "first accusations" in bringing the formal charges (19a9–b2), and the relevant "first accusation" is that Socrates is a nature-philosopher, an atheist. So, Socrates is assuming from the outset that if he is to be acquitted, he does not need to convince the jury that the gods he believes in are also the same gods they believe in.

He does actually make this point implicitly, however. Towards the end of the first speech, Socrates tells the jury in the most direct terms that he does "believe in the gods" and that it is precisely for that reason that he cannot encourage them to violate the oath they have taken to judge the case according to the laws (35c2–d9).[53] Here it is clear that Socrates thinks the gods who would be justifiably angry were he to encourage the jurors to violate their oaths are the very same gods to whom the jurors believe they have sworn their oaths. It could not be plainer that Socrates thinks that his pious obligation not to encourage the jury to violate their oath and the jury's pious obligation to be loyal to their oath are owed to the *same* beings.

There is yet another reason for skepticism that Socrates was in fact guilty of "not believing in the gods that the city believes in." It is doubtful that most Athenians would have regarded Socrates' conception of the gods as especially dangerous. Now there is no question that, at least as Plato portrays him,[54] Socrates differs from most Athenians with respect to their religious views in three significant and, perhaps, related ways. Most Athenians believed that the gods, motivated by such drives as cowardice, lust, envy, and revenge, sometimes committed all sorts of evils against mortals (and each other); in Socrates' view, by contrast, the gods are, by their very nature, thoroughly good beings. Socrates was driven to this conclusion by his convictions that the gods are thoroughly wise (23a5–6)[55] and that wisdom guarantees virtue.[56] Moreover, as we have already noted, Socrates says that he finds it hard to believe certain traditional myths about the gods and their exploits (*Euthyphro* 6a6–9). Third, Socrates rejects the notion that the gods can be moved to give mortals what they want by various sacrifices and offerings.

So, just how damaging would these views have been to Socrates had Meletus found a way to bring them out into the open before the jury? We believe that, in all likelihood, the jury would not have regarded them as especially significant and, in any event, they would not justify the charge that the gods Socrates believes in are not the gods that the city believes in. Regarding the second of Socrates' views we discussed, that Socrates rejects stories about the gods, nowhere does Socrates say that he rejects *all* traditional stories about the gods. We have no reason to think that Socrates rejects commonly held views about familial relationships among the gods making up the pantheon or tales about their physical prowess. What Socrates does deny are stories of the gods' failures to do what they take to be right or their failures to know what the right thing is. Nor is there is good reason to think that Socrates regarded all prayer and sacrifice as irrational. To be sure, he would suppose it is pointless (or worse) to ask the gods to do what is wrong or evil, but there is nothing about his beliefs that would have precluded requests of divine assistance as he tried to achieve worthy ends. Moreover, even though Socrates thinks that the gods cannot be benefited by mortals and thus he thinks that sacrifices aimed at making the gods better are pointless, he need not reject the practice of making sacrifices to the gods as a way of acknowledging their superiority or one's indebtedness to them as the cause of all good things (*Euthyphro* 15a1–2). Perhaps some of the jurors would have been puzzled about why Socrates believes what he does about the nature of the gods, but there is no reason to think that they would have regarded his opinions as in any way a serious threat to the city.

Finally, according to the interpretation we have been criticizing, Socrates was in fact guilty of impiety and so he escaped actually having to be confronted with clear evidence of his guilt only by Meletus' incompetence. But Socrates could not have known in advance that Meletus would blunder in the way that he did, and so if the interpretation we have been considering were true, Socrates himself quite needlessly blundered in inviting Meletus to articulate clearly the actual ground of Socrates' guilt. Socrates is saved from the effect of his own blunder, we are to suppose, only by the very fortuitous blunder Meletus makes.

We find this theory, to be frank, hopelessly elaborate and far-fetched. As we will see when we discuss the *Crito*, Socrates believes that he owes allegiance to the laws of Athens. Had Socrates believed that his own religious views were in conflict with the law forbidding impiety, his own theory of the citizen's duty would be that he must respond either by persuading the state to change the law, obey the law, or leave Athens. But since he neither undertook to persuade Athens to change the law, nor did he leave, and since he considers himself to have lived justly throughout his life (37b2–3), it cannot be the case that he harbors some suspicion that he really is guilty after all and that Meletus is simply too dim-witted to see how best to convict Socrates of his crime.

We are unable to find any ancient evidence that anyone regarded Socrates' belief in the gods as thoroughly wise and moral agents as a cause of any alarm at all. In the absence of such evidence, we have no reason to believe that his fellow Athenians would have regarded his religious views as grounds for punishment. We believe that many in Athens were indeed deeply troubled by what they thought was his attitude toward religion. But the threat he posed in their eyes is none other than atheism, which is what Meletus explicitly and plainly accuses him of and which is what Socrates assumes throughout the *Apology* is the charge against him. If we are right, there is no reason to think that Socrates takes advantage of Meletus' mistaken characterization of one of the formal charges. Instead, when asked by Socrates what the charge of disbelief in the city's gods amounts to, Meletus, relying on the "first accusation," says exactly what he means and what the jury suspects – and Socrates deftly refutes it.

2.6 DEFENSE OF THE PHILOSOPHICAL LIFE

2.6.1 *Return to the old prejudices (28a3–b2)*

Socrates concludes his interrogation of Meletus on a pessimistic note. After suggesting that it is so obvious that he is not guilty of the accusations Meletus brought that he does not need to say anything more about them, Socrates reiterates his despair about undoing the damage done to him by the "first accusations." If he is convicted – and he still thinks he will be – it will be because of the "hatred" so many people feel toward him (28a5–6). Prejudice has convicted many good men in the past, he says, and such injustices are not likely to end with his conviction (28a9–b2).

Before the interrogation of Meletus, Socrates' primary goal was to convince the jury that the "first accusations" made him a victim of mistaken identity: he had been mistaken for a nature-philosopher and a sophist. Now, after his interrogation of Meletus, his primary goal is to convince the jury that, despite the fact that few have recognized their value, the very activities that have angered so many have actually been a great good for the city. What this great good is, why Socrates believes he must provide it to the city, and how Socrates has gone about trying to bestow the great good become the central themes of Socrates' renewed attempt to dislodge the old prejudices.

2.6.2 *Doing the right thing is more important than merely living (28b3–d4)*

Instead of launching directly into an explanation of his value to the city, Socrates first imagines someone saying that he should be ashamed of the position he now finds himself in, for in all likelihood he is going to be put to death. He does so because he wants to challenge the widely held assumptions that it is shameful to suffer a great evil, especially at the hands of one's enemies,[57] and that death is the greatest of evils.

Socrates responds by arguing that such an accusation rests on a misunderstanding of what is really shameful. Socrates would have disgraced himself only if he had abandoned philosophical activities once he had recognized the vehemence of the animosity they were arousing. "You are mistaken if you think that it's necessary for a person who has any merit to consider the risk of life or of death and not to look only to this when he acts: is he acting justly or unjustly and performing the deeds of a good or a bad person?" (28b6–c1). To think otherwise, he says, would be to require the condemnation of the heroes of the Trojan War, including the "son of Thetis," Achilles, the greatest of the Greek warriors. Socrates is alluding to the touching episode in the *Iliad*[58] when Achilles' mother Thetis explains that it is his fate to die if he ventures forth to avenge the death of his friend Patroclus. Achilles, Socrates reminds the jury, "thought little of death and danger" and instead "had a much greater fear of living as a bad man" (28c9–d1).

By mentioning Achilles in this way, Socrates can effectively show the jury that his activities were motivated by a conviction they share once they think about it: one's first concern must always be to do what is right, or as Socrates sometimes says, "to act justly," even if that means one will have to die for it. It is shameful to do otherwise. Nowhere does Socrates say that he is indifferent to death. Instead, he is only asserting that if he must choose between death and injustice, he will choose death. Only in that way can he avoid doing what is shameful. We can now see why Socrates begins his explanation of his activities by responding to the charge that he should be ashamed of the way things have turned out for him.

He has now, in effect, put the jury on notice that he will not stop doing what he thinks is right even if it means he must die. The jury must not mistake his unwillingness to yield to injustice as in any way a sign of arrogance or disrespect.

2.6.3 Remaining at one's post (28d5–29a5)

Insisting that he is committed to being just is only the first step in Socrates' explanation. But instead of arguing that philosophy is just *per se*, that philosophy is by its very nature a just activity, Socrates next appeals to a second principle that the jury is likely to accept:

> For it really is this way, Athenians, that wherever someone stations himself, believing it to be best, or where someone has been stationed by his commander, I think, he must remain there to face danger, not weighing death or anything else more than disgrace.
>
> (28d5–9)

A few lines later, Socrates makes the same point in even stronger language. "But I do know that it is evil and disgraceful to do what is wrong and to disobey one's superior, whether it is god or man" (29b6–7). To make plausible that he is indeed the sort of person who remains at his post "to face danger," Socrates reminds the jury of his distinguished military record, where he "risked death" at Potidaia, and Amphipolis, and Delium (28d10–e4).[59] Similarly, he could hardly do otherwise when the god ordered that "[Socrates] must spend his life examining himself and others" (28e4–6). "That would indeed be terrible," he says, "and then someone might really bring me to court justly on the ground that I don't believe that the gods exist, since I disobey the oracle, fear death, and think I am wise when I am not" (29a2–5).

Socrates' explanation of why he has been engaged in philosophizing even though he has become the object of vicious hatred can be set forth schematically. The first two premises can be stated as principles, and the third as a factual claim.

1. It is always shameful to stop doing what is just in order to avoid death.
2. It is always just to obey one's superiors, whether divine or human.
3. The god has stationed Socrates in Athens to "examine himself and others," that is, to do philosophy.

If the jury believes that Socrates is sincere about (3), the factual claim that the god has ordered him to engage in philosophy, the jury can hardly fail to see that the principles they themselves share require Socrates to do what has been so badly misunderstood. To abandon the "post" the god has assigned him once it became clear that he could lose his life would have been the most shameful thing he could do.

2.6.4 Two questions

The way Socrates states the second principle raises two questions we can hardly ignore. First, what makes one a "superior" in the sense that it would be wrong to disobey his or her orders? Second, because Socrates actually says that he "knows" that it is wrong to disobey one's superior (29b6–7), how can he also claim that he lacks moral wisdom and that his own superiority over those who think they are wise resides in exactly those facts?

We might initially think that by one's "superior," Socrates means "moral superior," someone who is in a better position to judge what ought to be done.[60] This would explain why he thinks that the god counts as his "superior," for it is clear that he thinks that the god possesses moral wisdom that is "greater than human." If this is what he has in mind by "superior," then he is saying that one must always follow one's own judgment about what is right, unless that judgment conflicts with that of someone who has keener judgment about matters of good and evil, in which case one must yield to the better judge.

We think it is unlikely that this interpretation can be right. Whatever Socrates thought of the military expertise of those under whom he served during the campaigns he mentions, it is clear that he did not consider them to be his moral superiors. On the contrary, he has already informed the jury that during his attempt to discover the real meaning of the oracle concerning his wisdom, he has found no one wiser than he, a conclusion he never revises. Indeed, we have no reason to believe that his military commanders had any great moral insight at all. But the passage we are considering makes it clear that Socrates believes that one always has a moral duty to stay at the post assigned to him by his military commander because they are his superiors. Thus, we have to infer that Socrates thinks he has a moral duty to obey anyone in a position of legal authority, even if that authority's judgment conflicts with his own about what it is to be done.[61] So, Socrates does not get side-tracked by a lengthy discussion of the origins of authority. He is making the safe assumption that the jury agrees that the gods have authority over us and that various human beings have authority over us when they are given that authority by the position they hold in a legal structure. In both cases, the authority is legitimate and in both cases the authorities count as our superiors.

Although only this interpretation can make sense of the fact that Socrates believes that justice required that he obey his military superiors, it raises a vexing question of its own. What is the citizen to do when the citizen's judgment about what is just conflicts with that of his "superior"? Even if we think that the god could not make a mistake, surely human judgment is fallible. Is Socrates then suggesting that the citizen must follow the commands of his human superiors even when he believes they are in error? The same question arises again in the *Apology* when Socrates imagines the jury ordering him to abandon philosophy (29c6–d6), and although we will have more to say when we look at this passage, we must postpone our full discussion of the issue until we turn to the *Crito*, where the scope of the citizen's duty to obey legal authorities is the central issue.

Let's now turn to the second question we raised about the principle that one must always obey one's superiors. What makes the principle puzzling is the way Socrates states it: he says that he "*knows*" that it is correct. Before we try to explain how we can square such a bold assertion with his earlier claim that he is not really wise, we should note that we cannot dismiss this assertion as a slip or an unintended departure from what Socrates really thinks when he is speaking strictly, for Socrates immediately goes on to imply that there are other things that he knows are evil: "Rather than those things that I know are bad, I'll never run from nor fear those things which may turn out to be good" (29b8–c1). And when, after he has been convicted, he is given the opportunity to offer his counter-penalty to the jury, he makes it clear that he "knows" some of the options he could offer would constitute evils: "Can it be that I should suffer the penalty that Meletus proposes, which I say that I don't know whether it is a good or not? Or should I choose what I know to be an evil, making this my counter-penalty instead?" (37b5–8).[62]

We believe that the key to solving this puzzle can be found in what Socrates says about the "most important things," those things about which he questions others who claim to be wise. Somewhat later in the speech, he identifies what these "most important" matters are:

> For the only thing I do is go around trying to persuade you, young and old, not to care more about your bodies or money, nor so passionately as you do about the perfection of your souls, saying, "Virtue does not come from money, but money and all other good things for human beings, both in public and private, come from virtue."

> (30a7–b4)

Here we see that, for Socrates, the "most important things" are the moral virtues, or virtue, as Socrates often refers to them taken together. What his questioning of others has revealed is that no one, including himself, knows what virtue is. This is the respect in which he has found out that all human beings are deficient. So, this is the sense in which neither he nor anyone he has questioned is wise.

At this point, it may be helpful to distinguish between knowing something – perhaps even many things – about a body of knowledge, and actually possessing that body of knowledge. For example, we might know a great deal about medicine. We might know what its purpose is, how the knowledge of medicine is acquired, what tests to apply to see if one really possesses the knowledge of medicine. We might even know some of the same things that physicians know and demonstrate when they are displaying their medical knowledge. We might know, for example, that a fever is a sign of infection or that jaundice is a sign of a diseased liver. But for all that we might know of this sort, we will not actually be physicians if we do not possess the body of knowledge that is medicine. It is worth asking, then, what Socrates thinks the possession of such a body of knowledge requires.

Let us first notice that Socrates recognizes some individuals as possessing wisdom of a sort, namely the craftsmen (22d2–4), though of course, it is not wisdom about the "most important things." Although it would take us too far afield to discuss all of the various conditions of possessing a craft,[63] let us here point out only that Socrates believes that to qualify as a genuine practitioner of a craft, (a) one must be able to produce examples of the full range of things one has knowledge of, (b) one must be a competent judge of whether something is a good example of what it is one knows, and (c) one must be able to give an adequate explanation both of how to produce examples of one's craft and of the judgments one makes about examples that one's craft produces. The physician, then, can produce health, can reliably distinguish persons who are really healthy from those who only appear to be healthy, and can adequately explain how to produce instances of health as well as their judgments about who is healthy and who is not. Of course non-physicians can occasionally restore the ill to health too, but they do so only when they have seen health restored in that way by someone else or because they were experimenting on the patient and happened to hit upon a cure that worked. Physicians, by contrast, produce health in virtue of their medical knowledge of what is making the patient unhealthy and of what restores health.

If Socrates thinks that the wisdom he lacks and for which he is searching either is or is very much like a craft such as medicine, we can see how he can consistently claim that he knows many things of great moral import and yet not be "wise about the most important things." Now any discipline has a certain range or subject matter with which it is concerned. Medicine is concerned with health and architecture is concerned with the design of buildings, for example. Socrates lacks wisdom because he does not possess the body of knowledge in virtue of which he can reliably make and give the right account of the full range of correct judgments concerning "the most important things." As Socrates says in the *Gorgias* (508e6–509a7), he knows that anyone who asserts that being unjust is a good thing is wrong, but he does not know "how it is" that it is wrong. That is, Socrates is quite confident that being unjust does not really pay for the person who is unjust, but he cannot give the complete account of why this is true. Because he cannot fully explain his judgment, he does not qualify as possessing the craft-like knowledge required for wisdom about the "most important things." Like non-physicians who can correctly identify certain illnesses, Socrates possesses various pieces of moral knowledge. But like the same non-physicians, Socrates is not a moral expert and so lacks the wisdom so many others falsely profess to possess.

2.6.5 From where does Socrates' knowledge come?

In his speech to the jury, Socrates does not explain how he knows what few things he claims to know. But if we bear in mind the distinction between knowing that something is the case and knowing how it is that such a thing is the case, we can see why Socrates is so confident about some of his moral judgments. Now one way he might know that something is true is through inference. He can claim to know something if he derives it from premises that he also knows. This seems to be what he means when he says in the passage in the *Gorgias* just cited that arguments of "iron and adamant" have led him to believe that it is justice, not injustice, that is always good for its possessor.

Of course, this just raises the further question of how Socrates knows that the premises of his iron and adamantine arguments are true. Some propositions, no doubt, strike Socrates as commonsensical truths. "Virtue is always a good thing for its possessor" and

"It is always rational to pursue happiness as one's ultimate goal" would qualify in this category. No one would dispute claims such as these. Rather, they dispute what virtue and happiness are.

Another likely source of Socrates' knowledge is his examination of those who claim to be wise. For example, it is safe to say that his interrogations of others have shown him that anyone who says that virtue is really just wealth will end up contradicting himself by the time he finishes answering questions about what he really believes. At some point, Socrates would be justified in thinking that the claim that virtue is wealth is just not believable, because, after having been examined about it, everyone abandons that conception of virtue when faced with the problem it poses for their other beliefs. The *Gorgias* passage cited above suggests that it was by seeing over and over again that no one can successfully defend the notion that injustice is a benefit that Socrates came to the conclusion that justice is the real benefit.[64] Socrates' own conviction that virtue cannot be wealth, then, is likely to be only the product of an induction from the repeated failure of others to defend the contrary. Nonetheless, if the evidence for the induction is sufficiently strong, Socrates can claim to know that virtue is not wealth. In this respect, his claim to know is no different from any based on strong inductive evidence.

A third source of knowledge for Socrates involves his religious convictions.[65] He clearly believes that the gods communicate in various ways with human beings, and when they do, one can know certain things about what is communicated. As we have already seen, when he hears of his friend Chaerephon's trip to Delphi, Socrates never doubts that Apollo communicates with humans through oracles. Indeed, Socrates thinks that it is impossible for the god's intended message not to be truthful (21b6–7). Instead, he wonders what the intended message of the oracle could be, since the oracle said that no one is wiser than he and yet he is convinced that he is not wise in any way. Later, he explains to the jury that he has no doubt whatever that he has been ordered by the god to serve the city through philosophy. "I have been ordered to do this through dreams and oracles and in every way in which divine providence has ever ordered a human being to do anything whatever" (33c4–8). Of course, the dreams and oracles need interpretation too, just as did the oracle given to Chaerephon regarding Socrates' wisdom, and the interpretations placed on dreams and oracles, just as the interpretation of the Delphic oracle, are plainly fallible. Unfortunately, Socrates does not explain how he goes about testing various possible interpretations of divine communications through dreams and oracles to see which interpretation is the right one.[66] But as we will see when we examine his mission on behalf of the god, Socrates is so completely convinced that he has hit upon the right interpretation that he is willing to live the rest of his life in accordance with that interpretation. Prominent among the communications from the "divine" were warnings Socrates received which we have already seen he refers to as his *daimonion*, a sort of "voice" he has heard since childhood (31d2–3). Because it figures so prominently in Socrates' account of why he never entered into the political life of Athens, we will postpone for now our discussion of how it functioned to give Socrates guidance. Let us only note here that Socrates has no doubt whatever about the reliability of the warnings this "voice" communicates to him and that, as is the case with the other pieces of knowledge Socrates claims to possess, he cannot give a fully adequate account of why he is being warned. Once again, then, although Socrates *knows* that he ought not to engage in the specific action or action type that his *daimonion* warns him against, he lacks the wisdom to explain the full range of goods from which human beings can benefit and the full range of evils from which they can suffer. Only a craftsman of virtue, someone who possesses a wisdom greater than mere "human wisdom," could accomplish that. As he repeatedly insists, that is the sort of wisdom he lacks.

2.6.6 The fear of death is the pretense of wisdom (29a5–b7)

To this point, Socrates has argued that it would have been shameful for him to disobey the god and retreat from the "post" because he fears death. Even if death is an evil, doing what is unjust is a greater evil. Now Socrates argues that it is shameful to fear death at all as if one really knows what happens at death. Those who say death is something to be feared are star examples of persons who pretend to know what they do not.

> In truth, the fear of death, men, is nothing but thinking you're wise when you're not, for you think you know what you don't. For no one knows whether death happens to be the greatest of all goods for humanity, but people fear it because they're completely convinced that it is the greatest of evils. And isn't this ignorance, after all, the most shameful kind: thinking you know what you don't? But in this respect, too, men, I'm probably different from most people. If, then, I would say that I'm wiser than someone in some way, it would be in this way: while I don't really know about the things in Hades, I don't think I know. But I do know that it's evil and disgraceful to do what's wrong and to disobey one's superior, whether god or man. Rather than those things that I know are bad, I'll never run from nor fear those things that may turn out to be good.
>
> (29a4–c1)

Now we see the full force of Socrates' response to anyone who would say that he should be ashamed of having brought on his own death needlessly by engaging in philosophy. First, staying at his "post," even if it means he must die, is not shameful, for it is never shameful to avoid what one knows to be an evil in preference to what may, for all he knows, be a good. Second, it is the person who claims to know that death is a great evil who is guilty of ignorance of the "most shameful kind," for that person thinks he knows what he does not. Looked at in this way, we can see why Socrates thinks that his "human wisdom" really is preferable: he really is wiser than those who think they know about the things in Hades, for while he does not know about such matters, he does not think he knows (29b5–6).[67]

2.6.7 Socrates' commitment to philosophy (29b7–30a5)

Although he does not label it as such, Socrates explains his motivation to do philosophy in terms of his own self-interest. Since he knows that it would be shameful to disobey his superior, and since death may, for all he knows, turn out to be a good, it is better for him to stay at his post and face the possibility he may be killed. To underscore the firmness of his commitment to comply with the god's wishes, Socrates imagines the jury releasing him only on the condition that he stop practicing philosophy:

"Socrates, this time we won't do as Anytus says. We'll let you go, but on this condition, that you stop spending your time in this inquiry of yours and philosophizing. But if you're caught still doing so, you'll die." Thus, if, as I was saying, you were to let me go on this condition, I'd tell you, "Athenians, I respect and I love you, but I'll obey the god rather than you, and as long as I breathe and am able, I won't stop philosophizing and exhorting and pointing out to any of you I ever happen upon, saying just what I usually do, 'Best of men, since you're an Athenian, from the greatest city with the strongest reputation for wisdom and strength, aren't you ashamed that you care about having as much money, fame, and honor as you can, and you don't care about, or even consider wisdom, truth, and making your soul as good as possible?'"

(29c6–e3)

Is Socrates here saying that there is absolutely nothing that would make him voluntarily abandon his philosophical mission on behalf of the god? This passage is often interpreted in this way and thus is regarded as compelling evidence that, at least in the *Apology*, Socrates believes that any duty he has to obey the laws of Athens would never give him reason to cease philosophizing.[68] In other words, this passage is often interpreted to mean that a law or lawful command by a civilian authority issued to Socrates not to engage in philosophy will always be overridden by a more compelling moral or religious duty, owed to the god, to engage in philosophy. We will have much more to say about this issue in the next chapter, where we discuss the moral obligation to obey the law Socrates espouses in the *Crito*. Suffice it to say that, were Socrates stating his willingness to defy a jury directive that he cease philosophizing, he would be suddenly introducing a wholly new and complex issue into what had been upto this point a clear line of argument. The context, then, indicates that he is telling the jury that he will not abandon his mission on behalf of the god even in return for a guarantee that he will not be killed and that he can live out the rest of his life as he pleases. His message to the jury is that it is utterly pointless for them, or anyone else, to think that they could persuade him to stop irritating others with his questioning by threatening him with death. But it clearly does not follow from the single fact that the threat of death will not make him stop philosophizing that Socrates believes that one must violate the law when it commands one to do what one thinks is not right.

2.6.8 The nature of Socrates' mission (30a5–c2)

Having explained to the jury in the most direct way why he has been engaged in philosophy and why no coercion, no matter how strong the threat, will make him defy the god, Socrates turns to an explanation of what his mission on behalf of the god consists in. As we saw in our discussion of Socrates' attempt to refute the apparent meaning of the oracle by finding someone wiser than he, Socrates did find people, the craftsmen, who possessed wisdom of a sort: they possessed the knowledge that constituted their crafts. But Socrates declines to count their knowledge as being of any great importance because they were ignorant of "the most important things." Believing that they possessed the latter sort of knowledge when they did not is shameful, since they were apt to put the knowledge they did possess in the service of the wrong goals. In a passage we examined above, their mistake was to care about acquiring "as much money, fame, and honor" as they could, and not to make "wisdom, truth, and the perfection of the soul" their primary concern (29d9–e3). We should note that Socrates does not say that money, fame, and honor are always evils, or things we should inevitably avoid. But it is striking that Socrates seems convinced that it is shameful to pursue such things "as much as one can." It is the unlimited pursuit of these things, Socrates believes, that is evil. What turns these things that most people want into goods is "wisdom, truth, and the perfection of the soul," which he subsequently identifies with virtue:

> For the only thing I do is to go around trying to persuade you, young and old, not to care more about either your bodies or money, nor so passionately as you do about the perfection of your souls, saying, "Virtue doesn't come from money, but money and all other good things for human beings, both in private and in public, come from virtue."

(30a7–b4)

Socrates surely does not mean that virtue simply produces health, money, and so forth. Rather, he means that virtue is the power to identify what really is useful to one, and to make anything that one has into a good. That is, virtue is the power to make such things as money and health into things that contribute to living well – happiness.[69]

The idea that such things as honor, reputation, and money might actually be detrimental to someone is intuitively plausible. What would make them detrimental is their misuse, and they would be misused whenever we attach too high a value to them and so employ them in such a way that they undermine or conflict with other things that we want. Money, for example, can obviously be used to support activities that one will later regret. Similarly, we can certainly be concerned about how we are regarded by others to the point that we forego things that we later see that we want. The passage just cited, then, suggests that Socrates thinks that virtue guarantees that our possessions will not be mismanaged or misused.

So, what sort of thing, then, could provide this guarantee? Socrates does not tell us in this passage. But if our earlier discussion about the wisdom Socrates lacks is on the right track, Socrates thinks of the wisdom that he here identifies with the perfection of the soul as a kind of craft knowledge, or at least something very much like craft knowledge, for it is the power to perform some characteristic function or produce some characteristic product invariably and correctly. Just as what sets craftsmen apart from non-craftsmen is their knowledge of how to produce excellent examples of their crafts out of various materials, so virtuous people, Socrates thinks, are distinguished by their knowledge of how to turn such things as health and money into goods and thus how to make them contribute to a well-lived life. Of course, this expertise is one that he himself and all of his fellow Athenians lack. But we must count it as the "most important thing," for, clearly, by possessing it we will be able to manage unerringly all of the other things we want so that they will be goods for us. Without it, we are apt to pursue certain things at the wrong time, in the wrong way, or to the wrong extent.

Even though he also lacks this wisdom, we can now see why Socrates considers himself to be wiser than those who falsely believe that they possess virtue. Because he is aware that he lacks it and yet recognizes the supreme value of possessing it, Socrates understands the crucial importance of pursuing virtue in the only way it can be pursued, though philosophy. Because so many of his fellow Athenians falsely believe that they already possess it, they have no reason even to undertake to pursue it.

2.6.9 Is moral goodness by itself enough to secure happiness? (30c3–d6)

So, Socrates thinks of virtue as the best condition that the soul can be in, and that condition is wisdom about how to conduct one's life in such a way that one will be happy. Because it is the power to ensure that the other things one seeks will be good, wisdom is the most important good anyone can acquire. But it is unique in another respect, as well. It is the single thing that is unqualifiedly good, for unlike health or money, which plainly can be misused and so can become evils unless accompanied by virtue to guide them, wisdom is in need of nothing else to ensure that it makes its possessor better off. No one will ever be led astray by wisdom, for if one is truly wise, one is never deceived about what is truly good or evil. Are we to infer from this that Socrates believes that the possession of virtue affords an absolute protection against harm?

Socrates certainly says things in the *Apology* that have led many scholars to believe that he means just that.[70] Consider the following passage in which Socrates returns to his explanation of why he does not regard the very real possibility that he may be killed to be something he should fear.

> Neither Meletus nor Anytus could do anything to harm me; it isn't even possible. For I don't think it is divinely sanctioned for a better man to be harmed by a worse. Doubtless, he could kill me, or send me into exile, or take away my rights, and doubtless he and others also think these things are great evils. But I don't. In fact, I think that what he's doing now – trying to kill a man unjustly – is a much greater evil.
>
> (30c9–d6)

The passage is certainly confusing. Socrates begins by saying that it is not possible for Meletus and Anytus to harm him and concludes by implying that they could harm him after all, although the harm they would be doing to themselves thereby is much greater. So, which one does Socrates mean? Can he be harmed or not?

Unfortunately, there are passages that appear to count in favor of both answers to our question. For example, towards the end of the third speech, after Socrates has been sentenced to death, he tells those jurors who voted for his acquittal to be "optimistic about death and to think about this one truth, that no harm comes to a good man in life or in death, and his problems are not neglected by the gods" (41c8–d2). Since Socrates clearly thinks that he is a good man, it seems natural to understand him here as claiming that absolutely no harm can come to him in life or in death.[71]

On the other hand, in the second speech, when Socrates is explaining to the jury why he cannot propose any of a variety of counter-penalties the jury might well accept, he says: "Since I'm convinced that I've never been unjust, I am not about to treat myself unjustly and to say of myself that I deserve something evil and to propose that sort of penalty for himself" (37b2–5). Now, of course, the jury accepts Meletus' penalty, death, which Socrates is surely convinced will not be an evil for him.[72] As we noted in our introductory comments about the nature of the trial itself, the jury was prohibited by law from imposing on Socrates anything other than what Meletus had proposed or what he himself had proposed as a counter-penalty. Nonetheless, we can easily imagine that, instead of death, Meletus proposed – and the jury accepted – a long prison sentence, one of the penalties Socrates says would be evil for him. Thus, he seems to think that it is possible for him to suffer an evil after all. Add to this the fact that immediately after telling the jury that no harm comes to a good man, Socrates says that he is convinced that whatever happens at death, it is better for him to die for he will be "escaping these problems" (41d3–5). Socrates does not specific what "these problems" are but they cannot be dismissed as mere nuisances, since they are enough to make Socrates prefer his non-existence to continued existence.[73] Whatever he has in mind, then, since death, whatever it turns out to be, will be "better" for him, it seems "these problems" must be counted as evils. So, it appears that Socrates believes that a good person can suffer evils after all, and so it is not the case that absolutely no kind of harm comes to a good person. If so, moral goodness is not enough to guarantee happiness after all.

Socrates sometimes distinguishes between the good and bad condition of the soul and other goods and evils. Now if we think that, for Socrates, living well is living as one should – that is, living justly – and being badly off in one's life is living as one should not – that is, living unjustly – he can say that non-psychic goods are just those goods that help us to live well and non-psychic evils are those that hinder or prevent us from living well. When the soul is good, however, one will never live badly, for one will never do what one ought not. When the soul is corrupted, by contrast, one is bound to live badly.

We are suggesting, then, that in saying "no harm comes to a good person" Socrates need not be denying that a good person can suffer from all sorts of non-psychic evils, evils that might even prevent the good person from ever living well. What good people cannot suffer, as long as they remain good, is any harm that would make them live badly, since the only harm that could do that would be harm to their souls. But, given the way Socrates understands the good condition of the soul, causing his soul to be harmed is something Meletus can never do as long as Socrates values justice. Finally, because Socrates believes that being badly off with respect to one's life is living as one should not, we can see why Socrates would say that by killing him unjustly Meletus is doing greater harm to himself than he can possibly do to Socrates. By acting unjustly, however, Anytus and Meletus are suffering the worst thing that can befall anyone – living badly.

2.6.10 Can one be both good and ignorant?

Thus far we have been arguing that Socrates must believe that he is a good person and that whatever evils his prosecutors can visit on him, they are not evils of the worst sort. But we have also been arguing that, for Socrates, the best condition of the soul is virtue and that virtue is a craft-like wisdom about how to conduct one's life. But because he denies that he has wisdom, Socrates clearly denies that he possesses virtue. Can he consistently maintain that he is ignorant about the "most important things" and that he is a good person, who cannot be harmed by Meletus?

Nowhere in the *Apology* does Socrates see this as a problem for what he has been saying about himself. We think he does not because he sees as obvious the distinction between what he calls the "perfection of the soul," which he lacks, and (what is only an approximation of that perfection) the good condition of the soul, which he has been able to sustain throughout his life. The former, as we have seen, is moral wisdom (29e1–3). It is the best condition of the soul because its possession indemnifies one from ever forming false beliefs about how to conduct one's life. Just as a master craftsman can reliably identify any potential problems that arise in the exercise of his craft and knows how to avoid them, so a virtuous person's wisdom indemnifies him/her against making moral mistakes. Although good people generally possess right beliefs about how to live, they enjoy no such indemnity against wrongdoing, for, unlike those who are morally wise, not only can merely good people form mistaken judgments about what to do in particular cases, but, lacking the right account of their beliefs, they are apt to alter their beliefs when given any seemingly good reason.

It is testimony to the great care and steadfastness with which Socrates subjected his own beliefs to examination, along with the occasional warning of his *daimonion*, that Socrates has avoided injustice throughout his life (37a5–6). But although he has managed to maintain the right beliefs about the importance of acting justly and so has preserved the good condition of his soul, he still lacks wisdom. If this is right, the fact that he counts himself as a good person is evidence neither of a contradiction in what he says about himself nor of the insincerity of his denial that he possesses any wisdom about the "most important things."

2.7 SOCRATES' SERVICE TO THE CITY

2.7.1 *The god's gift – the human gadfly (30d6–31c3)*

To this point, Socrates has explained what has motivated his mission and what his mission is about. He now explains to the jury why it is in their interest not to condemn him. Certainly one sort of harm they will do to themselves is the harm that Meletus is doing to himself, "killing a man unjustly." But there is a second way in which they will harm themselves: Socrates is nothing less than a "gift given to them by the god" and if they kill him the god is not likely to send another such gift to replace the one they destroyed. The divine gift is his unceasing attempt to engage them in philosophy. In one of the most famous passages in the history of philosophy, Socrates compares himself to a "gadfly."

> For if you kill me, you won't easily find another person like me, simply put, even if it's funny to say so, who's been attached to the city by the god as if it were a large and well-bred horse, though one that's somewhat sluggish on account of its size and that needs to be disturbed by a gadfly. In some such way as this I think the god has attached me to the city – such a person who disturbs you and stirs you up and shames each one of you, I never stop landing on you everywhere all day long. Another one like me won't quickly come to you, men, and if you're persuaded by me, you'll spare me. But it's more

likely that you'll be angry, like those who are disturbed when they're drowsy, and swat me – having been persuaded by Anytus – and easily kill me, then you'd spend the rest of your life asleep, unless the god, in his concern for you, were to send someone else to you.

(30e1–31a8)

That stinging is, of course, his service to the god, from which "no greater benefit has ever come to the city" (30a5–7). It is a benefit precisely because it aims at making them attach the highest importance to *aretê*, the single thing that, as we have seen, can ensure that what they seek are real goods.

Socrates wants the jury to know that what he says about his labors on behalf of the god to benefit the city is not hyperbole. Many will think, he assumes, that it goes against human nature for a person to neglect his own affairs and the interests of his family as he has. He has set aside the sorts of concerns that other people have, Socrates says, because he labors to benefit those with whom he shares life in Athens, "going to each one in private, like a father or an older brother, trying to persuade you to care about virtue" (31b3–5). But he also wants the jury to know that he has conducted his life in this extraordinary way because it is a duty imposed on him by the god and not because he has ever gained any sort of material advantage from his philosophical activities. The evidence that he is telling the truth is the evidence that he has not been a sophist: his poverty (31c2–3), a fact apparently well known to all. Even his accusers, who are apparently prepared to say the most outrageous things about him, cannot claim that he has ever received pay for philosophizing (31b7–c1).

2.7.2 Socrates' labors as a private citizen and the role of his daimonion (31c4–32a3)

Socrates is well aware of just how skeptical many jurors are likely to be of his claim that he has lived a life of service for the benefit of the city. After all, the only public benefactors with whom they are familiar are political leaders, men who lived very public lives and who typically went before the Assembly to try to convince the mass of citizens that they knew best what would benefit Athens.[74] But all they know about Socrates is that he talks to people on an individual basis, usually accompanied by a crowd of rich young men who find great amusement in Socrates' interrogations of others (33b9–c4). He has never offered any sort of public lecture about how they ought to conduct their lives. If Socrates is to have any hope of convincing the jury that he really cares about their well-being, he must explain why he has always carried out his mission to improve them in private, going to each "individually, like a father or brother" (31b4–5) and never as a public speaker.

In what may well have offended the democratic sympathies of at least some of the jurors, Socrates explains:

> Don't be upset at me for telling the truth: no one will survive who genuinely opposes you or any other populace and tries to prevent many unjust and illegal things from happening in the city. Instead, one who really fights for what's just, if he's to survive even for a little while, must live as a private and not as a public man.
>
> (31e1–32a3)

Later, he repeats the same bleak assessment of the possibility of engaging in politics and yet remaining a good man. It simply is not possible, he says (32e2–33a1). Socrates apparently had not always believed that politics has a corrosive effect on one's character. In one of the most famous passages in the *Apology*, he tells the jury that there was a time when he actually considered entering the public forum but was turned away by his *daimonion*, the divine voice we mentioned earlier that sometimes warns Socrates about doing things he ought not do.

This is not the only passage in Plato's writings in which reference is made to the "divine something" Socrates hears.[75] He refers to this same "voice" again in the *Apology*, toward the end of the third speech, when he explains why he is convinced that the outcome of the trial will not be an evil (40c2–4). But because the passage here at 31c7–d6 gives us some insight into how the voice actually functioned and how Socrates made sense of its warnings, we should look closely at just what Socrates says about how it warned him against going into politics.

Some scholars have worried about Socrates' argument here, and about his attitude towards what he calls his *daimonion* generally. The problem is that the Socrates who refers so often to the influence and effects of this *daimonion* on his life is presumably the same one who insists at *Crito* 46b4–6 that "I'm not just now but in fact I've always been the sort of person who's persuaded by nothing but the reason that appears to me to be best when I've considered it." How can *this* Socrates, a model of the life of reason, be so illogically committed to following the dictates of something as repugnant to modern rationality as a divine sign?[76]

Because Socrates spent his life exhorting people to subject their own beliefs to examination and rational reflection, it is perhaps tempting to try to understand what Socrates experiences as the voice of conscience or moral intuition.[77] But our text makes it clear that neither is what Socrates is talking about. Whenever our conscience bothers us about something, we already have reason to believe that it is the wrong thing to do. We do not have a twinge of conscience and then see that what we are thinking about is the wrong thing. Moreover, most of us would say that our moral intuitions are defeasible. That is, we think that our as yet unexplained belief that something would be wrong can easily be overturned by a good reason to the contrary. Even if we think we have pretty good intuitions and so require relatively strong reasons for thinking we are mistaken about them, we still treat them as beliefs that may turn out to be mistaken in the light of further evidence or reflection. While it is surely the case that Socrates came to believe that his *daimonion* is always correct whenever it turns him away from his past experience in responding to it, he never suggests that it has ever turned him away from something that, later, he became convinced would have been, on balance, good for him. Nor does he ever suggest that he even questioned the reliability of the voice once he came to believe that it was of divine origin. He never thinks about the voice's warnings, as we would about our intuitions. Any warning from his *daimonion* is sufficient to turn him away.

No doubt, the indefeasible character of these peculiar warnings is tied up with the fact that Socrates regards them as having divine authority. That having been said, it would be a mistake to try to identify the *daimonion* with the voice of any specific god, such as Apollo, the god who communicates to human beings through the oracle at Delphi. Whenever Socrates talks about what he inferred from the oracle's pronouncement regarding his wisdom, he always refers to his understanding of what "the god" wants of him (e.g. 23c1, 28e4–5, 29d3–4), which, in this case, was that he should devote his life to a particular cause. The "voice" only steers him away from particular courses of action. If Socrates believes that the *daimonion* is the voice of the god of Delphi, he would surely say so. Doubtless, Socrates believes that the sign is divine because only a divinity has the power to see what the future holds, and the voice has so consistently looked into the future to turn him away from some evil he was about to become involved in. But just how this divinity, which communicates with him by means of the "voice," differs from other divinities, Socrates nowhere says. Indeed, it is remarkable that this is a question about which Socrates shows a complete lack of interest.

Even those scholars who are (however reluctantly) inclined to accept that Socrates' report of this uncanny phenomenon is not to be reduced to conscience or intuition attempt to defend Socrates against the charge of irrationalism by insisting that even if the phenomenon itself did seem divine in origin to Socrates, he nonetheless subjected it entirely to his own ability to interpret its messages according to the strict dictates of reason.[78] Others, however, have resisted this rational sanitizing of Socrates, insisting, on the contrary, that Socrates himself seemed to find no contradiction in claiming always to be a man of reason, but also (apparently supposing it to be reasonable) following his perception that "something divine" would sometimes oppose something he was about to do.[79] This latter position is our view of the matter.

We have offered many arguments for this view elsewhere, but for our purposes here it is perhaps enough simply to sketch the textual grounds of our position. On the one hand, the view that we have called "reductive" (according to which Socrates' *daimonion* is

really not an extra-rational phenomenon at all) does not sufficiently account for the quite evidently religious descriptions
Socrates frequently provides for the phenomenon.[80] On the other
hand, the view that we have called "sanitizing" (according to which
the phenomenon itself may be extra-rational, but whose role in
Socrates' life is wholly governed by independent rational interpretation) presupposes that there can be no cases in which the inter-
ference of the *daimonion* is itself what explains something that
Socrates does. We have argued[81] that the example of Socrates' *daimonion* opposing his engaging in politics (*Ap.* 31d4–5), however,
cannot be explained in the "sanitizing" way. The main advocate of
the "sanitizing" view, Gregory Vlastos, however, was not at all won
over by our citation of this text against the view:

> The impression persists in the mind [*sic*] of some readers of the
> *Apology* that Socrates does allow his "sign" to trump a decision he has
> reached on rational grounds. The impression is articulated as a formal
> thesis by my friends, Thomas Brickhouse and Nicholas Smith. ... To
> support their thesis that Socrates does allow it they refer to *Apology*
> 31D–E. But does that passage really provide evidence for their thesis?
> It certainly would if what is said there were, as they claim ... that
> Socrates had "already decided to engage in [political] activity" and the
> "sign" supervened to oppose the decision. ... But is this said in the
> text? Does Socrates say he had decided to go into politics, had *resolved*
> to do so, and had *tried* to do so? No. Not a word there to indicate that
> he had done any of these things. All he says is that the *daimonion*
> "opposes my engaging in politics" (31D5) and that he sees good rea-
> son for its doing so (31D6–E2). When the text is closely read all we
> learn from it is that his "sign" opposes his going into politics, and that
> so does his reason. "Sign" and reason are in accord. There is no
> trumping.[82]

In Vlastos' view, the opposition of the *daimonion* never
"trumps" some deliberation or decision that Socrates has made,
and even where there is such an opposition from the *daimonion*, it
is never that opposition that actually explains why Socrates ceases
or desists from what the *daimonion* opposes – the explanation,

rather, is that Socrates has some *other* reason(s) for ceasing and desisting from what the *daimonion* opposes. Now, we continue to think that this provides a very implausible reading of *Apology* 31d4–5, despite Vlastos' resistance: after all, in that passage Socrates quite explicitly and directly identifies the opposition of the *daimonion* as the explanation of why he has not engaged in political activity ("*This* is what opposes my engaging in politics"). If the opposition of the *daimonion* is not really the reason why Socrates has desisted from engaging in politics, then it is simply misleading for him to say that it was. The picture that emerges from Socrates' explanation of how he conducts his mission on behalf of the god, then, is this: there was a time when he was seriously considering going into politics, but before he could actually do so, he experienced his "divine voice," which "turned him away." At that point, because he had already experienced such warnings before, he knew that he must not continue with his plan to enter politics. About that he could be quite confident. In fact, there is an important sense in which the "voice" actually overruled his reasoning. At that point, however, we must assume that Socrates was baffled about what it is about politics that makes it an evil, for presumably the result of his own initial deliberation about it was that participation in politics was something he should do. It is only by *further* deliberation, this time not about whether to enter politics, but what it is about politics that would make it an evil for him, that Socrates came to see that a good person simply cannot survive in the political arena. Warned against what he intended to do, he concluded that his trying to serve the city as politician would have resulted in his having been killed "long ago," having done neither himself nor the city any good.

Moreover, later, at *Apology* 40a4–6, Socrates explains that his *daimonion* has opposed him "on quite trivial matters if I was about to do something that wasn't right." And at 40b4–5, we learn that the *daimonion* would interrupt Socrates in mid-speech on many occasions, but he notes that on the day of his trial, the *daimonion* "hasn't opposed me at any point in what I was doing or saying" (*Ap.* 40b5–6). It seems to us to be beyond cavil that the way in which the *daimonion* is said to operate in all of these passages – and, indeed, in every other one in which we find one of its appearances described – is that it does not oppose Socrates when he is merely *in the process* of deliberating about some course of action. Rather, it operates by opposing Socrates when he is either actually engaging in the action it opposes (for example, when it stops Socrates in mid-speech), or else when he has made up his mind and is on the verge of undertaking the action. And when he does cease and desist from the opposed action, Socrates says that it is the opposition of the *daimonion* that explains his own reversal. It is true that he generally then does find some reason as to why the opposition (and his unflinching acquiescence to it – we know of not one case where Socrates presumes to act in defiance of his *daimonion*'s opposition) was appropriate. But the plain sense of what Socrates says in such cases, we claim, is that such rational explanations of the *daimonion*'s oppositions are inevitably *subsequent* to them, and that were it not for the opposition of the *daimonion*, Socrates would not have had any reason to look for these reasons. Instead, he would have gone right ahead and done what he later agrees he was lucky to have been warned against by his *daimonion*.

In all of the other cases in which Socrates cites the *daimonion*, it is because this strange phenomenon has made its appearance to oppose something he was either actually doing or was about to do. But at the end of the *Apology*, it is the *non-appearance* of the phenomenon that his jurors are supposed to find "wonderful" (40a4). Unless we are prepared to convict Socrates of frequently acting without deliberation (so that the frequent appearance of the *daimonion* would oppose no actual reasoning that Socrates has undertaken), we must suppose that what is "wonderful" about the fact that the *daimonion* made no opposition at any time during Socrates' day in court shows that, despite his considering his words as thoughtfully as he ever does, the fact that he has not had his thoughts and plans opposed at any time is surprising to Socrates. Given all that seemed to be at stake, and everything he has said and done on this day, his *daimonion* has not even once had to save him from some misstep he would otherwise have made. Only if we actually suppose, therefore, that the *daimonion* could and often actually *did* act in such a way as to "trump" Socrates' own reasoning can we understand at all why its inactivity on this important day counts as "strong evidence" (40c2) against the common view that death is an evil and in favor of the view that the outcome of the trial will be a good thing for Socrates.

As we try to understand just how the *daimonion* served to warn Socrates not to engage in a certain activity, it is important to grasp two features of the way it operates. First, Socrates cannot use the voice to which he has access as a way of testing the permissibility of whatever he is about to do. It should be kept in mind that although he says that he has heard the voice ever since he was a child and so has heard it with sufficient frequency and witnessed the results of acting in accordance with its warnings that he finds it utterly reliable, it does not follow that he experiences the divine sign *whenever* he is about to do something that would be an evil. All Socrates says is that "whenever it speaks, it turns me about from what I am about to do" (31d2–3), from which it obviously does not follow that absolutely every time he is about to do something evil he hears the *daimonion*. Consequently, he cannot rely on it as a test, nor does he ever try to employ it as one, for its silence as he is about to do something is consistent with his being about to set off on a disastrous course. Second, the "voice" does not provide him with the reason why the action he intends to perform ought to be avoided. Instead, it leaves it to him to discover through his own deliberation what it is about the contemplated action that will yield an evil. Once again, we see that Socrates can know *that* something is the case, in this instance, that he ought not to engage in some specific action. But even when he discovers what it is about the action that would make it an evil, he obviously cannot thereby claim that he can fit that explanation into a full account of the human good and all that contributes to and detracts from that good. Only a craftsman of virtue can do that, someone who possesses the very sort of wisdom Socrates lacks.

Having said all of this, however, must we not now conclude that Socrates' uncritical acceptance of this strange "voice" shows that he is not really committed – at least not fully committed – to leading the fully rational ("examined") life after all? After all, we have just seen that when its warning conflicts with Socrates' own judgment about what is best, Socrates defers to the "voice." Does it not show us that, in fact, he had a superstitious streak every bit as much as did the typical Athenian? And if so, how are we to square such a willingness to accept superstition with Socrates' claim (quoted above) to be such a rational fellow in the *Crito* (46b4–6)?

As much as other scholars have worried about such questions, we believe they can all be easily answered. In the first place, Socrates never says that one must scrutinize *every* one of his beliefs in order to lead a thoroughly "examined life." Unlike the school of philosophical skeptics who followed him, Socrates sees no reason to scrutinize the non-moral beliefs that he and everyone else take to be commonsensical. We never see him questioning his perceptions or his memory, for example. But he is also remarkably like his fellow Athenians in other ways, as well. He does not doubt that there are gods and, as we have seen in connection with the ora-cle regarding his wisdom, he believes that the god of Delphi com-municates with human beings. Indeed, he is convinced that his conclusion that the god has "stationed" him in Athens to philoso-phize has been confirmed "through dreams and oracles and in every way in which divine providence has ever ordered a human being to do anything whatever" (33c4–5). To this extent, he is, to modern readers, remarkably uncritical. It is important to notice, however, that what he calls the "voice" that warns him is not merely a strange feeling from which he leaps to the conclusion that it must be a divine communication of some sort. Recall that he says that he has heard the "voice" since childhood. It seems likely that, however puzzled Socrates may have been as a child when he first heard these warnings, over time, as he came to see that the warn-ings were entirely reliable, he concluded that only a divinity could be sending them. Thus, he connects such experiences with divinity through evidence. What else, he must have thought, could explain their prescience? Once he is satisfied that he understands the ori-gin of the warnings, he does not continue to pursue the issue. Given his past experience with the voice and his understanding of the fallibility of his own reasoning about how to act, Socrates thinks he has reason to defer to his *daimonion* when it conflicts with his own deliberations. His daimonic warnings are simply more reliable. If we moderns have a criticism of Socrates in this regard it is that he should have been more careful about how he construed the experiences he calls "warnings." But we see no reason to think that he was a mindless dogmatist about any aspect of his life, including his religious beliefs.

It is understandable that modern readers are left quite uncomfortable by Socrates' claims to have a "sign from the god" interfering in his life and "trumping" his deliberations. In so many other ways, we are led to find Socrates an icon of the life of reason, and his own words at his trial, that "the unexamined life is not worth living for a human being," might well be the perfect motto for advocating the rational life in opposition to other ways of living that too liberally allow extra-rational considerations to take precedence over the proper rule of reason in human life. But as uneasy as we may feel about Socrates' quite obvious willingness to blend both rational and extra-rational elements in the way he led his life, we cannot understand well or appreciate rightly this charismatic philosopher unless we recognize the different – and in his view, entirely compatible – roles both sorts of elements played in his life. It may not seem "rational" to us to allow "signs from the god" to stop us in mid-speech, or to force us irrevocably to change our course from what our best reasoning had persuaded us to do only moments earlier. For Socrates, however, it seems obvious that the phenomenon he called a "sign" or "voice" provided compelling reasons for these sorts of reversals. But then, to those who do believe in divinities, it would never qualify as reasonable to oppose or neglect clear indications of the wills of such divinities. Worries about Socrates' "irrationalism" on this issue, then, we suggest, are likely to be only expressions of a more general form of skepticism about the rationality of religion in any human life.

2.7.3 The first "great proof" – the trial of the ten generals (32a4–c3)

As if to underscore the depth of his commitment to doing what is right, Socrates cites what he calls "great proofs," two incidents in which he refused to commit an injustice even though in each he might well have paid for his decision with his life. The first concerns a famous trial that took place in the aftermath of a naval battle in which the Athenian navy defeated the Spartan fleet near the Arginusian Islands in the northeastern Aegean Sea. Fate, as it turned out, gave Socrates a central role in the affair.

> My district, Antiochis, was in charge of the Council,[83] when you wanted to judge as a group the ten generals who failed to pick up those who died in the sea-battle. What you wanted, though, was against the law, as you all realized some time later on. At that time, I was the only one of the Councilors in charge who opposed you, urging you to do nothing against the law, and I voted in opposition. And though the orators were ready to denounce me and arrest me, and though you urged them to do so by your shouting, with the law and justice on my side, I thought that, though I feared imprisonment or death, I should run the risk rather than to join with you, since you wanted what's not just.
>
> (32b1–c2)

This is what appears to have happened.[84] Although the Athenians were victorious in the naval battle, stormy conditions and perhaps fear of reengagement with the Spartans persuaded the ten Athenian naval commanders in charge[85] not to remain at the site of the battle, and this decision led to their failing to retrieve the bodies of those who had been killed and to rescue those on ships that had been disabled. Because Athenian losses during the battle were significant, there were many in Athens among the friends and families of the lost men who wanted the generals brought up on charges. The Council turned the matter over to the Assembly, where, after considerable debate and legal maneuvering, a proposal was made to the Council that it order the generals tried as a group, not individually. It is to his service on the Council when it received the request from the Assembly that Socrates is referring in this passage. He openly opposed what the Assembly wanted the Council to do and he continued to object even after some vowed to have all dissenting members of the Council tried along with the generals. Socrates remained undeterred, but was outvoted. As a result, the generals were tried as a group. Now it is not entirely clear that Socrates' interpretation of the law was in fact correct. What ancient sources do make clear, however, is that feelings were running extremely high at the time, and so Socrates is not exaggerating when he says that he was risking his life by refusing to vote for a single trial for all of the generals. Ancient sources also agree that after the single vote was taken and the generals were executed, the majority of Athenians soon came to regret what they had so vehemently urged the Assembly to do and agreed with the legal position Socrates had all along insisted upon. Because the episode had occurred relatively recently and had been so controversial, it is likely that many jurors at his own trial would have known about Socrates' refusal to yield when he was serving on the Council. Moreover, they must have known that Socrates had nothing whatever to gain personally from the way the trial of the generals was conducted. The only conclusion they could reach was that he was indeed willing to risk his own life to do what he thought was right. It also seems likely that to some jurors this was indeed a very "great proof" that he would never choose his own personal safety over doing what he thought justice required.

2.7.4   The second "great proof" – defiance of the thirty (32c3–e1)

The second of the "great proofs" concerns an event that took place even more recently, after the war, when the democracy had been suspended:

> when the oligarchy came to power, the Thirty summoned me and four others to the Rotunda and ordered us to bring Leon from Salamis to be put to death.[86] They often ordered many others to do such things, since they wanted to implicate as many as possible in their causes. At that time I made it clear once again, not by talk but by action, that I didn't care at all about death – if I'm not being too blunt to say it -- but it mattered everything that I do nothing unjust or impious, which matters very much to me. For though it had plenty of power, that government didn't frighten me into doing anything that's wrong. So when we

left the Rotunda, the other four went to Salamis and arrested Leon, and I left and went home. I suppose I'd have been killed for doing so if that regime hadn't been deposed shortly thereafter.

(32c4–d8)

Socrates is referring to the period during which the Spartans suspended the democracy in Athens and the Thirty Tyrants ruled the city. As we mentioned during our discussion of whether there were more specific slanders about Socrates that he was reluctant to discuss at his trial, soon after they were put into power by the Spartan occupation, the Thirty began confiscating property and arresting those they suspected of opposing their reign. Now one such person was a certain Leon, who lived on the island of Salamis. When the Thirty ordered Socrates and four others to arrest Leon, Socrates says that he alone defied the order and returned home. As is true of his assessment of the risk he took by opposing the Assembly's wishes regarding the trial of the ten generals, Socrates is probably not exaggerating when he says that had the Thirty not been overthrown soon after his act of defiance, he himself would have been arrested and executed for his defiance. Like the first, the second "great proof" is likely to be one with which the jury was familiar, for Socrates says that there are many witnesses who can testify about this matter (32e1).

Ostensibly, Socrates cites the case of Leon because he wants to convince the jury that the fear of death would not lead him to act contrary to what he thinks is right. But he had at least two other reasons for bringing up the famous case. First, as we noted in our earlier discussion, it is likely that many jurors believed that Socrates had at one time been on friendly terms with Critias, the person who emerged as the leader and most violent of the Thirty, and perhaps also with Critias' nephew, Charmides, who was also one of the Thirty. By recalling his refusal to participate in the arrest of Leon, Socrates shows the jury that whatever friendship he may have had at some point with Critias, it could not induce him act unjustly. Indeed, he says that he was called upon not out of any continuing friendship, but because the Thirty wanted to implicate as many as possible in their vicious schemes (32c7–8).

Second, recall that after the Thirty were installed, hundreds of Athenians (of various political sympathies) who were uncomfortable with their extremism left Athens and formed an armed force under the leadership of Thrasybulus. After eight months, the democratic faction overthrew the Thirty, killing Critias and Charmides in the process. Now many of the jurors were aware that Socrates chose not to leave the city and thus did not choose to share the dangers of trying to overthrow the tyranny of the Thirty. It is reasonable to think that those who left viewed those who stayed behind in Athens with deep suspicion, if not open hostility – despite the fact that Socrates was already an older man in his late sixties at the time. No doubt, they suspected either that those who stayed were sympathizers with the Thirty or else were simply cowards. By reminding the jury that the Thirty would have surely killed him had they not been overthrown, Socrates effectively shows that it was neither support for the causes of the Thirty nor fear for his life that persuaded him to stay behind.

2.7.5   *Further concerns about sophistry (32e2–34b5)*

Of course, it does not follow from the fact that Socrates thinks the Thirty became corrupt that he was not a significant cause of their corruption. Before ending his defense, then, Socrates returns to what he clearly assumes is the most damaging charge against him, namely, he corrupted the young through his sophistry. His response at this point is two-fold. First, he flatly denies that he "has ever given in to anyone contrary to what is just, not even to any of those whom my accusers say are my students" (33a3–5) and then he denies with equal directness that he has "ever been anyone's teacher" (33a5–6). Once again he readily admits that he converses with people. Indeed, he talks to anyone at all who wishes to hear what he has to say, young or old, rich and poor alike (33a7–b3). He cannot be a teacher because, as he has insisted throughout the speech, he simply has no knowledge to convey. He readily concedes again, as he must, that there are those who follow him and listen to him examining others who think they are wise. But they do so because they find it enjoyable, not because they are being taught anything. His denial that he has ever taught anything, Socrates believes, absolves him of any responsibility for how those who listen turned out:

> If any of those who listen becomes good or not, I couldn't rightly be held to be the cause, since I've never promised any of them any knowledge, nor have I ever taught anyone anything. If anyone says that he's ever learned anything from me or heard in private something that everyone else hasn't heard, you can be sure that he's not telling the truth.

> (33b6–8)

We might wonder at this point whether this part of the defense provides evidence that Socrates' past association with Critias and perhaps other members of the Thirty was mentioned by at least one of the individuals who spoke against him as part of the prosecution. The fact that Socrates' denial that he ever gave into any one, "not even to any of those whom my accusers say are my students," comes immediately after his account of his behavior at the time of the arrest of Leon certainly suggests that Socrates is referring to an allegation that he had been Critias's teacher and that it was through what Socrates taught him that Critias was corrupted. Socrates doesn't actually repeat whatever names his accusers mentioned, so anything we have to say about who these people may have been must necessarily be speculative. But the passage we are now considering is at least consistent with the idea that Socrates was aware that his jurors might believe that some of those who later became members of the Thirty had been his students at one time.

But even if some of the jurors do indeed have this specific concern about Socrates and his past associations, it does not follow from this that Socrates believed that his past association with any of the Thirty was the primary source of the suspicion that he was a wrongdoer and that he must specifically deny having been *their* teacher if he is to have any hope of persuading the jury that he ought not be convicted. As we said, there was at least one other person who was not a member of the Thirty, Alcibiades, yet who was well known to have associated with Socrates and who turned out to be a spectacular moral failure. Knowing this, Socrates could not have believed that the real accusation he needed to answer was that he was responsible for having spawned the Thirty. We see no reason, then, to abandon or to revise the conclusion we reached earlier that Socrates did not consider his past associations with any particular individuals to be the actual reason he was placed on trial. If the first accusers mentioned Critias at all, they mentioned him as an example of the great harm Socrates did by teaching his students to reject the old values on which Athens' greatness had been built. And as we have seen, this charge is one that Socrates directly takes up in his defense.

But even if Socrates did not profess to know anything and so did not teach anything to anyone, might he not have been responsible for their corruption in another way? Readers are often troubled by the fact that Socrates is so quick to deny any responsibility for the effect his examinations had on those who heard them. Might not some of those who enjoyed listening to him conclude that there simply is no such thing as the right way to live, or even if there is, no one can *know* that it is the right way to live?[87] Indeed, would this not be a reasonable conclusion for one to reach after one had witnessed countless individuals being made to look ridiculous after being subjected to Socrates' relentless questioning? But then, regardless of his good intentions, was Socrates not producing moral nihilists or moral skeptics and should he not have recognized that fact and taken steps to counter it?

It is not clear to what extent Socrates anticipates this specific accusation, but it is interesting that he does not qualify his assertion that he is not responsible for the effect his interrogations have on those who hear them. Instead, he tries to convince the jury that, as a matter of fact, no one who followed him around was corrupted in any way. Socrates does not deny that some of those "wealthy young men" who enjoyed listening to his investigations of others may have turned out to be very wicked indeed. But if they did, nothing he said or did not say was the cause. He makes this point very effectively by inviting anyone who wishes to come forward to testify either that he was himself corrupted or that he had a relative who was corrupted by Socrates (33c9–d5). No one does. From the unwillingness of anyone to step forward, whatever stories people have heard about Socrates' corruption of specific individuals such as Alcibiades or Critias now seem implausible. Since no one accepts Socrates' invitation to make an accusation, including Meletus himself (34a3–5), who apparently called no witnesses to say that they knew of someone who had been corrupted by Socrates, Socrates proceeds to mention the names of some seven men (and he says he could name many others) whose sons or brothers associated with him (34a7–b1). Once again, no one comes forward. On the contrary, Socrates claims that "all of the relatives" of those whom he is supposed to have corrupted are actually "ready to help me, the guy who [allegedly] did bad things to their [sons or brothers]" (34a7–b1). What reason could they – men who never associated with Socrates and so who could not have been corrupted by him – possibly have for wanting to testify *on Socrates' behalf*? They are willing to do so, Socrates infers, only "because they know that Meletus is lying and that I'm telling the truth" (34b4–5).

2.8 THE END OF SOCRATES' DEFENSE SPEECH

2.8.1 *Why Socrates will not beg the jury to release him (34b6–35d9)*

Having shown that no one is willing to say that he harmed one of their relatives, Socrates announces that he has said all that he can say in defense of the activities that have been so tragically misunderstood. He does not end his speech here, however. That he would want to conclude with final remarks about his character would not have taken the jury by surprise, for closing remarks that did not specifically address the evidence presented were not at all unusual. What must have surprised and perhaps even shocked the jury, as Socrates recognizes, is what he actually says in his final remarks. He announces that he will not beg for mercy, nor will he allow his children and relatives to appear before the court in the hope that it will arouse pity for what will be their plight if Socrates is convicted (34c2–7). He knows full well that at least some of the jury

will be ashamed and angry when they compare how he has conducted himself during the trial with how they have behaved in
court about some "much less serious matter" (34c1–2). In explaining his refusal, Socrates manages to remind the jury that he has a
family, which includes an adolescent son and two small boys
(34d7–8). Quoting Homer, he says that he was not born "from oak
or rock" (34d5–6).[88] Thus, the jury is to understand that he has
the same feelings for his family that any person has. Nonetheless,
even the thought that he will be taken from them is not enough to
make him bring them before the jury to sway the jury with their
mournful cries for mercy. Why can Socrates not bring himself to
do this?

Socrates gives two reasons why he will not engage in such
manipulative tactics. First, he says he has a reputation for being
superior to the run of people and that anyone who also thinks he is
superior "whether in wisdom, or courage, or in any virtue whatever" (35a2–3) and yet who engages in such shameless tactics
brings disgrace to Athens. What is odd about this is Socrates'
expression of concern for a "reputation for superiority." Even if in
his own case his reputation for superiority is deserved, it is clearly
undeserved by so many of his fellow citizens who mistakenly think
they possess virtue. In any case, why would Socrates say that anyone who has a mere *reputation* bears a special obligation not to
engage in raw appeals to pity?

The answer, we believe, is that Socrates is concerned about the
effect such a reputation, whether deserved or not, may have on
others. If one believes that an individual really is superior with
respect to virtue and then one sees that person engaging in shameful behavior out of a fear of death, one will naturally but falsely
conclude that virtue is not strong enough to master such a powerful fear. Now Socrates believes that it is disgraceful to encourage
others to hold false beliefs about virtue and he is convinced that no
one who really is virtuous can be mastered by a fear of death. Thus,
even though neither he nor anyone else in Athens actually possesses
virtue, it would be disgraceful to encourage anyone to believe that
virtuous people engage in "pitiable scenes" and thereby make a
"laughing-stock of the city" (35b7–8). What is disgraceful is not

reducing the city to ridicule; rather, it is encouraging anyone to think that if the circumstances are sufficiently dire, the virtuous are not better than cowards.

The second reason Socrates refuses to appeal to the jury's sense of pity concerns his commitment to justice and piety. As we will see when we turn to the *Crito*, Socrates believes that it is never right to undermine the legal institutions in Athens. This is not to say that he thinks Athens' legal institutions are perfect as they are; he does not. In fact, he criticizes the Athenian legal system for requiring that capital cases be tried in one day (37a8–b1). Nonetheless, he believes that it is fundamentally unfair for any citizen, even one who is convinced of his innocence, as he is, to try to thwart the outcome of a duly constituted legal process. Thus we see that he repeatedly tells the jury that he is telling them only the truth (instead of saying whatever he thinks they want to hear), and that it is their job as jurors to listen only to the truth. In this passage, we find Socrates reminding the jurors that each has taken an oath "not to make gifts to whom each wants, but not judge the case according to the laws" (35c4–5). Thus, were he to appeal to them to cast their vote out of pity for him and his family and not because the truth demands it, he would be encouraging them to violate their oath, which, as he says, would make them both impious (35c6–7). Then he really would deserve to be charged with encouraging people not to believe in the gods. But because, as he so emphatically insists, he does believe the gods exist (35d6), he must not encourage others to break oaths they have sworn.

Here we see that Socrates' commitment to justice and piety requires that he not encourage anyone else to do what is unjust or impious. With respect to the jurors, it is not enough for Socrates to encourage them to do the right thing, which is not to convict an innocent person. He must also try to persuade them to do the right thing for the right reason: they must acquit an innocent person because the truth of which they have been made aware requires that he be acquitted. Whatever reasons Socrates has to desire one outcome of the trial rather than another, they must be compatible with the requirement of justice that Socrates do all that he can "to instruct and persuade" (35c1–2) the jury about the truth of the charges. Having done all that he can to discharge that duty, the time has come for him to "leave it to you and to the god," as he tells the jury, to decide "what is best for you and for me" (35d8–9). If they decide the case in accordance with their oath, and judge according to the truth, they will do what is best for everyone concerned.

2.9 THE SECOND SPEECH

2.9.1 The vote to convict Socrates (35e1–36b2)

At the beginning of his defense speech (18e5–19a7), Socrates recognizes that the task he faces, in trying to persuade the jurors of his innocence, is a difficult one. He is not at all surprised, then, when the jury returns the verdict of "guilty." What does surprise him, he says, is that he was convicted by such a narrow margin (36a3–5). Indeed, had only thirty of those voting against him voted in his favor, he would have won the case.[89]

In Plato's account, Socrates announces to his jurors that the closeness of the vote proves that he actually defeated Meletus, who avoided having to pay the 1,000-drachma fine levied against prosecutors who fail to win one-fifth of the final votes only by having Anytus and Lycon assist him in the prosecution (36a8–b2). (The point of such a fine was to deter people from undertaking frivolous prosecutions.) Even as recently as twenty years or so ago, scholars generally agreed that Socrates made no serious effort to defend himself against the charges he faced, or to win an acquittal from the jurors, and some scholars persist in maintaining this view of the defense speech Socrates offers in Plato's *Apology*. Such a view, however, makes very poor sense of the closeness of the vote to convict Socrates – unless, of course, we are to suppose (contrary to all of the historical evidence we have about Socrates) that the jurors began the trial unaffected by any of the prejudices to which Socrates refers early in his defense speech. In fact, unless we are to prefer the very implausible account of the vote to convict given by Diogenes, the relative narrowness of the vote to convict Socrates is at least strong *prima facie* evidence that his defense speech was quite effective – indeed, nearly effective enough to win acquittal from jurors likely to have begun the trial already suspicious and possibly hostile to Socrates, and to the pursuits that had made him notorious in Athens.[90]

2.9.2   What Socrates really deserves (36b3–37a2)

As we said in section 2.1.4, Socrates' trial was an *agôn timêtos* – a trial procedure for which there was no penalty set by law. So, after expressing his surprise at how very nearly he had won the case, Socrates settles into the business of formulating a counter-penalty. The prosecution had called for the penalty of death in the indict- ment itself, though we may speculate that the prosecutors were hoping or at least assuming that Socrates would offer exile as the counter-penalty. If so, what Socrates actually says in his second speech surprised and disappointed them.

The way in which Socrates begins his deliberations about the penalty he should offer has confused many readers. Here is how he puts it: "Well, what should I propose to you as a counter-penalty? Isn't it clear it should be what I deserve? So, what would that be?" (36b4–5). What seems peculiar about this is that, in any case in which a convicted defendant had argued for his innocence of the alleged crime or criminal activity, it may simply be assumed that the defendant would suppose he deserved to pay no penalty whatever. Given that Socrates had already made it abundantly clear that he regarded himself as innocent of any wrongdoing, why begin his consideration of a counter-penalty with the condition that what he should offer be what he deserves?

Of course, the traditional answer to this question is that Socrates was using this part of the speech to add to the ways in which he had already sought to annoy and alienate the jurors. But as we have just said, this general view of Socrates' behavior at his trial does not at all accord with the closeness of the vote to convict him. So what other reasons might there be for beginning his deliberation in this way?

Any answers to this question must obviously be quite specula- tive, but at least two possibilities seem compatible with what we know about Socrates and the trial. One possibility is that in fram- ing the deliberation in this way, he was simply mimicking the way in which the actual law was written. We know that those convicted in proceedings of this sort were given the opportunity to propose a counter-penalty, but we do not know exactly how the law expressed this. It is possible, we suggest, that the law may have stated that the newly convicted criminal in a procedure of this sort "will then propose what he deserves as an alternative penalty," or something of this sort. In beginning his thoughts about the counter-penalty, then, Socrates may simply be literalistically following the actual letter of the law.

But another possibility may also be considered. At the end of his deliberation, Socrates actually does offer a considerable fine as his counter-penalty. During his defense speech, not only did Socrates proclaim his innocence of the charge and each of its specifications, he also insisted that the good man should never allow the fear of death to lead him into doing anything shameful or dishonorable. If, indeed, he really was innocent of any of the allegations against him, and he had no fear of death – which he says might even be "the greatest of all goods for humanity" (29a7–9) – then why should he offer any counter-penalty at all?

In fact, Xenophon's account of the trial directly contradicts Plato's on this very issue. According to Xenophon, at this point in the trial, Socrates actually refused to offer any counter-penalty at all. He also forbade his friends from offering anything, precisely on the ground that doing so would imply some acknowledgment of guilt (Xenophon, *Ap.* 23). But in Plato's version, Socrates plainly avoids this implication precisely by formulating his counter-penalty deliberation in the way that he does. By starting out with a consideration of his "just deserts," Socrates makes sure he reminds the jurors that he continues to regard himself as entirely blameless of the crime the jurors have now convicted him of committing. Plato's version of the counter-penalty speech, then, shows how and why the account we get in Xenophon was *not* required by Socrates' insistence that he was innocent. Accordingly, we have good reason to prefer Plato's version of Socrates' counter-penalty to what Xenophon says about the matter. It is possible that Xenophon did not understand why Socrates did not actually refuse to offer a counter-penalty. We do know that Xenophon was on a military campaign in Asia at the time of Socrates' trial and had to rely on others' accounts (see Xenophon *Ap.* 2, 10, 14; *Mem.* 4.8.4), whereas Plato represents himself as actually present at the trial itself (see 34a2, 38b7).

In Plato's version, at any rate, Socrates seems to wish to make it very clear, at the start of his second speech, that whatever counter-penalty he should select will in no way amount to a confession of guilt. He begins his second speech, accordingly, by telling them that – if he were to offer a counter-penalty he "deserves," he would propose free meals at the Prytaneum (36d7–8, 37a1–2) – the civic honor reserved for the city's greatest benefactors (generally, leaders of successful and important military campaigns, victors at the Olympic games, and such). Scholars who argue that Socrates' discussion of this would have outraged many jurors seem to miss the fact that Socrates' comment about what he "deserves" follows naturally from his having already proclaimed himself in his first speech as a gift to Athens from the god (30d8).

We may still wonder, however, why Socrates does not simply insist that the jurors should not mistake any offer he makes for a confession of guilt, rather than going into what looks like the extravagant detail of considering his just deserts. The problem Socrates faces in this situation, however, is somewhat more difficult than just continuing to insist on his innocence, for it has also been his view that his "divine mission" puts very significant demands upon him:

> I didn't go where I would've been no help at all to you or to me, but went, instead, to each one of you in private[91] to do the greatest good. As I say,[92] I went there undertaking to persuade each of you not to care about your possessions before you care about how you will be the best and wisest you can be, nor to care about what the city has, before you care about the city itself, and to care about other things in just the same way.

> (36c4–d2)

Even if we find it difficult to accept that Socrates regarded his activities as a mission on behalf of the god, that is how he actually characterized those activities in his defense speech. And even if we suppose for the sake of argument (and we are not at all suggesting that we should interpret his words in such a way) that he was not really serious in making such claims, certainly nothing in what he now faces, as he considers his counter-penalty, suggests that he is now permitted to make radical changes to the values that have shaped his life thus far. Accordingly, even now, convicted of a very serious crime, the logic of what he had said about himself in his first speech requires that he continue to try to get the jury – and anyone else who might be listening to him – to take what he has been trying to do seriously and to understand it in the proper light. Of course, he cannot simply *expect* the jurors suddenly to find sympathy for the very activities which they have just judged to be criminal. So, although he risks antagonizing even further those who are already antagonistic to him and his activities, he continues to tell them nothing but the truth, and continues to show them, by word and deed, just how important his mission and his exhortations are. The upshot of such considerations, then, is obvious to Socrates:

> There's nothing more appropriate, Athenians, than that such a person [as I am] be given meals in the Prytaneum; in fact, it's much more appropriate than for one of you who had won at Olympia with either a pair or a team of horses. For he makes you think you are happy, but I make you happy, and he doesn't need the food, but I do. So if I'm supposed to propose a penalty in accordance with what I deserve, I propose to be given meals in the Prytaneum.
>
> (36d6–37a2)

2.9.3 Other possible penalties (37a3–38b1)

Obviously, Socrates is not so foolish as to suppose that the same jurors who had just found him guilty by a majority vote could now be persuaded to award him the city's highest honor as the "penalty" for his wrongdoing. In Plato's account, therefore, Socrates goes on to consider what sorts of punishments the judges might be induced to accept, in lieu of the death penalty proposed by the prosecution. But as we noted earlier, our ancient sources are not at all consistent about this part of the trial. Xenophon, as we have already noted, simply has Socrates refuse to offer a counter-penalty of any kind. Diogenes Laertius offers yet another account. Immediately after reporting the first vote in the garbled way we have already discussed, here is what Diogenes has to tell us about Socrates' actual counter-penalty offer:

> And when the jurors were demanding what it is necessary for him to suffer or to pay, he said he would pay 25 drachmas. Eubulides says that he agreed to pay 100 drachmas. And when the jurors made an uproar at this, he said, "For my services, I am proposing free meals at the Prytaneum."
>
> (D.L. 2.42)

We will have more to say about the fine Socrates offers as his counter-penalty in the next section, but it is worth noticing here that in Diogenes' account, free meals at the Prytaneum is Socrates' actual final offer of a counter-penalty. Some scholars seem to have been persuaded by Diogenes' account of what Socrates did at this point, by stating that Socrates' actual counter-penalty was free meals at the Prytaneum.[93] But, as in the case of the differing reports of the vote to convict Socrates, most scholars accept Plato's account of Socrates' counter-penalty offer. And in Plato's version, the discussion of free meals is clearly framed as a preface to what comes next, which is Socrates' deliberation of possible penalties the jurors might actually recognize *as penalties*.

The possibilities Socrates considers and rejects are, in order of appearance: imprisonment (37b8–c2); a fine with imprisonment until the fine is paid (37c2–4); and exile (37c4–38b1). Socrates gives very brief arguments as to why the first two alternatives are unacceptable, but given everything he has already said, his reasons for rejecting them are clear enough not to have to be discussed at length. He has already told his jurors not only that he thinks he is innocent, but also that he does not regard himself as in a position to tell whether death is a good or a bad thing (37b2–7). Imprisonment, however, which would prevent him from going about his customary activities in Athens – activities Socrates regards, recall, as a mission on behalf of the god – is something that Socrates is in a position to recognize as an authentic evil (38b7–c2). Accordingly, it is plain that if Socrates offers this as his counter-penalty, he risks encouraging the jurors into assigning a penalty he knows to be evil, in place of one that, for all he knows, is the "the greatest of all goods for humanity."

The risk, moreover, is not just to Socrates. Obviously, he risks suffering an evil that he might otherwise avoid. But by encouraging the jurors to subject him to that evil, Socrates would therefore encourage them to harm another person. One of Socrates' most important ethical claims, repeated in several dialogues, is that one must never harm another, or trade evil for evil (see, e.g. *Crito* 49a4–c11; *Rep.* I.335b2–e5). Those who do wrong, and choose to harm others when better courses of action are available, risk damaging their souls (*Crito* 47d8–48a4; *Grg.* 478c3–e5, 511c9–512b2; *Rep.* I.353d3–354a7). If his jurors choose a penalty that is worse and more harmful to Socrates than the alternative, they accordingly risk harming their souls. And if Socrates encourages them to do this wrong, he risks harming his own soul. For the jurors' sake, then, no less than for his own, Socrates must avoid offering a counter-penalty that would add to the wrong already done to him by the unjust verdict (see also 30c7–e1).

The same considerations as those that apply to the possible offer of imprisonment apply to the next possibility Socrates considers: a fine with imprisonment until he pays it. The problem here is that Socrates' poverty (see 23b9–c1) is such that he cannot afford to offer much of a fine (about which, see next section), and so if he offered to pay a substantial fine, with imprisonment until he paid it, he could never meet the condition that would allow him to get out of prison. This option, accordingly, would end up being the same as a proposal of imprisonment for some unspecified period.

Socrates next considers a penalty that many think he might have persuaded the jurors to accept: exile. Exile was, in fact, quite commonly offered as an alternative to the death penalty, and some scholars have even speculated that the prosecutors themselves were really hoping that Socrates would propose this penalty and have it accepted. All of this could be, of course, but there is no way to know it, if so. We do have excellent reasons for believing, however, that exile was an option that Socrates could never propose or accept, and for the very reasons he gives here in the *Apology*:

> I'd really have to be in love with living, men of Athens, to be so illogi-
> cal as to suppose that if you, who are my fellow citizens, weren't able
> to bear my activities and arguments – but they became so burdensome
> and hateful that you're now seeking to be free of them – yet others
> will endure them easily. I think that's pretty unreasonable, Athenians.
>
> (37c5–d4)

Despite the many troubles in its recent history, everyone in the courtroom that day realized that Athens remained the most free and most liberal place in the world in 399 B.C.E. If *Athens* would not permit Socrates to continue his "mission" of philosophizing, it is implausible to suppose that anywhere else Socrates could go would tolerate his "activities and arguments" – activities and arguments, let us recall, that put everyone's most basic ethical beliefs under intense critical scrutiny. Even if his jurors might be willing to allow him to go into exile, there is no good reason to suppose that other cities would show Socrates any greater tolerance than he now found in Athens.

Of course, the problems Socrates would face in exile would be the result of the same "activities and arguments" that had landed him in court in Athens. It is natural to wonder, accordingly, how Socrates might fare in exile if he ceased and desisted from those "activities and arguments." In fact, we know from the *Crito* (see 44e1–46a9) that Socrates might well have had some support for going to live somewhere else. Just a few days before his execution, according to that dialogue, Socrates was given yet another opportunity to escape and flee Athens to go elsewhere – in this case, to Thessaly (*Crito* 53d2). In that instance, too, Socrates declined the opportunity. But mightn't the Thessalians at least allow Socrates to live there?

> Perhaps, if you don't disturb anyone. But if that's not the case,
> you'll hear many terrible things about yourself. You'll live a life of

> fawning and serving all people – what will you do in Thessaly other than feasting? – as if you traveled to Thessaly for dinner! And what'll happen to our arguments about justice and the other virtues?
>
> (*Crito* 53e2–6)

In hastening off to live in such a place "filled with disorder and self-indulgence," as Socrates puts it in the *Crito* (53d3), he would give the lie to his brave claims that death is nothing to fear, and to everything else he has for all his life. If we take seriously, as he so explicitly claims he did, that he regarded himself as having a divine mission to philosophize, then continuing to live – in Athens or anywhere else – where he was not allowed to "disturb anyone" was simply not an option, lest he end his life becoming guilty of the very charge for which the Athenians wrongly convicted him. But more than that, Socrates is now willing to proclaim, philosophizing is not just a divine mission for him; it is a condition of living a life with any value whatsoever. In perhaps his most famous pronouncement, Socrates flatly rejects the option of going away somewhere to "live quietly" and stop his "activities and arguments":

> If I say that this is disobedience to the god and that's why it's impossible to keep quiet, you'll think I'm not being sincere. And if I say that this is really the greatest good for human beings – to engage in discussion each day about virtue and the other things you have heard me talking about and examining myself and others, and *the unexamined life is not worth living for a human being* – you'll be persuaded even less by what I say. These things are true, as I say, but it's not easy to persuade you.
>
> (37e5–38a8).

2.9.4 The fine and the final vote (38b1–10)

There remains but one option, then, if Socrates is not to offer a counter-penalty that is actually worse than the death penalty called for by the prosecution. He must offer to pay a fine.

If I had money, I'd offer what I could afford to pay, for I wouldn't be harming anything. But as it is, that isn't possible, unless you want to impose a penalty on me that I can pay. I suppose I could probably offer to pay you a mina of silver. So I offer this amount. Plato, here, Athenians, and Crito, Critobulus, and Apollodorus bid me to pay a penalty of 30 minas, and they'll guarantee that it's paid. I offer that much, then, and they'll be guarantors of the silver for you; they're good for it.

(38b1–10)

For many years, the standard view in the scholarly literature was that the amount of the fine, even when supplemented by the offer of Socrates' four friends, was so small that it could only have annoyed the jury.[94] As we have already noted, Socrates' poverty was such that he could not by himself offer any very substantial fine. But poverty was not a condition we would associate with Socrates' very wealthy friends (Plato included), and it is senseless to think that four of these wealthy friends would provide the sort of assistance to Socrates that would allow him to raise the amount of the fine he could offer *by 3000 percent* unless they supposed that the fine they could thereby help Socrates to offer would, indeed, be (at the very least) no offense to the jury. In fact, a mina of silver was enough to pay for 100 days of labor from a free Greek worker; 30 minas, then, would pay for 3,000 days of labor – over eight years' worth of wages, not counting holidays! The question, then, is why the jurors would not accept the fine Socrates offered – since its adequacy as a substantial penalty to pay cannot any longer be seriously questioned.

Once again Diogenes Laertius' account has been the source of considerable confusion. According to Diogenes, after Socrates offered his counter-penalty (recall that in Diogenes' account, Socrates' final offer was to demand free meals at the Prytaneum), the final vote to condemn Socrates to death was by an even larger majority than the vote to convict had been, by an accession of an additional eighty votes (D.L. 2.42) – all but thirty, in other words, of those who had found Socrates innocent in the first vote (according to the calculation we provided earlier in section 2.6). Despite not accepting any other part of Diogenes' obviously confused account of the trial in preference to Plato's, some scholars continue to write as if this part of that account were true.[95]

In Diogenes' version, Socrates plainly made no attempt to offer any reasonable alternative to the death penalty. As we have seen, however, in Plato's version, a substantial fine is offered. Diogenes makes no reference at all to the very sizable fine reported by Plato, and our view is that it makes no sense to accept Diogenes' account of the final vote against Socrates unless we also jettison all the rest of Plato's account. For one thing, it strikes us as wholly implausible that eighty jurors who (by originally voting for his innocence) were willing to allow Socrates to walk out of the court without paying any penalty at all would not be willing to allow him and his friends to pay 30 minas in order to enjoy the same privilege they were willing to provide for free. Even if the first vote were as lopsided as Diogenes claims it was (which Plato also denies – and Plato was actually there, let us recall), those jurors who found Socrates innocent could hardly be supposed to be more eager to put him to death than to allow him to pay a fine. The *only* way to make sense of Diogenes' account of the final vote, accordingly, is to reject completely Plato's account of the counter-penalty offer. Scholars willing to do this, we contend, are required to present some argument as to why they are willing to prefer what is only found in a very garbled story from over six centuries later in antiquity, to the detailed and plausible account we find in Plato, an eyewitness at the trial itself.

In the next section, we will argue that Plato's account actually suggests that there was no change whatever between the first and second votes at the trial, on the basis of the way in which Socrates distinguishes only two groups of jurors in his third and final speech.[96] This, moreover, is what we might expect. If we assume that the jurors who voted against Socrates in the first vote did so because they thought that his "activities and arguments" in Athens must be brought to an end (whether as impious, as the charge had it, or simply as irksome, as Socrates seems to recognize), then we can well understand why they would not be won over by the offer of even a very substantial fine. Socrates, after all, had made it abundantly clear in both his defense and counter-penalty speeches that he would never abandon his philosophizing until and unless he were permanently silenced. Those, on the other hand, who were willing to find Socrates innocent, as we argued above, would surely be willing to accept any fine Socrates might offer – especially if the amount of the fine were respectfully substantial. Accordingly, we should find nothing surprising – despite the last-ditch intervention by Socrates' wealthy friends – in that none who had found him guilty were willing to accept the proposed fine as an alternative to the death penalty.

2.10 THE FINAL SPEECH

2.10.1 *The start of the final speech (38c1–39e5)*

The last of the three speeches in Plato's *Apology* is supposed to be given to the jurors "while the officers are taking a break and I'm not yet going to the place where I have to go to die" (39e2–4). From a historical point of view, it seems at least possible that there might be time at a trial for the convicted person to address the jurors in this way – both in Plato (here in the *Apology*) and in Xenophon (also in his *Apology*, 24–26), Socrates does make such a final address to the jurors. Our knowledge of Athenian law, unfortunately, provides no clear evidence of what sort of "break" this may have been for the authorities, or of how customary it might have been for those convicted to make such a final speech.

In Plato's version, Socrates divides the jurors into two groups and addresses each group separately. The first group he addresses is identified as "those of you who voted for my execution" (38d1–2), as "those of you who voted against me" (39c1–2, 39d9), and as "you who are putting me to death" (39c4). The second group is identified as "those who voted to acquit me" (39e1).[97] In the last section, we considered the claim (found only in Diogenes Laertius) that the second vote – that Socrates should be executed – went against him by an even wider margin than had the vote to convict him. We suggested that there was no reason to accept Diogenes' claim about this. The actual way in which Socrates divides the jurors, in Plato's version, moreover, gives us further reason to doubt Diogenes' account.

Note that if Diogenes were right about this, there would actually be three groups for Socrates to address at this point: (1) those who voted to convict Socrates, and then went on to vote to execute him; (2) those who voted to acquit Socrates, but then went on to vote to execute him; and (3) those who voted to acquit, and then voted in favor of the counter-penalty he proposed. Those in the first of these groups might well be described in the way that Socrates describes the jurors antagonistic to him, and those in the third of these groups would plausibly be described and addressed as Socrates describes and addresses the jurors friendly to him. But what about the second of the three groups Diogenes' account requires? In our view, if there were jurors who had voted for Socrates in the first vote, and then against him in the second vote, they could not sensibly belong to either of the only two groups of jurors Socrates describes and addresses in his third speech. They would indeed be jurors who had "voted to execute him" and would be "putting him to death," but could not be understood to belong to the second group he mentions, because they would in fact be jurors who had voted to acquit him, and so they would have to fall into the first group. Yet the jurors whom Socrates identifies as "those who voted to acquit me" he calls his "friends" at *Apology* 40a1, and says they are "judges" in the true sense at 40a3. These terms plainly would not apply to jurors who had just voted to put him to death. The fact is that Socrates plainly distinguishes the two groups of jurors whom he addresses in his third speech from one another, and the second group of jurors imagined by Diogenes Laertius' account would belong to *both* groups, which would make nonsense of Socrates' distinction between them. Perhaps some few did change their votes for some reason. However, we are suggesting that the numbers on both sides must have been approximately the same in order for Socrates to suggest that he is addressing the same groups. As a result, either we must reject Diogenes' account of the final vote then – along with everything else he tells us about this moment in the trial that contrasts with what Plato tells us – or we

THE APOLOGY OF SOCRATES

must reject Plato's account (including, therefore, the entire third speech) in favor of Diogenes'. We cannot imagine any good reason to take the latter strategy in preference to the former, and so we assume that none of "those who voted for my acquittal" went on to be among "those who voted for my execution."

2.10.2 "Those who voted for my execution" (38c1–d10)

As we have said, the first of the two groups of jurors Socrates addresses are those who voted against him both times. To these jurors, Socrates' words are quite harsh: he predicts that they will become "notorious and blamed by those who want to revile the city" (38c1–2), where such contempt might easily have been avoided by the simple application of patience. At his advanced age, Socrates would surely not have lived much longer anyway (38c1–7).

According to Socrates, those who had voted against him must suppose that he might have won their favor if he had only been willing to resort to the more familiar tactics of playing to their pride and sympathy by acting in shameless and pathetic ways (38d3–e2). Socrates reminds them that it is sometimes easy to avoid death, if one is but willing to do anything, no matter how shameful it might be, and notes how much worse it is to behave in such a way than to die through acting well:

> In battles it often becomes clear that one could avoid death by throwing down his weapons and turning to plead with his pursuers. And there are many other ways in each sort of danger to escape death if one would resort to doing and saying anything. For, men, it's surely not difficult to flee from death, but it's much more difficult to flee from evil; for evil runs faster than death. And now, being slow and old, I'm caught by the slower one, but my accusers, being clever and sharp-witted, are caught by the faster one, evil. And now I go away, having been sentenced by you to death and they go away, sentenced by the truth to evil and injustice. I'll stand by my penalty and they, by theirs.
>
> (39a1–b7)

To anyone who is familiar with Socratic philosophy, the sense of these words could not be more ominous: as we have seen earlier, Socrates is not at all convinced that death is anything to be feared. But evil and injustice, he is convinced, are ruinous to the soul (see sections 2.44 and 3.8–3.9). Despite appearances, then, there is no doubt in Socrates' mind who has suffered the worse fate as a result of his prosecution and condemnation: his fate, death, is not merely *slower* than the swifter fate of evil that his accusers have incurred; their "sentence," too, is very much the more damaging, as well.

It is by no means clear just how accurate Socrates was in this "prophecy." Of course, one can say that it has been fulfilled, at least in a sense, through the centuries of sympathetic readers of Plato's *Apology*. There is also some evidence that the Athenians themselves soon changed the way they regarded Socrates. As little as we are inclined to credit the tales we find in Diogenes Laertius' biography of Socrates, he alleges that the Athenians soon regretted their decision and closed down the palaestras and gymnasia because they were in mourning. Socrates was soon honored by a bronze statue designed by the renowned sculptor Lysippus (copies of whose surviving works are well known and continue to be widely studied). The statue of Socrates was said to be placed in the Pompeion (The Hall of Processions) in Athens; but if it did ever exist[98] (like most other bronze sculptures of that era), it was later lost or recycled for the usable metal. On the other hand, the Athenians voted to banish Anytus and Lycon, and put Meletus to death (D.L. 2.43). When Anytus, in exile from Athens, went to Heraclea, he was also banished from there on the same day as he arrived. But Diogenes' stories of the fates of the prosecutors cannot be found corroborated by the more likely reliable ancient authorities. Xenophon says only that Anytus later suffered because of the depravities and alcoholism of his son (a result of Anytus' neglect of his proper education), and for this, and because of his own lack of judgment, was reviled by the Athenians even after his death (Xenophon, *Ap*. 30–31).

After rebuking and condemning his accusers, Socrates goes on to make a prophecy about what his jurors will face after he is gone, as well. Those jurors who voted against him will face "a much worse penalty, by Zeus, than the one you've imposed on me by killing me" (39c4–6). For they suppose that by killing Socrates, they will escape having the bothersome old man harassing and examining them and their lives. But in fact, Socrates foresees, the opposite will be the case, and younger, harsher men – whom Socrates has held in check until now – will take up the same task even more vigorously, and with greater irritation to the Athenians (39c6–d3).

> If you think that by killing people you'll put a stop to anyone criticizing you because you don't live as you should, you're not thinking clearly. Escape is neither really possible nor admirable; the best and easiest course is not to restrain others, but instead to do what you need to do to be as good as possible.
>
> (39d3–8)

One could hardly have a clearer advocacy of a policy of free political speech than is found in these words, and it is something of a bitter irony that Socrates' two best-known younger associates, Plato and Xenophon, became (if they were not already, during Socrates' life) such bitter ideological opponents of the Athenian democracy and its institutions – such as, for example, the popular court by which Socrates was tried and put to death. At least in these two men, Socrates' prophecy to his jurors came true – in the younger generation of Socratics, the Athenians truly did face harsher critics of them and their ways than they had ever faced in Socrates.

2.10.3 "Something wonderful has happened to me" (39e1–40c4)

After making his prophecy to the jurors who had voted against him, Socrates turns to those who had voted in his favor, and seeks to reassure them that what has happened should be no source of anxiety to them on his behalf. Instead, as he puts it, they have "good reason to be hopeful" (40c5; see also 41c8) about what has happened at the trial. He arranges his argument to support this conclusion into three parts: (a) he tells them that "something wonderful" has happened to him (40a4), whose meaning can only be that "I'm about to have good luck" (40c3–4); (b) he offers what in logic is called a "constructive dilemma" intended to compel the conclusion that whatever death might be, it is something a good man like Socrates should look forward to with some happy antici- pation; (c) he asserts that the gods do not neglect good people. Let us go through each of these parts of Socrates' reassurance to his supportive jurors.

The "wonderful" thing that has happened to Socrates, it turns out, is what has *not* happened to him, which he supposed might have been so likely under the circumstances. As he left his home at dawn to make his way to the court, when he arrived at the court itself, and during his entire speech, not once did his familiar "divine thing" or "sign" (the *daimonion* – see also 31c8–d4, and our dis- cussion in section 2.7.2) interrupt him to signal that he was about to do something wrong (40a4–b3). Yet, in the past, this uncanny disturbance has made itself felt by Socrates, as he says, "on quite trivial matters if I was about to do something that wasn't right" (40a6–7), and might even hold him back even when he was in the middle of what he was saying (40b4–5). On this day, by contrast, it has left him unopposed at every point, despite all of it leading to what (though Socrates himself doubts it) is generally considered to be the greatest of evils (40a7–b1). Even if Socrates cannot be absolutely certain that the *daimonion* would oppose him absolutely every time he was about to do something evil or harm- ful, it has, as it were, missed too many opportunities for interfer- ence on this day for Socrates to conclude anything else than that this private warning from divinity he has enjoyed (or struggled with) since childhood has foreseen nothing in what has happened on this day against which to warn him:

> What, then, do I take to be the explanation? I'll tell you. What's hap- pened to me will probably be something good, and it can't be that we're right in supposing that death's an evil. I've got strong evidence that this is so. It can't be that I haven't been opposed by my usual sign unless I'm about to do something good.
>
> (40b6–c4)

We have already discussed how we should understand the role and consequence of Socrates' *daimonion* in his life, and also how his mention of the *daimonion* in this and other passages should be understood. Here in the third speech of the *Apology*, the role of the *daimonion* is rather different than it is in the other cases in which Socrates explains its effects on him and what he does, for, as we discussed earlier, it is the *non-appearance* of the *daimonion* that Socrates notices in this case. The obvious sense of this, however, is that given how often the *daimonion* alerted him in the past, its non-interference in this case can reasonably be supposed to show that nothing he has done or said on this day has led him into something bad. For those jurors who are inclined to take Socrates at his word about this strange phenomenon, then, the fact that he has not been disturbed by it today can indeed count as a reason to be hopeful on Socrates' behalf.

2.10.4 "Death is one of two things" (40c5–41c7)

Socrates' next strategy is to argue that the outcome of the trial should be no source of grief to those jurors who voted in his favor. Instead, he contends, there is "good reason to be hopeful" (40c5), for, he says,

> Death is one of two things: either it's like nothingness and the dead have no awareness of anything, or it's as they say, a change and the soul migrates from this place to another place.
>
> (40c6–10)

Either way, Socrates avers, it is nothing to fear.[99] If it is "like nothingness," then it may be compared to the deepest and most dreamless sleep. "If death's like this," Socrates proclaims, "I'd say it's a gain; for the whole of time seems no more than a single night" (40e4).

Socrates' argument for this possibility is familiar enough even within our own culture, which sometimes characterizes death as "the big sleep," or as "eternal rest." His description of death-as-nothingness as "better and more pleasant" than what we experience

during most of our lives (40d6), however, has struck some commentators as simply absurd: "The only reason that a night's
dreamless sleep is pleasant is because one wakes from it in the
morning refreshed and vitalized. Only then can one look back
gratefully to the night."[100] But this does not, in fact, seem accurate
of our actual experience. When we go to bed at night, we do not
simply look forward to waking up the next day "refreshed and
vitalized." We may well do this (and we often do hope that our
sleep will not be so poor as to leave us unrefreshed and drained on
the following morning), but it also seems evident that those who
are sleepy actually do look forward to *sleeping*, without particular
or explicit consideration of how they will feel when they wake up.
Even if the predictable consequences of a good night's sleep (by
which we generally do mean a deep and undisturbed period of
unconsciousness) were to be denied to us – as, for example, they
might be if we knew that as soon as we awoke we would be given
some form of sedative that would leave us feeling lifeless and
enervated – we would still prefer and indeed hope for a long, sound,
and dreamless rest before the advent of the new day. Sleep, in short,
is attractive to the sleeper not just for its anticipated benefits in the
next period of waking, but just for its own sake. If death really is
just like a deep sleep, then, Socrates does seem to be right to claim
that fearing it is senseless.

The other option that Socrates offers is more interesting – and
more controversial. If death is not "like nothingness," then it would
seem to follow that our consciousness somehow continues to exist
after death. It cannot remain with the body, since the body is eventually destroyed; so it must go somewhere else. But if we assume
that it does migrate to some other place, what should we think
about what that might be like? The picture of an afterlife Socrates
provides in the second "horn" of his constructive dilemma is not
exactly like any of the other afterlife stories that have come down
to us from the ancient world.[101] It may be true that the picture of
an afterlife Socrates provides to his jurors (lively philosophical discussions with the other dead) leaves nothing to fear (though some
students in philosophy courses might demur from Socrates'

description of an eternity of philosophizing as an "unimaginable happiness" at 41c4). But does migration "from this place to another place" not, after all, include any number of terrifying prospects? What if that migration, for example, transported us into an eternity of torture in hell?

There were several quite scary stories of the afterlife in Greek folklore, but we need not fault Socrates for ignoring them in this instance. First, let us recall that it is another aspect of Socrates' religious views that the gods are completely wise and completely good – indeed, he goes so far as to say that human beings enjoy "nothing good that they don't provide us" at *Euthyphro* 15a1–2. So Socrates is certainly not ready to consider stories about the gods – or about how they have arranged the fates of mortal men – that would characterize them as gratuitously sadistic or cruel. Second, let us be clear that Socrates is not here considering what might be the afterlife fates of evil or unjust human beings. There is, of course, some plain threat in the fact that he imagines what he calls "real judges" (41a2) waiting there to judge those who enter into the next world. But Socrates has nothing to fear from a "real judge," for as he has said of himself (and as those jurors who voted in his favor seem ready to concede), he has never willingly wronged anyone (37a6–7), is convinced that he has not done anything wrong (37b2–3), and does not deserve anything evil or bad (37b3–4, 38a8–b1). So what should he expect, if, as some of the stories have it, he will be judged by "real judges" in the afterlife? We know what he thought he should receive for his "crimes" from the actual judges he faced at his trial, for he has already told his jurors that at the beginning of his second speech – that his life philosophizing with his fellow mortals should be supported by free meals at the Prytaneum (36b3–37a2)! His vision of the afterlife, where the distractions of "making a living" are now unnecessary, and where others can't kill you a second time for philosophizing, seems, indeed, very like what he supposed was his proper due for the life he has led. There may, of course, be other visions of an afterlife that are possible – and Socrates all along readily concedes that no one really knows what may happen after death – but he sees no reason to consider any conception of the afterlife other than one that is like an endless sleep, or one in which the souls of good men like Socrates are given proper rewards for having lived as they should.

2.10.5 Was Socrates agnostic about the afterlife?

In making his argument to his jurors as he does, Socrates does not in any clear way signal which of the two options he presents about death – "nothingness" or migration – seems more likely to him. Accordingly, some scholars have concluded that Socrates' considered view about what follows death is simply agnosticism: it is not simply that death *might* be one of two things; it is that anyone who thinks he has good reason to believe that it is one rather than the other of these options is irrational.[102] If the *Apology* were the only text we could rely upon to determine what Socrates' beliefs about death and the afterlife might be, it is likely that this view is the one that would most recommend itself to us. But in the *Crito* (54c6–8), Socrates has the personified laws warn that he will receive harsh treatment from the laws in Hades if he seeks to damage the laws of Athens – and this, plainly, implies that there is an afterlife. And in the *Gorgias* (523a1–526d2), Socrates tells a remarkably long and detailed myth of the afterlife, and insists that Callicles (to whom he tells the myth) will probably think it is only a myth, but insists that he himself counts it as an "account" (523a2), which Socrates says he regards as true (523a2, 524a8–b1), and finds persuasive (526d3–4). Scholars have considered various reasons why we should not consider these other texts as justifying us in supposing that Socrates actually did believe in an afterlife, but for our purposes here, it is enough to note that they raise the question: could Socrates argue as he does in the *Apology* if he really did believe in an afterlife?

At *Apology* 29a4–b6, Socrates says he regards it as "the most shameful ignorance" to fear death as if they knew it was the greatest of evils, when for all they know it might in fact be the greatest of blessings. It obviously follows from what he says in cautioning his jurors in this passage that whatever he or anyone else may suppose about death and the afterlife, no view of these matters (or, at any rate, no view held by living human beings) will qualify as *knowledge* about these matters. When one claims that human beings have no knowledge of some issue, however, one might be making the very strong statement that our ignorance of the subject is so complete that no opinion will be any better justified than any alternative to it, or one might be making the much weaker claim that even the best and most justified opinions of human beings will not rise to the very exacting standards required for knowledge. One of the most often repeated claims we find Socrates making in the early dialogues is that he lacks knowledge or wisdom.[103] In making this disclaimer, however, Socrates plainly does not at all mean to say that everyone else's opinions on this subject are as just as good as are his own opinions! By taking seriously the fact that we do not know, we allow ourselves to consider reasons for all sides of an issue. But the whole point of being open to consider reasons for all sides is not simply to avoid formulating any opinion at all, but rather to ensure that any opinion we might form will be as well informed (and well formed) as it can be. Socrates thinks that all human beings lack knowledge and wisdom about what he calls "the most important things" (22d7–8); he does, however, quite evidently manage to hold several famous opinions on such matters.

Similarly, we should not suppose that just because Socrates describes the pretense of knowledge about death and the afterlife as "the most shameful ignorance" it follows that he would condemn all opinions on the matter as equally ignorant and insupportable. Nor does his argument that "death is one of two things" force us to conclude that he supposes that no reason could be given for thinking that one of these possibilities is more probable or more plausible than the other. In the *Crito* and the *Gorgias*, as we have said, Socrates seems to betray an opinion on such matters that favors the view that there is an afterlife. In these dialogues, he does not, however, offer any arguments to support such a conclusion. In some of Plato's later dialogues, we do find the character Socrates providing a variety of such arguments. The most famous of these arguments can be found in the *Phaedo*, which (according to the stylometric method of dating the dialogues) has been argued to be from the same general period of Plato's writings as those dialogues we have been calling the early ones. But few scholars find they accept that the arguments of the *Phaedo* fit with the views of the "Socrates" expressed in the (other) early dialogues of Plato. In the first place, the "Socrates" we find in the *Phaedo* seems to characterize the nature of the afterlife so differently. Moreover, many of the arguments of that Socrates rely on a sophisticated metaphysical and epistemological theory – the "theory of Forms" that Aristotle attributed to Plato and not to Socrates (*Metaph.* VIII.4.1078b30–32). So if Socrates did regard the belief in an afterlife as more justified than the belief that death is the permanent extinction of consciousness, he never actually offers any explanation of why he does in Plato's early dialogues.

We need not be deceived, however, by the fact that Socrates is willing to allow that death might be "one of two things" into supposing that he thus regarded each of them as no more probable than the other. When he makes this final argument to his jurors, he has already made it plain that he does not regard anyone as knowing what happens after death. But he is aware that people fear death – and that is not because they actually know what will happen, but because people *don't* know. To counteract this fear, Socrates creates his constructive dilemma. Either death is annihilation, or if it is not annihilation, then the soul goes somewhere else. Socrates assumes that his jurors don't *know* which of these two options it will be, and their anxiety on his behalf is based upon fear of the unknown. By forming a constructive dilemma, however, he tries to show them that according to the best reasoning available to them (that is, thinking of annihilation in terms of sleeping, and thinking of the migration of the soul in terms of what they have heard about this in myths), no matter what death turns out to be, there is reason to be hopeful on his behalf. Now, if Socrates were instead to lecture them about which of the two options he personally found more probable, he would be less likely to reassure his jurors about *their* fears, and more likely to convince them (especially if they are inclined to believe the *other* option) that his own fearlessness is only a product of his own faith in a conception of the afterlife they find themselves unable to share with confidence. The virtue of employing a constructive dilemma at this point is that it serves to address the fears of his jurors no matter what their understanding of what happens at death. It plainly does not follow, however, that Socrates himself has no specific beliefs about the afterlife.[104] Rather, Socrates' specific beliefs (or those of any specific juror, for that matter) are not what are at issue here, for if Socrates' argument is a good one, no matter which "horn" of the constructive dilemma one judges to be the more likely, the same conclusion may be reached.

2.10.6 "No harm comes to a good man" (41c9–d2)

Socrates concludes his argument as to why he thinks that those jurors who are well disposed towards him should not be concerned on his behalf with the words "you should be optimistic about death" (41c8–9). He then offers his final argument as to why his fate is nothing to fear: "No harm," he proclaims, "comes to a good man in life or in death, and his problems are not neglected by the gods" (41c9–d2). These apparently straightforward confident words have proven somewhat difficult to interpret. Many scholars have taken these to be a plain and explicit statement of what is called the "sufficiency of virtue" thesis, which claims that those with virtue simply cannot be harmed – virtue, all by itself and with no further requirements, assures its possessor of at least some positive overall happiness in life (and in death).[105] As strongly as this passage suggests such a view, however, reading it this way creates other problems. For one thing, unless Socrates has his own case in mind (or at least supposes that it is an example to consider in accordance with the doctrine he announces here), his assertion at this point would be senseless. We may assume, therefore, that in telling his jurors that "no harm comes to a good man," he means to reassure them that no harm is coming to *him*. But even if it seems clear that Socrates regards himself as a good man, there are very good reasons for thinking that Socrates *does not* regard himself as a *virtuous* man. For one thing, in many places throughout the early dialogues, Socrates makes it clear that he supposes that no virtue is possible without wisdom.[106] But, as Socrates' interpretation of the oracle from Delphi to Chaerephon makes clear, Socrates does not regard himself as in possession of wisdom. If he lacks wisdom, then he cannot be a virtuous man, no matter how much he might aspire to be one, and no matter how good he may be, relative to other human beings. If the doctrine is to apply to *Socrates*, then, and must be understood as a doctrine about absolute indemnity from harm, then it would have to be understood as the claim that merely being a good person indemnifies one absolutely against harm.

But this claim is not only philosophically implausible, if we are to understand "harm" in any ordinary way; it also seems to go directly against all of Socrates' considerations in the second speech about the relative merits of the death penalty sought by his prosecutors and other penalties he considers and rejects as alternatives. Some of these other penalties, recall, Socrates rejected explicitly on the ground that they would *harm* him. So, it simply cannot be that Socrates thinks that *no kind of harm* can befall good people. He must, accordingly, have some special sense of "harm" in mind when he utters these words in his final speech.

Let us consider once again what kinds of harms Socrates thinks he could suffer from others. According to what he said in his second speech, he might have been harmed if he had proposed imprisonment for life and had this accepted by his jurors, or if he were exiled from Athens. We may assume that none of these fates would change anything in Socrates' character (for which reason he predicted that he would be exiled from everywhere else he might go), so the harm he would receive from imprisonment or exile would be harm to his way of life only. In the *Crito*, as we'll see, Socrates understands that one's life may be so destroyed by disease or other bodily infirmity as not to be worth living (*Cri.* 47d8–e6). But in the next breath in that argument (*Cri.* 47e7–a4) he distinguishes this bodily kind of harm from harm to the soul, proclaiming the latter to be vastly worse than the former. If we identify the person with his or her soul, as Socrates plainly does (since his conception of an afterlife plainly imagines the survival of the same person – and not some new and different being – after the death and disintegration of the body), we can thus distinguish between the kinds of harms that may damage one's hopes of being able to act in the ways one would wish (acting, that is, in the sorts of ways that will make one's life a happy one), and the kinds of harms that would actually be

THE APOLOGY OF SOCRATES 183

directly destructive of one's soul or self. The destruction of the soul or self may not cause the end of the soul's or self's actual existence (if, as Socrates seems at least to believe as a possibility, the soul is immortal), but at least one thing is certain: judging from Socrates' cheerful willingness to die rather than to damage his soul, he plainly regards damage to his soul as a fate worse than death. Because the only thing that harms a person in this especially devastating way is wrongdoing, none of *this* kind of harm can ever happen to a good person. It is *this* most devastating harm, we suggest, that Socrates has in mind in saying that "no harm can come to a good man."

Socrates also supposes that the gods do not neglect the sorts of problems good people can sometimes have. In adding this to his claim that "no harm comes to a good man," Socrates also at least strongly suggests that he does not accept the sufficiency of goodness (or virtue) for happiness. After all, if goodness were all by itself sufficient to guarantee that the good person would be happy, the gods would have no need to watch over the good person, and provide some relief or protection against whatever problems they might have. The most the gods could contribute, we must suppose, if goodness were sufficient for happiness, would be to make a person already absolutely assured of happiness (no matter what their problems might be!) perhaps even more happy. This understanding of Socrates' claim about the concern of the gods here in the *Apology*, however, seems most implausible. It seems far more plausible to suppose that Socrates means his jurors to understand that the gods watch over good people precisely in order to prevent such good people from suffering too greatly.

Now for these two claims – that "no harm can come to a good man," and that "his problems are not neglected by the gods" – Socrates offers his jurors no arguments. He has already emphasized in his first speech just how important he regards what he has called the "care of the soul" (see 29e2), and so there is little need for him to construct an argument here in the last few minutes he has to speak to his jurors about why one who has undertaken to take care of his soul can be assured that his soul is not in danger of harm from wrongdoing. Again, everything Socrates has said about the gods (at his trial or in any of Plato's other early dialogues) shows that he regards them as flawlessly good and beneficent. In his view, their wisdom assures their beneficence.[107] So we may be entirely confident that Socrates really does believe that the gods take good care of good people. If his jurors can share his confidence about these matters, these considerations can be counted as additional reasons to those he provided earlier in this speech for them to be hopeful even though Socrates has been condemned.

2.10.7 "The time has come to leave" (41d3–42a5)

In the last few moments before he leaves the courtroom, Socrates sums up his encouragements to his jurors. He concludes, on the basis of everything he has said to the jurors who voted on his behalf, that what has happened to him did not simply happen "by chance" (41d3), but instead shows that dying now and being spared of further troubles will be a good thing for Socrates. This is why his *daimonion* did not interrupt him in anything he said or did on this day, and this is why, he now explains, that he is not at all angry with the jurors who condemned him, or even with his prosecutors. They did attempt to do him some harm, it is true – and for this they should be blamed (41d7–9). But as a matter of fact, Socrates is now convinced, their attempt to do him harm has backfired, for far from harming him, they have actually turned out to serve his interests well.

His last request to those who had condemned and prosecuted him is, we may assume, both ironic and also entirely sincere: Socrates requests that they "punish" his sons in exactly the way he had "punished" those who had become so angry with Socrates as to put him on trial and condemn him to death. He asks his adversaries not to allow his sons to suppose that anything is more important than virtue, and to reproach them if they suppose they have amounted to anything when they haven't. "If you'd do this," Socrates contends, "I myself and my sons will have been treated justly by you" (42a1–2). We may suppose that there is little chance that those hostile to Socrates will undertake any such "care" for the souls of Socrates' sons. Nonetheless, we may also suppose that Socrates would indeed approve of anyone undertaking to do for his sons after his death what he has done as Athens' gadfly for so many years before it.

No doubt because the officers have done whatever had occupied them earlier, Socrates sees that the time has come for him to go to the jail, where he will await his execution. Despite his confidence in thinking that there was nothing at all for him to fear in his future, Socrates concludes his final speech with characteristic modesty:

> But now the time has come to leave, me to die and you to live on; which of us is going to the better fate is unclear to anyone except the god.
>
> (42a2–5)

NOTES

1   The English "apology" is derived from the Greek "*apologia*," which means "defense."

2   Xenophon, *Ap.* 1–2.

3   For a highly speculative account that argues that at least parts of the *Apology* were written as late as 387, some twelve years after Socrates' death, see de Stryker and Slings 1994, 16–21.

4   An excellent, brief discussion of this distinction can be found in Harrison 1971, vol. II, 76–78.

5   This can be inferred from the probable location of the prison in which Socrates was held until his execution and one of the public courts, together with Plato's remark (*Phd.* 59d2–4) that "the court where the trial took place" was close to the prison. For a discussion of the probable location of courts and the prison in which Socrates was held, see Camp 1992, 107–8 and 113–6.

6   MacDowell 1978, 35.

7   Roberts 1984, 56.

8   This is implied by *Ap.* 36a8–b2. See also MacDowell 1978, 64.

9   D. L. see 2.41.

10 Ibid., 2.40.

11 See MacDowell 1978, 37–39; Burnet 1924, note on 36a5.

12 Aristophanes, *Wasps* 291–311.

13 For more on the composition of Athenian juries, see MacDowell 1978, 34–35.

14 This possibility is suggested by Burnet 1924, note on 23e3. It is, however, only a mere possibility.

15 See Andocides, *On the Mysteries.*

16 It is noteworthy that no ancient source on Socrates' trial mentions the Meletus who is Socrates' prosecutor in connection with the arrest of Leon. See Andocides, *Myst.* 94.

17 Socrates' remark may also simply mean that he attributed one-third of the votes against him to each of those who had participated in the prosecution. Each of these thirds, given the final vote of 280 to convict, would have fallen short of the 100 votes necessary to avoid the fine.

18 See Xenophon, *Mem.* 1.1.1.

19 D. L., 2.40.

20 Burnet 1924, 63–64. Much the same point is echoed by Vlastos 1971, 3. Another, more recent proponent of this view is Charles Kahn 1996, 88–89, who claims that the *Apology* "can properly be regarded as a quasi-historical document, like Thucydides' version of Pericles' funeral oration" and that "there are external constraints that make his *Apology* the most reliable of all of our testimonies concerning Socrates." Unlike Burnet and Vlastos, Kahn relies on similarities between the Socrates of Plato's *Apology* and what we know of Aeschines' description of Socrates.

21 We make the same point in Brickhouse and Smith 1989, 4.

22 Emile de Stryker in de Stryker and Slings 1994, 7–8.

23 de Stryker and Slings 1994, 6–8, for example, advance this argument.

24 Gorgias' *Defense of Palamedes* is perhaps the best example of this genre.

25 See Hutchinson 1999, 603.

26 This fact was noted in Riddell 1877, xxi, and is discussed by Burnet 1924, notes on 17a1–18a6. See Brickhouse and Smith 1989, 48–59 for full discussion.

27 See, for example, Thrasymachus' assessment of Socrates at *Rep.* I, 336e–337a and Callicles' accusation that Socrates deceives his opponents at *Grg.* 483a2–9.

28 One mina was equal to 100 silver drachmas, and one drachma was a typical daily wage for an unskilled laborer, which many of the jurors probably were. For more on the value of one mina, see section 2.38.

29 See, for example, *Birds* 1281–4.

30 See Brickhouse and Smith 1989, 71.

31 Polycrates, Isocrates, and Xenophon; see Brickhouse and Smith 1989, 72.

32 Burnet 1924, 181.

33 A reconstruction of this work is undertaken in Chroust 1957, 69–100.

34 See D. L., 2.39.

35 Critias and Charmides were killed during the fighting that resulted in the overthrow of the Thirty and the restoration of the democracy in 403 B.C.E. The circumstances of Alcibiades' death are less clear, but it appears that he was assassinated in northern Greece in 404 B.C.E.

36 Of course, Plato, a near relative of both Charmides and Critias, twice indicates that he was present at the trial (34a1, 38b6), but he would not have been willing to speak against Socrates.

37 In his version of the speech, Xenophon also reports that Chaerephon journeyed to Delphi to inquire about Socrates' wisdom. According to Xenophon (*Ap.* 14), however, the oracle replied that "no one is more liberal minded, more just, or temperate than [Socrates]." We think that because both Plato and Xenophon make reference to the story in connection to Socrates' wisdom, it is more likely than not that Socrates actually referred to Chaerephon's journey in his speech.

38 For a full discussion of this aspect of Socrates' philosophy, see Brickhouse and Smith 1994, 103–36.

39 See *Euthphr.* 13d5–8.

40 For an excellent, extended discussion of the Delphic oracle and the origin of Socrates' mission, see McPherran 1996, 208–46.

41 Similar statements of the formal charges against Socrates can be found in Xenophon, *Mem.* 1.1.1 and in D.L., 2.40. Diogenes' account, which purports to be based on Favorinus' claim that Meletus' actual sworn statement was still hanging in the Metroon, a building in Athens which served as the legal archive, is virtually identical to Xenophon's. Both differ from Socrates' statement of the charges principally in the order in which they are presented.

42 See, e.g., Allen 1976, 34, 1975, 11; Beckman 1979, 61; Burnet 1924, notes on 24c9, 28a4, 26d4; Hackforth 1933, 104; and Taylor 1952, 100.

43 We have already seen Socrates' reliance on the analogy in the *Euthyphro* at 13b9–c1. As we will see in the *Crito* (47a2–48a11), Socrates is convinced that the majority of Athens' citizens are not capable of improving anyone and that their opinions are to be disregarded.

44 Some commentators have reached this conclusion. See, for examples, Taylor 1952, 164; West 1979, 137.

45 Socrates argues that all wrongdoing is the product of ignorance at *Meno* 77b6–78b8.

46 For evidence that the general population in Athens was hostile towards the sophists, see Kerford 1981, 15–23.

47   According to Plutarch (*On Pericles*, 32.1), the decree (or *psephism*) of
      Diopethes was passed at about the time hostilities broke out between
      Athens and Sparta. This decree, which was probably aimed at
      Anaxagoras, made it an actionable offence "not to believe in divine
      things (*ta theia*) and to teach doctrines concerning the heavens."
      Whether anyone was actually prosecuted under the decree is not
      known. Moreover, it was annulled under the conditions of the general
      amnesty passed at the time the democracy was restored. However,
      the fact that Meletus is relying on what the *psephism* of Diopethes out-
      lawed in order to charge Socrates with violating the law forbidding
      impiety shows that the Athenians regarded this sort of atheism as
      quite serious.

48   See, for example, Seeskin 1987, 84.

49   Plato has Socrates explicitly shy away from providing alternative
      accounts of divinities and their sometimes unusual offspring at *Phdr.*
      229c6–230a6.

50   This reading is required by the *de* that introduces the charge "[believing]
      in other new divinities" at 24c1.

51   Although they offer somewhat different reasons for this conclusion
      from each other, this assessment of Socrates' guilt can be found in
      Vlastos 1991 157–78; McPherran 1996, 156–60; Burnyeat 1997, 1–12.

52   Xenophon, *Ap.* 12.

53   It would be extremely misleading, at best, for Socrates to make this
      claim if he understood or supposed that the gods he says he believes
      in were *not* the same gods that the jury believes in and, hence, the
      gods that the city believes in.

54   Although Plato and Xenophon provide evidence that Socrates
      engages in orthodox religious behavior such as making sacrifices,
      Xenophon, somewhat implausibly, holds up Socrates as a model of
      conventional Athenian piety. For an excellent discussion of this issue
      and the relevant texts, see McPherran 1996, 77–82.

55   See also Xenophon, *Mem.* 1.1.19.

56   One of the hallmarks of Socrates' philosophy is the view that every
      action aims at what the agent at least believes to be good for him. It
      follows from this that whenever one does what is, in fact, not good for
      himself, the explanation can only be that, at the time the agent acted,
      the agent mistakenly believed that the act would yield a good for him.
      When we couple this with Socrates' view that virtue is always a good
      thing for its possessor, we can see why he believes that one who is
      wise about what is good will do what is good. And since, as Socrates

believes, virtue requires wisdom, the person who possesses wisdom about good and evil is the same person as the virtuous person.

57 We hear this commonly held opinion echoed in the *Crito* (45c6–9) when Socrates' friend Crito urges him to escape from prison.

58 *Iliad*, Book 18, lines 95–104.

59 These battles took place in 432, 422, and 424, respectively. Plato makes much of Socrates' valor in the first and third. In the *Laches* (181b1–3), in describing Socrates' heroism during the retreat from the battle, the general Laches actually says that the Athenians would not have been defeated had the rest of the army behaved as courageously as Socrates did.

60 This is the interpretation adopted by Kraut 1984, 23 n. 38, and Woozley 1979, 49.

61 We will have more to say about why Socrates would think that the citizen has a moral duty to obey legal authorities in our discussion of the *Crito* in the next chapter.

62 Socrates' claims that he possesses knowledge are not limited to the *Apology*. In the *Ion* (532d8–e3), he characterizes some of the things he knows as "trivial and commonplace," the sort of thing anyone could know. For example, he seems entirely confident that he knows the definition of quickness in the *Laches* (192a8–b3) and the definition of "figure" in the *Meno* (76a4–7). But he also claims to know something of moral relevance in the *Euthydemus* (283c4–5), where he says that he has known for "a long time" that good people are not unjust. See also *Euthyd.* 293b7–8 and *Meno* 98b2–5.

63 For a more complete discussion, see Brickhouse and Smith 1994, 5–10.

64 For a detailed account of how Socrates derived beliefs about moral propositions from the failures of his interlocutors to answer his questions, see Brickhouse and Smith 1994, 16–21.

65 For an extended discussion of the ways in which Socrates' religious beliefs were orthodox and the ways in which they were not, see McPherran 1996, 130–74. We do not share McPherran's view that such unorthodoxies played a role in Socrates' trial and execution, however.

66 An interesting discussion of how this process might work is offered in McPherran 2002.

67 It would be a mistake to think that Socrates believes that we can say nothing at all about what happens at death. Later he tells the jury that he does not believe that it is "even possible for a better person to be harmed by a worse" (30d1–2). In his third speech, immediately before he is taken away to prison to await his execution, he tells those jurors

who voted for his acquittal to be "hopeful about death" and that "no harm comes to a good man in life or in death" (41c8–d2). We will have more to say about each of these claims below.

68 This interpretation of the passage qualifies as the standard view. Recent expressions of this view can be found in Kraut 1984, 13–17; Reeve 1989, 115–16; Weiss 1998, 7–38; and Colaiaco 2001, 139–47.

69 We offer a detailed analysis of this power in Brickhouse and Smith 2000.

70 See, for example, Irwin, 1995, 273–75; Vlastos, 1991, 209–32; Burnyeat 1971, 211–12.

71 We discuss this passage and its relevance to the issue we raise here at length in section 3.4.4.

72 We will have more to say in section 2.10.4 about what Socrates thinks will happen to him when he dies.

73 As we will see, Socrates believes that death may turn out to be annihilation, a kind of "dreamless sleep" (40c9–d1).

74 In Athens even military leaders, those in command of the army and the navy, were political leaders who were elected and who spoke regularly before the Assembly.

75 Socrates also refers to the "divine sign," or "voice," or "divine something," at *Ap.* 40b2, 40c3–6, 41d6; *Euthyd.* 272e4; *Euthphr.* 3b5–7; *Rep.* VI.496c4; and *Phdr.* 242b8–9, 242c2.

76 For similar versions of this statement of the problem, see Vlastos 1991, 157, and Reeve, 1989, 71–72.

77 See Nussbaum 1985, 234–35. The same very implausible reduction of the phenomenon may be found promoted as one of the two correct ways to understand the phenomenon in Vlastos 1991, 283.

78 This is the other correct understanding of Socrates' reactions to his *daimonion*, according to Vlastos 1991, 283.

79 Examples of this view may be found expressed in Brickhouse and Smith 1989, 237–57 and 1994, 189–95, and in McPherran 1991 and 1996, 185–208. A lively correspondence between the main participants in the debate about the epistemological role of Socrates' *daimonion* may be found in Woodruff 2000.

80 For examples of Socrates' descriptions of the phenomenon as a "sign from the god" at *Ap.* 40b2, a "divine sign" at *Ap.* 40c3–4, 41d6, *Euthyd.* 272e4; *Rep.* VI.496c4; and *Phdr.* 242b8–9, or where he calls it a "something divine" at *Ap.* 31c8–d1, 40a4–6, *Euthphr.* 3b5–7, *Phdr.* 242b8–9).

81 In Brickhouse and Smith 1989, 168–69 and 1990.

82 Vlastos 1991, 286.

83 Each district had fifty representatives (selected by rotation and lot) on the Council each year and each group of fifty took a turn being in charge of the Council. The Council had a number of important functions, including the preparation of legislation to be presented to the Assembly. But it also had oversight in all matters involving the public officials charged with misconduct.

84 For an excellent account that judiciously weighs the evidence from the various ancient sources on the trial of the ten generals, see Andrewes 1974, 112–22.

85 There is some disagreement in the ancient sources about whether there were actually ten generals in charge or fewer. For more on this dispute, see Brickhouse and Smith 1989, 175 n. 25.

86 The arrest of Leon was by no means the only such illegal arrest that took place during the reign of the Thirty Tyrants, but it must have been especially egregious in the eyes of many Athenians. See Xenophon, *Hell.* 2.3.39.

87 This accusation is made in Nussbaum 1980.

88 Socrates is referring to the *Odyssey*, Book XIX, line 163.

89 For our reasoning that the jury at Socrates trial was probably 500 and not 501, as is sometimes claimed, see section 2.6 above.

90 See Brickhouse and Smith 1989, 214.

91 See 31e2–32a3.

92 See 29d7–e3.

93 See, e.g., Fox 1956, 231; Guthrie 1971, 64; A. E. Taylor 1952, 166; West 1979, 255.

94 In our first article on Socrates, we argued that, in fact, earlier accounts of the actual value of the fine Socrates offers as his counter-penalty grossly under-appraised the actual value of the fine. For those who maintained that the value of the proposed fine is insignificant and our refutation of that claim, see Brickhouse and Smith 1982 and 1989, 225–30. The subsequent scholarly literature, we are pleased to see, no longer repeats this error. See, for example, the change from the earlier Grube translation of the *Apology* (Grube 1975, 39 n.12), to the revised translation in the third edition (Grube 2000, 24 n. 6 and 39 n. 17).

95 See, for example, C. C. W. Taylor 1998, 14.

96 See also Brickhouse and Smith 1989, 231–32.

97 The term in Greek that Socrates uses to identify this group at 39e1 is a form of ἀποψηφίζομαι. Socrates uses the same term at 34d9 in a way that makes its meaning plain. See Liddell et al. 1996, 228, who

actually cite these two uses of the term in Plato's *Apology* to document their understanding of the meaning, "vote an acquittal."

98   At least one major authority on Greek sculpture seems to suppose that a portrait sculpture of Socrates by Lysippus did exist: see Boardman 1985, 195.

99   A very clear and plausible reconstruction of Socrates' argument may be found in Rudebusch 1999, 65–79. Our own formulation of the argument follows, but does not duplicate the admirable detail of Rudebusch's interpretation, which was partly motivated by his disagreements with our earlier characterization of the argument in Brickhouse and Smith 1989.

100 See, e.g., Roochnik 1985, 214. A contrasting view may be found in Rudebusch 1999, 68–72.

101 For a sample of these, see Rice and Stambaugh 1979, 217–55.

102 A thorough and detailed expression of this position may be found in McPherran 1996, 247–71.

103 See, for examples, *Ap.* 20c1–3, 21d2–7, 23b2–4; *Charm.* 165b4–c2, 166c7–d6; *Euthphr.* 5a7–c5, 15c12, 15e5–16a4; *La.* 186b8–c5, 186d8–e3, 200e2–5; *Lys.* 212a4–7, 223b4–8; *Hip. Ma.* 286c8–e2, 304d4–e5; *Grg.* 509a4–6; *Meno* 71a1–7, 80d1–4; *Rep.* I.337e4–5.

104 *Contra* McPherran 1996, 266–67.

105 An example of this view may be found in Irwin 1986, and Vlastos 1991, 200–32.

106 At one point, he seems even to argue that all virtue – and anything else of value, for that matter – must be either wisdom itself, or at least under employment by wisdom. See *Euthyd.* 278e3–281e5. In the *Protagoras*, Socrates appears to argue for what is called the "unity of the virtues," according to which all of the virtues are in some sense all the same. In this view, there can be no (other) virtue without wisdom. For a discussion of the interpretation of this doctrine, see sections 1.4.3–1.4.5.

107 For a reconstruction of how this follows, see Brickhouse and Smith 1994, 179–81. See also the letter by Vlastos in Woodruff 2000, 203 n. 15, quoting N. Smith.

3

THE *CRITO*

3.1 INTRODUCTION TO THE *CRITO*

3.1.1 *The general structure of the* Crito

There is a broad consensus among scholars that the *Crito*, the shortest of Plato's works, belongs to the earliest, or "Socratic," period. One reason for thinking this is the relative simplicity of its structure and the directness of the language employed. The *Crito* is set in Socrates' room in the prison to which he was sent immediately after the conclusion of his trial. His old friend Crito has come to Socrates' room in the prison to urge him to escape. After a brief introduction that explains why Socrates' execution was delayed and why his death is now imminent (43a1–44b5), Crito makes his case for escape (44b1–46a6). Socrates then undertakes his own review of the reasons that he thinks require him to remain in prison to await his execution, undeserved though his sentence is (46b1–50a3). To help Crito better understand his reasoning, Socrates asks that they imagine what the laws of Athens would say to them if they could articulate their position. Using the device of personified laws,[1] Socrates lays out the case against the moral permissibility of escape (50a6–54d1). It is often noted that with the introduction of the Laws the tone of the work changes markedly. At this point any real dialogue between Socrates and Crito ceases as the Laws present what amounts to a lecture to Socrates and Crito in which they assert their political superiority over all citizens. After the speech of the Laws, the dialogue ends quickly when Crito indicates that he cannot refute their case (54d2–e2).

3.1.2 Some general interpretative problems

The *Crito* is one of the most widely read of Plato's works, doubtless because it concerns some of the most basic issues in political philosophy. Can the citizen ever justify disobedience, if undertaken in a peaceful manner, to laws of the state that the citizen considers to be immoral? Why does the citizen have a moral obligation to obey any laws of the state? From what does the state get its moral authority to make any demands of citizens at all? But although no one disputes the importance of the issues Plato is addressing in this work, and in spite of the relative simplicity of the dialogue's structure and language, the range of opinions about how Plato addresses these issues is remarkably diverse. Difference of opinion about how to interpret the *Crito* has been motivated by three issues in particular. First, it is not at all obvious how to reconcile the view of the moral duty to obey the law advanced by the Laws with the stance Socrates is often seen as taking on this issue in the *Apology*. As we saw in the last chapter, at his trial Socrates is often understood to be asserting that any legal order to cease the practice of philosophy must give way in the face of his god-imposed duty to philosophy. The *Crito*, by contrast, seems to suggest that for Socrates the duty to obey the laws of Athens admits of no exceptions. If that is indeed what Socrates is arguing in the *Crito*, it would be his moral duty to obey a law forbidding the practice of philosophy. A second puzzle arises from what we find inside the *Crito* itself. As we will see, Socrates appears to be claiming that one must never willingly do an injustice. But if we also assume that the Laws express what Socrates himself believes,[2] it seems that

Socrates thinks that one's duty to obey is absolute. But surely even the best-intended law-makers can make mistakes and order a citizen to do what the citizen correctly recognizes to be an injustice. If one must always obey the law and the citizen believes the particular law to be unjust, then the position developed in the *Crito* is contradictory. Finally, apart from the apparent internal inconsistency of the *Crito*, the very idea that the citizen is morally obligated to obey every legal requirement that impinges upon him strikes many as flatly incompatible with the sort of respect for individual autonomy that is required of any acceptable view of political obligation. While many modern readers will allow that a person who intentionally breaks the law of the country in which he or she has chosen to live must be willing to pay the legally prescribed penalty, they will also insist that no acceptable account of the citizen's obligation to the state can morally require that the citizen act against the dictates of his or her conscience. As we explore the *Crito* in this chapter, we will develop each of these puzzles in some detail and will try to assess the various responses to each that have been prominent in the secondary literature.

3.1.3 Who is Crito?

Actually, Crito is mentioned twice in the *Apology*. In the first passage (33d9) he is named as the father of Critobulus, one of the young men who were often seen in the company of Socrates. There we learn that Socrates and Crito are from the same *deme*, or district, in Athens and that they are about the same age. In the second (38b8), he is named as one of the four men who are willing to guarantee payment of the 30 minas that Socrates offers as his counterpenalty. This fact alone suggests that Crito is a man of some means. Further evidence for this comes from Crito's suggestion that his money could assure Socrates' safe escape (44c1–2). That Crito was indeed a wealthy man is also supported by Xenophon's testimony (*Mem*. 2.9). Some of his money must have come from a farm he owned (*Euthyd*. 304c3).

It is clear from the opening of the *Crito* that Plato is portraying Crito and Socrates as life-long friends. Xenophon lists Crito as a member of the Socratic circle of friends. But it is also reasonable to think that Crito was Socrates' most trusted and faithful companion. Otherwise, in the *Phaedo*, the Platonic dialogue that takes place on the final day of Socrates' life, we would not find Crito playing the role he does. It is Crito who escorts Socrates' wife and children out of the prison when Socrates' friends arrive (60a7–8). It is Crito alone who accompanies Socrates for his final bath before execution (116a2–3). And it is to Crito alone that Socrates gives his final instructions before he dies (118a7–8). But even though there is good reason to think that Socrates and Crito were close friends as a matter of historical fact, we have no independent reason to think that the historical person Crito ever actually urged Socrates to escape or that Socrates declined to escape for the reasons presented in Plato's dialogue *Crito*.

Commentators have pointed out that in the *Phaedo* Crito shows little interest in the philosophical argument developed by Socrates, but is instead only concerned with the mundane details of Socrates' last day. Couple this with Crito's evident concern with his own reputation, expressed in the *Crito* (44cb9–c2), and we might wonder whether Crito should really be counted as a devoted Socratic at all. But doubts of this sort are almost certainly unjustified. As we will see, the *Crito* itself is ample evidence that Crito has long espoused the same principles as Socrates and that, in spite of his initial desire to see one outcome from the discussion, he yields when the stronger case is made for a contrary outcome. Moreover, Crito's concern for his own reputation is not incompatible with a deep concern for Socrates' well-being. Certainly, there is nothing in the *Crito* to suggest that Crito is prepared to sacrifice what he thinks is in Socrates' best interest in order to advance his own. Indeed, as we will argue, Socrates himself does not think that the loss of a reputation is never an important consideration. While it may be true, then, that Crito does not fully grasp why the practice of philosophy is of such fundamental importance to Socrates and that Crito is certainly not the most adept practitioner of Socratic examination, there is no reason to doubt his devotion to Socrates the man or to Socratic principle.

3.2 THE OPENING SCENE

3.2.1 *The first exchange (43a1–44b5)*

According to Plato, the prison in which Socrates was held, the Prison of the Eleven, was "close" to the court in which he had stood trial (*Phd.* 59d3–4). If we assume that the trial took place in what is now generally believed to be a Heliastic court located at the southern side of the Athenian *agora*, the prison was probably located only several hundred feet to the southwest of the court itself. As the dialogue opens, it is just before dawn (43a4). Socrates awakes and finds Crito already in the chamber. Crito has been there for some time (43a9). A guard, it seems, who has seen Crito come there often and who has been "helped out" by Crito in the past had let him in (43a7–8).[3] Plato effectively uses the opening lines to contrast Crito, who is "restless and disturbed," with Socrates, who has been sleeping quite peacefully (43b3–5). Plato doubtless wants the reader to understand that Socrates' claim, expressed at the end of the *Apology* – "no harm comes to a good man in life or in death" (*Ap.* 41c9–d2)–was not bravado. The picture of Socrates that Plato is drawing for us is that of one who, convinced of his goodness, has nothing to fear at the approach of death.

Socrates surmises that Crito is there so early because he has news and assumes that the "ship has returned from Delos," which means that his execution is imminent. Crito confirms the "terrible news." Indeed, the ship has already reached Sounion, the tip of the Attic peninsula, not far from Athens itself. It seems that some who were on board disembarked at Sounion and have reached Athens on land ahead of the ship. By Crito's calculations, then, the ship will be back in Piraeus, the port of Athens, that very day. Socrates' execution will then be scheduled for the following day.[4]

The reference to the return of the sacred ship requires a bit of explaining. As it turns out, the day before Socrates' trial marked the beginning of a religious festival celebrated annually in Athens to commemorate the safe return of Theseus, a legendary king of Athens, from Crete, where he had been imprisoned in a labyrinth with the Minotaur. As Plato tells the story in the *Phaedo* (58a10–c5), the Athenians promised the god Apollo that if Theseus and the seven young men and women who accompanied him were allowed a safe return to Athens, Athens would every year send a group to make a pilgrimage to the island of Delos as a way of commemorating the great goodness the god had bestowed on the city. The Athenians remained loyal to their word.[5] Until the ship returned, the law forbade any executions, which explains why Socrates was not executed on the day after his trial. Plato fails to specify just how long the boat's journey took in the spring of 399, saying only that there was a "long time" between the trial itself and the execution (*Phd.* 57b8). However, Xenophon (*Mem.* 4.8.2) says that it took a month. In any event, because Crito believes that the ship will return that very day, he believes that Socrates has no more than two days to live.

3.2.2 Socrates' dream

Socrates quickly lets his friend know that he is not convinced that the ship will actually make port that day. Just before he awoke, he tells Crito, he had a dream in which a beautiful woman, dressed in a white tunic, approached him, telling him that "on the third day to fair Phthia you will arrive" (44b2).[6] The woman is referring to a line in Homer's *Iliad* (IX, 363) in which Achilles, the greatest of the Greek warriors, speaks of his own return to Phthia, his home. Socrates, like most Greeks of his time, took dreams to be important and reliable ways in which divinities communicate with mortals, and so there is every reason to think that he takes the dream he describes to Crito with complete seriousness. Some scholars[7] take Socrates to mean that at death his soul will in three days literally return to its place of origin. As we argued in Chapter 2, we think it is likely that Socrates did believe in the separation of the soul from the body at death and the migration of the soul to another realm. But we have no independent reason to think that Socrates held the view so closely associated with the Orphic cult that at death of the body the soul returns to its place of origin, whatever that might be. It is more likely that Socrates interprets the dream to mean that his death is something that will be a great good for him, something he can look forward to with hope and anticipation *as if* he were returning home after being away for a long time.

3.3 CRITO'S CASE FOR ESCAPE

3.3.1 *Crito's first argument (44b1–46a9)*

We soon learn that Crito has not arrived at the prison so early merely to inform Socrates that the sacred ship will soon be back in port. Crito wants Socrates to escape. Knowing his friend as he does, Crito is well aware that the mere news of the ship's impending return will not cause Socrates to do anything at all. Crito will have to persuade him that there are better reasons for escape than there are for remaining in prison to be executed. Crito's first argument is that if Socrates refuses to escape, Crito himself will suffer irreparable harm, and according to Crito, "it will not be a single disaster" (44b7). Not only will he himself be losing an irreplaceable friend, but also most people, who will think that Crito could have saved Socrates by bribing the right people and making escape possible had he only been willing to spend the money, will view him with contempt. Most people, or "the many" (*hoi polloi*), as Crito calls them, will never believe that it was Socrates who refused to escape in spite of the best efforts of Socrates' friends to persuade him to leave.

Socrates' response is perhaps predictable. "What," he asks, "do we care about the opinion of the many? For the best people, about whom we ought to think most highly, will think that things were done just as they should be done" (44c6–9). Although his rejoinder is what we would have expected Socrates to say, we should note, first, that it shows that Socrates has apparently already given the entire matter some thought and concluded that it is better for him to stay in prison, for that will be doing what the "best people" will think should have been done. The second point is that Socrates' rejoinder only asserts that we should (rightly) disregard what the many *think*, a point Socrates will develop in some detail momentarily. Discussion of this passage often misses the fact that Socrates has not shown that one should not be concerned about what the many can *do* to us.

Crito is quick to pick up on the fact that he needs to clarify why he thinks we should be concerned about the many. As the trial and impending execution of Socrates amply show, Crito believes that the many can produce "virtually the greatest evils" for those on whom they have turned for some reason (44d3–5).

To this different point, Socrates offers the following, initially perplexing reply:

> I only wish, Crito, that most people were capable of the greatest evils so that they'd be capable of the greatest goods. That would be fine. But as things are, they're able to do neither. For they're not able to make anyone wise or ignorant, but instead they act randomly.
>
> (44d6–10)

Here it is clear that Socrates thinks that the greatest good is wisdom and the greatest evil is ignorance. But why does Socrates think that the many are not able to produce either, and why does he think that if they could produce ignorance, then they could produce wisdom? The answer to the first question is easy. When Socrates says that most people are not able to produce the greatest good or the greatest evil, he means that they lack the knowledge, or what he usually calls a "*technê*," or craft, to produce either one. Someone who possesses a craft of something is able to produce its distinctive products in a reliable manner that the practitioner of the craft could explain to someone else. But the many, because they lack the requisite knowledge, cannot produce results that meet this standard.

To find the answer to the second question, we need to look beyond the *Crito* itself. In Book I of the *Republic* Socrates indicates that if someone really knows how to produce an effect of some sort, that person will also know how to produce the opposite effect (*Rep.* I 333e3 ff.). The skillful healer, he says, will also be able to inflict disease, just as the skillful guardian will also be an expert thief. Since wisdom is the opposite of ignorance, then if most people did have the knowledge of how to make people ignorant, they would have the knowledge to make them wise, too. Thus, since the many lack the *technê* that yields the one, they must lack the knowledge that yields the other. When Socrates says that they act "at random," then, he means that they act without any principled understanding to guide them when they act. They just do one thing and see what happens and then do something else and see what happens.

Before we turn to Crito's second argument, it is worth emphasizing that even if Socrates can successfully show that the many have the power to produce neither the greatest good nor the greatest evil, Socrates has not refuted Crito's point that most people *can* harm, indeed, do great harm, even if they cannot do so as a matter of *technê*. It seems reasonable to think that Socrates is aware of the limitations of his response. Thus, we would do well to regard his point about the inability of most people to do either the greatest harm or the greatest good as an aside and to look for a more adequate response later in the text. As we will see, Socrates later does meet Crito's point head on.

3.3.2 Crito's second argument

Crito's second argument is really an attempt to remove any hesitation Socrates may have about harm coming to those of his friends who aided in the escape. Crito sees that Socrates may well realize that if the "blackmailers" (*sykophantai*) discovered them, his friends risk the confiscation of all of their property, the payment of a heavy fine, or some other punishment (44e5–6). The blackmailers to whom Crito is referring were people who made it their business to find out who had broken the law or even appeared to be engaged in some sort of unlawful activity. Because the Athenian legal system made no provision for a public prosecutor but instead allowed any citizen to bring legal action against another, the blackmailers would threaten to initiate prosecution unless the party threatened with legal action paid them to remain silent. The real concern, then, which Socrates admits he has (45a4–5), is that if the blackmailers find out which of Socrates' friends abetted the escape, his friends would either have to suffer a severe punishment or pay these unprincipled individuals an exorbitant sum in return for their silence.

Crito concludes that such fears are simply unfounded. In the first place, the blackmailers will not require much money. In fact, Crito himself has enough to ensure their silence (45a6–b1). And if Socrates is still worried that Crito's involvement will somehow be discovered, Crito informs him that there are foreigners present in Athens, who are presumably beyond the reach of Athenian law, who will be quite happy to pay whatever is necessary. He refers to Simmias and Cebes, both Theban followers of Socrates, by name,[8] though, interestingly, Crito says that there are a "great many other" foreign Socratics who are also willing to offer financial assistance. There is no reason to doubt that Crito is right.

Before offering additional reasons in favor of escape, Crito next tries to remove one additional concern Socrates may have. At his trial Socrates said that he could not propose exile as a counter-penalty because he would not be able to practice philosophy in any other city, but would be driven from one city to the next (*Ap*. 37d4–6). Here Crito paraphrases Socrates' concern, quite misleadingly, in fact, as "not knowing what to do with himself" if he went into exile. But according to Crito, Socrates is simply wrong about what exile would be like. In fact, he says there are "many places" he could go and that he himself has friends in Thessaly who will make sure that he is not disturbed (45b9–c4). Crito's confidence on this point would make little sense unless he was entirely confident that his friends would protect Socrates from harm even after Socrates began to engage in philosophical discussion, as he surely would.

By appealing to what he thinks will be Socrates' sense of what is right, Crito presents what he no doubt thinks are his strongest arguments. First, Socrates is throwing his life away when he might have saved it and he is allowing his enemies to do just what they want to him (45c5–8). Second, he is deserting his children, whose upbringing and education he has an obligation to see through to the end (45c8–d6). Finally, he is bringing shame on himself and on his friends, for it will certainly appear that this entire disaster could have been avoided – the trial could have been avoided, the conviction could have been avoided, and now it will appear that it was a failure of courage on the part of his friends that ensured his execution when he could have escaped (46a2).

3.3.3 Socrates' response – doing what seems best (46b1–c6)

In spite of Crito's attempts to convince Socrates that there is no time for deliberation about *whether* Socrates should escape and that they need to start immediately setting a plan in motion for Socrates to leave the prison that night (46a4–9), Crito should probably not be surprised that Socrates must discuss it. The following brief speech nicely captures Socrates' commitment to philosophical reflection:

> My friend, Crito, your concern will be worth a great deal if it is on the right side of this issue. But if not, the greater it is, the more difficult it makes things. So we need to consider whether we must do this or not. Because I am not just now but in fact I've always been the sort of person who's persuaded by nothing but the reason that appears to be to me best when I've considered it. I can't now, when I'm in my present circumstance, set aside reasons I was giving earlier. If they seem to me to be virtually the same, I'll respect and honor the ones I did before. Unless we can come up with something better in the present circumstance than these, rest assured that I won't give in to you. Nor should the majority of people have any greater power to scare us in these present circumstances as if we were children by sending us to prison and death and confiscating our money. How, then, is it most reasonable for us to consider these things?
>
> (46b1–c6)

Apart from the fact that this passage provides a clear statement of Socrates' unyielding commitment to philosophical reflection and action from the best principles, it also helps us to understand his response to the case Crito has just made for escape. As Socrates sees it, nothing Crito has said concerning why he ought to escape has convinced him that he ought to abandon the principles he has long held, and his own review of those principles, which presumably has taken place while he has been in prison and has led him to conclude that it is best that he remain in prison to await execution. The fact, then, that Socrates does not begin by addressing each of Crito's arguments is not evidence that Socrates does not take them seriously. He simply did not find that they forced him to abandon anything he had previously considered. Socrates is, of course, willing to consider escape. But before he will go down that path, he will need to be convinced either that one or more of his principles is misguided or that he is mistaken about their applicability to his present circumstances.

3.4 SOCRATES' OWN POSITION

3.4.1 *Socrates' method of inquiry (46c7–47d7)*

Before we begin our examination of Socrates' case against escape, we should note that Socrates says that he "want[s] to consider in common with you" to see whether he should change his mind about what he should do (46d4–6). This may well strike us as puzzling because Socrates proceeds simply by asking Crito whether he, Crito, still agrees with him about some point. Once Crito says that he does indeed accept a proposition, Socrates feels free to use that proposition as a premise in an argument he is apparently constructing and then moves on to ask Crito whether he agrees with some other proposition. Surely Socrates does not think that Crito's mere assent to a proposition is enough to secure it and that when they draw an inference from some propositions that they have agreed to that they have necessarily brought some important truth to light. After all, Crito might assent to something that is false. Why, then, would Socrates have any great confidence in the argument he is about to construct?

To see why, we should recall that Socrates has apparently already considered what he should do, and the case for escape that Crito has made has given Socrates no reason to question the principles that led him to conclude that he ought to stay in prison. Now, as he enlists Crito's aid in this inquiry about what he ought to do, he makes the same point as follows: "I can't now, when I'm in my present circumstance, set aside reasons I was giving earlier. If they seem to me to be virtually the same, I'll respect and honor the ones I did before. Unless we can come up with something better in the present circumstance than these, rest assured that I won't give in to you" (46b6–c3). So when he asks Crito to consider the matter with him, Socrates is really asking Crito to try to give him a good reason for giving up something that until this point he always believed that he should accept. If this is what is going on, it is not Crito's assent that secures a proposition for Socrates; the argument is secured by the reasons Socrates already has for adopting them in the first place. If Socrates is to persuade Crito, however, Crito, too, must accept the premises of the argument. This, then, is why Socrates is so interested in Crito's assent, and it is important to notice that until 50a1, where, as we shall see, Crito first appears not to understand Socrates' question, Crito quite readily endorses again what they have said they believed in the past. Unfortunately, Socrates does not say in the *Crito* what his own reasons are for believing the premises to which he gets Crito to assent.[9] Scholars have often argued, however, that these can be inferred from what Socrates says in other works.

3.4.2 Whose opinions should matter? (46d7–47d7)

Socrates suggests that they start with Crito's point (*logos*) about the importance of opinions (46c7–8). "Were we right or not each time we said that one ought to pay attention to the opinions of some but not of others? Or, were we right before I was obliged to die, but now it's become clear after all that it was all done merely for the sake of argument and was really just for play and fooling around?" (46c8–d4). Actually, Socrates is asking two questions, and it is not entirely clear just how we are supposed to sort out them out. What Socrates probably has in mind, however, is this: in the past he and his fellow Socratics, including Crito, have always said that they ought never concern ourselves with what the many think about how one ought to act. Now, he asks Crito, should the fact that the many are about to kill me make us abandon what we have always said before? Put this way, we can see that Socrates is not denying that the many can do us great harm; nor is he denying that the many might well be right about how we ought to act. He is merely asking whether the *fact* that the many can harm us gives us reason to look to them to find out how we ought to act.

As we have seen, once Socrates has gained Crito's assurance that he would answer the questions Socrates put to him as Socrates apparently has, Socrates feels free to use the propositions agreed to as premises. Thus, when Crito responds to Socrates' question about whose opinions ought to be respected, Socrates sees that he has reason to believe, and no reason not to believe that one should not honor all the opinions people have, but only some of these opinions and not others, and one should not honor the opinions of all people, but those of some people and not others (47a3–4). Crito can hardly deny that we should respect the good opinions but not the bad ones (47a7). The obvious question, then, is whose opinions are good and whose are bad. Crito is just as quick to agree that the good opinions are those of the wise and the bad are those of the foolish (47a10–11).

Socrates next turns to an illustration of the point on which they have just agreed. When it comes to physical training, although the many will doubtless have much to say to us about how to train, we should reject their advice in favor of what the wise in such matters tell us, the doctor or trainer (47a13–b3). The opinions of the many, then, at least when it comes to physical training, are not to be respected. Of course Socrates is not denying that the advice of the many about how best to train might coincide with that of the physical trainer and so the advice of the many might happen to be right. Socrates' point, however, still stands: even if the many happen to be right, we still have no reason to heed their advice, for lacking expertise, they lack good reason for what they tell us to do. Given Crito's agreement on this last point, Socrates is ready to turn to the harm we risk when we follow the advice of the many. Those who listen to the uninformed opinions of the many run the risk of harming their bodies (47c5–7).

Socrates' next move is to apply the general point on which they have agreed, that we ought to listen to the expert and reject the opinion of the uninformed, in regard to actions of moral significance, "the just and unjust, shameful and the noble, and the good and the bad." Socrates asks:

> Should we follow the opinion of most people and fear it, or that of the one, if there is anyone who understands, whom one ought to respect and fear rather than all of the others? If we don't follow this one individual, won't we corrupt and destroy what becomes better through justice but is destroyed by injustice? Isn't this so?
>
> (47d1–6).

Although Socrates does not say so explicitly, we can safely assume that he thinks it is the soul that "becomes better through justice but is destroyed by injustice."[10]

3.4.3 The appeal to an expert

Who is this "one person of understanding" with respect to justice and injustice? Certainly it is not Socrates, for one of the salient features of his speech to the jury in the *Apology* is his profession that he lacks any special moral expertise (23a7–c1). And though he has discovered no shortage of people who think they are wise about "the most important things," Socrates has never found anyone else who possesses moral expertise.

In fact, however, Socrates never says that there actually is a moral expert to whom one ought to turn. Instead, he is asking whether we ought to respect the opinion of such a person, *if* there is such a person. As long as Crito accepts the possibility of moral expertise, then, since by definition most people lack moral expertise, we have no good reason to respect their opinions about the just and the unjust. This is a purely negative conclusion – the injunction, "Do not trust *those* people" does not tell us whom we *should* trust. So what do we do if there *are* no moral experts in whose judgments we can place our trust? Socrates seems to be suggesting, in answer to this question, that as long as we understand a significant number of the relevant features of experts whom we do recognize – experts such as trainers and doctors – as Socrates clearly thinks we can, then we can try as assiduously as we can to reason as we think an expert would, were we to find one. Here the idea is that even if we may not have medical expertise itself, if we wish to restore someone to health, we would be better off trying to treat that person in the way we think a doctor would rather than listening to the opinion of most people. By the same reasoning, if we lack moral expertise, if we wish to do the right thing, we would be better off trying to approach the issue as we think a moral expert would rather than just listening to the opinion of the uninformed many. In both cases, because we lack expertise, we are vulnerable to the sort of grave errors that a true expert would unfailingly recognize. Nonetheless, we would be more likely to achieve our goal by eschewing the opinion of most people and trying as best we can to act as we think an expert would. And one difference between experts and the many is the very one Socrates has already pointed out to Crito: the many change their views and actions all the time, whereas the expert thinks and acts in a consistent manner. One acts more like an expert, then, if one "won't give in" and won't change one's views or actions without good reasons for doing so.

3.4.4 What we value most (47d8–49a3)

Once Socrates has established what the effect of injustice is on the soul, it comes as no surprise that Crito and he think it is undesirable. But how much should we disvalue it? Here we see that Socrates does not think that harm to the soul is self-evidently evil. Instead, he thinks that we want to avoid it for the same reason we want to avoid crippling and chronically painful diseases. When the body is corrupted in these ways, life is not worth living (47e3–5). So, when the soul is corrupted by injustice, life is not worth living (47e6–7). But because the soul is more valuable than the body (47e7–48a2), injustice is an even greater evil than chronic and debilitating disease.

Socrates clarifies the point concerning why one should always avoid injustice by making explicit how it conflicts with what we ultimately value, namely, what he here calls "living well." What we have always valued most, he says, is not living but living well (48b3–6), and living well is the same thing as living justly (48b8–9). Although the phrase "living well" may strike us as perhaps somewhat quaint, Plato often uses it as a synonym for *"eudaimonia"* ("happiness"). It is worth pausing here to note that it is *self-interest* that makes Socrates think that injustice is always to be avoided. It is because we value *our own happiness more than anything else* and injustice makes happiness impossible by corrupting the soul that we should always avoid injustice. It is also worth noting here that Socrates is not denying that the many can do us great evil, for they can destroy our prospects of even being happy – for example, by inflicting crippling and agonizing punishments on us. Thus, it would be a mistake to think that Socrates believes that justice, or even the whole of moral virtue, is sufficient for having a life that is worth living or that it can protect us from every grave evil. But because the many can only harm the body and the soul is more important than the body, it is more important, Socrates concludes, that we avoid injustice than that we avoid any evil the many can do to us.

Unless they have some reason to abandon the views they have long held, the argument to this point shows that if one had to choose between no longer having even the prospect of a life that is "lived well" and not living at all, they should choose the latter. And since living well and living justly are identical, they think they would be better off dead than not living justly.

With the great evil injustice causes us now out in the open, Socrates can deal directly with the issue that caused Crito to go to Socrates' prison cell so early in the morning: unless Socrates escapes, he will very soon be killed. As Socrates says at 48c1–2, if it seems just, he should try to leave; but if not, he should refuse Crito's proposal. We can also see why Socrates thought earlier that Crito's concerns about "the confiscation of money, reputation, and the training of children" were premature. When Socrates says that they are "really the considerations of most people, who readily kill people and would bring them back to life if they could and would do so without even thinking about it" (48c4–6), he does not mean that they are of no importance at all to him. Were that his position, the Socratic view of what we ought to value would be far more counter-intuitive than we believe it is. We can now see that that the supreme value Crito and he place on living justly requires that before they decide to do anything at all, they must first decide what justice requires.

> But since our reasoning requires this, we must consider only what we were saying just now: would we, the ones who are escaping and the ones who're helping out, be doing what's just in paying our money and thanking those who'll get me out of here? Or would we really be acting unjustly by doing all of these things? If we'd clearly be bringing about an injustice, we shouldn't give any consideration to whether we

need to remain behind to be killed and keep quiet about it or suffer anything at all rather than the injustice we'd be doing.

(48c6–d5)

Insofar as we care about money, reputation, friendships, and all of the other things Crito mentioned, we must do so *only* in a way that is just. In valuing our reputation, for example, we may not lie to protect it. In caring about our friends, we may not promote their well-being by stealing from others. In caring about our children, we may not give them unfair advantages to help them achieve their goals.

3.4.5   *The basic moral principles (49a4–e2)*

Socrates now begins to set forth the premises of his argument in the form of principles, always being careful to ask for and receive Crito's agreement. In light of the immediately foregoing discussion, the first principle, which we might call "the prohibition against injustice" principle, comes as no surprise.

- **One ought never act unjustly** (49b9–10)

To emphasize the universal scope of the prohibition, Socrates makes explicit that the fact that suffering unjust treatment is never a reason for acting unjustly. So,

- **One ought never to return injustice with injustice** (49b10–11)

Crito, of course, indicates that he agrees that such has been one of their principles as is another one, which we might call "the prohibition against evil principle," with a parallel corollary:

- **One ought never do evil** (49e2–3) and
- **One ought never return evil with evil** (49c4–6)

Socrates indicates (49c7–9) that he regards the two prohibitions as equivalent and so in what follows he will feel free to consider any evil that might be done to the city by escaping as an injustice to the city. But he also feels the need to make sure that Crito understands just what he is endorsing, for, Socrates says,

I know that these things seem and will seem true only to a few people. But to those to whom it has seemed right and to those to whom it

hasn't, there is no common ground, but they can't avoid having dis-
dain for each other when they see each other's conclusions. Consider
very carefully then whether you agree and share the same opinion
with me and let's begin by deliberating from that point, namely that
it's never right to do what's unjust or to retaliate or for one who has
suffered an evil to avenge it by retaliating wrongly, or do you reject this
and not share my opinion about where to start?

(49d4–9)

3.4.6   The just agreements principle (49e2–50a5)

Before applying the two basic principles to the question of his
escape, Socrates asks Crito about what we might call the "just
agreements principle."

- **One must keep one's agreements provided that they are just**
  (49e6–8)

It is worth noting in passing that Socrates is careful to qualify the
agreements one must keep. Even if he had made the agreement
with Crito to escape, were Socrates to discover that escape would be
unjust, subsequent to the making of the agreement, he would not
be violating the just agreements principle if he then refused to go
along with the agreement he made with Crito, since it requires
only that we keep *just* agreements.

Armed with these five principles, Socrates seems to think that he
has all that he needs to decide whether his escape would be morally
permissible.

Now observe what follows. If we go away from here without having
persuaded the city, would we be doing anything wrong to anyone, and
what's more, would we be doing it to those whom we ought least of
all be doing it to, or not? Do we stand by what we agreed right, or not?

(49e9–50a3)

It turns out that the questions were premature, for Crito claims
not to understand what Socrates is asking (50a4–5). At first, we

might wonder whether Crito is being sincere since an affirmative answer to the first question certainly will destroy his case for escape altogether. Alternatively, we might wonder whether Crito is simply demonstrating that he is just too stupid to follow the argument Socrates has been so carefully developing.[11] We think that Crito's bewilderment is both sincere and justified. First, just who are those "whom they least ought to harm"? If Socrates has the city of Athens and its citizens in mind, we might well wonder why Socrates would count them as among "those he ought least to harm" since they, after all, did everything in their power to kill him unjustly. We can now see why he must not retaliate against them. That is ruled out by the corollary to the "prohibition against evil" principle. But why should Socrates regard them as among those he *least* ought to harm? Moreover, why should he think that by escaping he would be harming *anyone*? After all, it is not as if there is any real danger that other prisoners will suddenly start following Socrates' example. No doubt, if Socrates escapes the city will go on pretty much as before. Why should Socrates think that he would be violating a just agreement? An agreement with whom? Finally, Socrates poses two questions. What is the relationship between them? Could they be doing harm to those whom they least ought to harm without also violating an agreement that they have said is right?

3.5   THE ARGUMENT OF THE LAWS

3.5.1   *The Laws of Athens make their case (50a6–c5)*

To help Crito better understand what he has in mind by these two questions, Socrates asks Crito to consider what "the laws and the state"[12] would say, could they speak to them as they contemplate escape, and so he asks Crito to imagine the Laws, as he calls them, suddenly speaking to them. Despite a few scholars' recent expressions of skepticism on this issue,[13] there is very good reason to believe that the Laws express Socrates' views. The introduction of this device serves at least two important functions, both psychological. First, having Crito think of the laws of Athens as flesh and blood persons, as opposed to airy legal abstractions, makes it easier for Crito to imagine that escape will actually harm them, a key point in the Laws' case against Socrates' escape. Second, the Laws express their views with a tone of moral superiority. In fact, it is clear that they become morally indignant at the very thought that Socrates is even contemplating escape. Since the Laws speak for Socrates, we have to think that he himself finds the idea of escape morally outrageous. By having the Laws speak as if they were addressing him as well as Crito, Socrates can convey to Crito the sense that escape, in spite of Crito's good intentions, is deeply offensive to him.

3.5.2   Destroying the Laws

Straightaway the Laws challenge Socrates: "Are you intending to destroy us and the whole city for your part? Or, do you think that the city can still exist and not be destroyed when the decisions handed down in the courts have no force but are left without authority by private citizens and are destroyed?" (50b1–5). Many readers find the presumptions in these questions puzzling. First, it is not plausible to think that by escaping Socrates would actually succeed in destroying the city. And second, it seems false that by escaping Socrates is "intending to destroy the city for his part." In what sense could his escape pose an actual threat to the city and its legal institutions?

In response to the first question, the Laws are probably relying on the notion that anyone who performs some action intentionally also intends the foreseeable consequences of the action. So if the destruction of the city is a foreseeable result of escape, then the destruction of the city is intentional also. But what about the second question? Why should anyone think that by escaping Socrates would be destroying the city for his part? Again, the Laws do not spell out what they have in mind, but they are probably relying on what is usually called the generalization principle:

- If it is permissible for one person to perform an action X, it is permissible for each similarly situated person to do X also.

But clearly, where X is escape from prison after having been convicted of a crime, it is not permissible for every person convicted of a crime to escape from prison. The reason it is not permissible is just what the Laws say: the city simply cannot exist "when the decisions handed down in the courts have no force but are left without authority by private citizens and are destroyed" (50b2–5). Allowing each convicted person to escape would harm the city, in violation of "the prohibition against evil" principle. Therefore, it is not permissible for Socrates to escape.

Socrates sees that this argument may not be convincing (50c1–3), for it is still open to someone to say that we ought to distinguish between those who have been rightly judged guilty by the city and those who have not. Although it would be unjust for those in the former group to escape, one might argue, *everyone* in the latter group, as Socrates himself surely is, is morally permitted to escape if the opportunity presents itself. After all, we are assuming that they do not deserve to be in prison. The Laws, then, need to show that even the innocent would be acting unjustly and harming the city if they escape.

3.5.3   The respect argument (50c6–51c5)

The Laws' argument that even the innocent are not morally permitted to escape is not always as carefully marked off as it might be. The Laws begin by apparently relying on the just agreements principle, informing Socrates that he, and by implication all citizens, have indeed entered into an agreement with them "To abide by the decisions that the city hands down" (50c7–8). The implication is that the agreement emphatically was *not* that those who believe that they have been wrongly convicted are free to escape from prison if and when the opportunity presents itself.

The Laws seem to recognize that Crito will be puzzled at the claim that they have ever entered into an agreement with the city. But rather than first explaining why it is reasonable to think that there is an agreement between the citizen and the Laws, the Laws develop a different line of argument, one aimed at showing that even those who have been wrongly convicted would be harming the city were they to escape. In this argument, the Laws appeal to the fact that through them and them alone extraordinary benefits have been conferred upon the citizens of Athens. First, the laws governing marriage legitimize birth, thereby conferring the benefit of future inheritance (50d1–5). Then, the laws overseeing the upbringing of children insured that the citizen is given a proper upbringing and education. The Laws claim at least that they instructed Socrates' father to give Socrates the traditional education in music and reading to prepare the mind and physical education to train the body[14] (50d5–e1).

3.6 THE "OBEY OR PERSUADE" DOCTRINE

3.6.1 *Respect and obedience (50e1–51c4)*

From the facts regarding their regulation of the citizen's birth and upbringing, the Laws draw a startling conclusion.

> Well then, since you were born and raised and educated by us, could you say in the first place that you're not our offspring and slave, you and your ancestors? And, if this is so, do you think that what's just for us and you is based on equality? And whatever we try to do to you, do you think it's right for you also to do in return? What's just for you in relation to your father, or to your master, if you happened to have one, wasn't based on equality, so that you could do in return the very thing you suffered, whether to talk back when criticized or to strike back when struck, and many other such things? Yet, on the other hand, are you empowered to do such things against your fatherland and the laws, so that if we try to destroy you in the belief that it's right, you'll try to destroy us, the Laws, and the country in return in so far as you're able? And do you, who really care about virtue, maintain that in doing this you're doing what's just? Or, are you so wise that it's escaped you that, compared to your father and mother and all of your ancestors, your country is more honorable, more revered, more sacred, and to be held in higher esteem by the gods and by people with sense, and that you should revere your country and yield to it and cajole it when it's angry more than your father, and either persuade it or do what it orders

and you should suffer in silence if it orders you to suffer something, whether it's to be beaten or to be imprisoned, and whether it leads you into war to be wounded or killed, you must do this, and it's just that you do so, and you shouldn't yield, or retreat, and abandon your post, but in war and in court and everywhere, you must do what your city and country orders, or persuade it as to the nature of what's just. But it's impious to use force on your mother and father; it's much more impious still to use it on your country."

(50e1–51c4)

In this passage the Laws are addressing one of the most difficult questions in political philosophy, namely: why is the state justified in ordering its citizens to act and to forebear from acting under the threat of punishment if they do not do as they are ordered? More succinctly put, what justifies the state's political authority over its citizens? They are not claiming that they are somehow morally better than the citizen, nor are they suggesting that they know more about how the state ought to conduct its affairs – if they were, then they would leave no room for the citizen to *persuade* the state when the state errs and the citizen recognizes the state's error. The Laws' argument suggests that necessary and sufficient for the state's authority is its having provided for the good of their citizens in the way that good parents provide for the well-being of their children and good masters provide for the well-being of their slaves. The benefaction, which takes place over time and presumably involves significant sacrifice on the part of the benefactor, gives rise to a claim on the beneficiary. The idea seems to be that just as an offspring owes his or her parents "honor, respect, and reverence," so the citizen owes these same things to the state, only the citizen owes the state more "honor, respect, and reverence," presumably because the benefits the citizen receives from the state are greater than those a parent can bestow on children. We have a duty, in other words, to show the proper respect to those who have provided us with the most important goods we enjoy. The citizen demonstrates the appropriate respect, it appears, when he either persuades or does what the state orders. The citizen fails to show the appropriate respect when he fails either to "obey or persuade."

As the final line makes clear, just as it is impious to do violence to one's parents, so it is impious for the citizen to do violence to the state that has provided benefits. The violence, we must assume, can take a variety of forms, including treason and insurrection. But one form, it seems, is to fail to "obey or persuade."

3.6.2 The argument from just agreements (51c6–53a8)

The Laws' assertion that the citizen is obligated to "obey or persuade" is at the very center of their argument against the moral permissibility of Socrates' escape. As we will see, however, it is far from clear just what the doctrine of "obey or persuade" amounts to. Nor it is clear that it is consistent with things Socrates says elsewhere. It should not be surprising, then, to find that the secondary literature on the *Crito* is filled with attempts to clarify just what the "obey or persuade" doctrine really means. But before we turn to the most influential of these accounts, let us examine the second, independent argument that the Laws construct in favor of the same doctrine.

Recall that Socrates introduced the Laws into the discussion because he supposed that he had entered into a just agreement that precluded escape, but Crito professed not to understand why (50a4–5). Having established that the citizen who has benefited from the State in fundamental ways must respect the State, Socrates now undertakes to explain why it is reasonable to think that he has entered into a just agreement not to escape. The Laws set the stage for the second argument by reviewing a number of conditions that have obtained during Socrates' life in Athens. They first remind Socrates of the many important benefits he has received from them, the same benefits that gave rise to the duty of the citizen to respect the Laws in the "respect argument." Indeed, the Laws go so far as to say that they have given Socrates and all other citizens "a share of all the good things that they could" (51c9–d1). The Laws also remind Socrates that had he become dissatisfied with them, he was free to leave and go wherever he wanted, taking his possessions with him (51d6–e1). They return to this point somewhat later in speech, saying that he never even left the city except to go on military duty (52b4–6), that although the jury might have allowed him to leave the city as his punishment, he said he "preferred death to exile,"[15] and that although Socrates "often said that Sparta and Crete were well governed," he never chose them or any other Greek or foreign city over Athens (52e5–53a1). They remind him that he "chose" to have children in Athens (52c2). Nor can Socrates say that he was rushed into a decision about whether the legal and political arrangements of the city suited him. He has had more than seventy years to think about the matter (52e2–3). The Laws take all of this to be "proof" that Socrates was pleased with the city and its legal arrangements (52b1–2).

But merely having been pleased with the city and having chosen not to leave is not sufficient for an agreement. The Laws point out that they did nothing to hide the way they conducted their trials and managed the city (51e2–3). They make it clear that each person who enters into citizenship (*dokimasthai*) sees "the ways of the city and the laws." Nothing of relevance to the citizen's decision about whether the city is just or pleasing to him is hidden. Moreover, Socrates' reference to entering citizenship is significant. As Richard Kraut points out,[16] not only was the process carefully regulated, with the credentials of each candidate carefully scrutinized by members of his deme, but the candidate had to *apply* for citizenship. Citizenship, then, was by no means automatic once the male child born in Athens became of age. Kraut's point is that the fact that citizenship expresses the wish of the candidate considerably strengthens the Laws' case that the obligations of citizenship are something that the citizen has chosen.

We can now see why the Laws think that they and the citizen have indeed entered into an agreement even though the agreement is made "by the citizen's actions" (51e4), not words, and so it is tacit, not explicit. Citizenship brings with it great benefits and, for its part, the city promises to continue to confer them, to the extent it is possible, on all of its citizens. Moreover, there is evidence both that the citizen initially wanted to receive these benefits and was pleased with these benefits, for it was open to him to leave the city were he not pleased. There is, in addition, nothing surreptitious about the way the city conducts its affairs. Finally, the citizen is never coerced into accepting the agreement. The citizen is free to leave at any time before a law actually calls upon him to discharge some duty. But because the city cannot exist unless it has rules and procedures for defining offices and forbidding some actions and requiring others, it is reasonable for the city to say that any person who has accepted the benefits of citizenship under the conditions just outlined has entered into an agreement with respect to those rules and procedures. That agreement is to "obey or persuade" (51e6–52a3). It is important to notice that the Laws emphasize that agreement is not to obey blindly. "We do not order you savagely," they say. They invite the citizen to persuade them about "what we have ordered that is not right." Thus, this option to show why some particular legal command is wrong is a crucial part of the agreement. Once all of these conditions have been met, the citizen has entered into an agreement with the state.

But exactly when does the agreement begin? At one point the Laws give the following answer:

> Whether someone wishes to emigrate to a colony or to go somewhere else and live as an alien, if we and the city should fail to please him, no law stands in his way or forbids him to go where he desires and keep his things. But he among you who stays, seeing the manner in which we dispense justice and conduct the affairs of the city in other ways, we say that this person has already agreed with us by his actions that he'll do what we command ...
>
> (51d6–e4)

The Laws are not saying that the citizen must actually have been tempted to leave the city and decided to stay, nor must he have a full understanding of the way the city conducts its affairs. The Laws understand that one may never be tempted to leave. Instead, they mean that the agreement is struck as soon as the candidate understands that he is free to leave, that he has received great benefits and will continue to receive the great benefits of citizenship, and that he has enough of an understanding of the ways of the city to make an informed decision as to whether he will be better off in Athens or somewhere else. But it is important to note that the Laws sometimes speak of "compacts and agreements" (in the plural) between the state and the citizen (e.g. 52d2, 52d8–e1). What this means, we think, is that the Laws do not regard the agreement as a one–time affair, something that, once struck, binds the citizen to the state for as long as the citizen is alive. The citizen, in other words, is free to change his mind if he thinks that the country is initiating unjust policies or otherwise pursuing goals that it ought not. But as various changes in the legal structure of the state take place and the citizen becomes aware of them and is at least not displeased, it is not misleading to say that there is a new agreement between the citizen and the state. Whether we call it a new agreement or we say that the former agreement has been agreed to again is perhaps immaterial. What is important, though, is that the citizen is free to leave even after the agreement has been struck. As we will see in a moment, however, the freedom to leave if one is dissatisfied is not unconditional.

3.6.3 Obey or persuade – the strict compliance interpretation

We have now seen that the Laws present two different but compatible arguments for what we are calling the "obey or persuade" doctrine. Each is intended to show that if Socrates escapes, he will have neither obeyed nor persuaded. As the Laws put it at one point, "we say that the one who does not persuade us acts unjustly in three ways: because he doesn't obey us who produced him; because he doesn't obey those who raised him; and because, having agreed to obey us, he neither obeys nor persuades us if we're doing something that's not right" (51e4–7). The first two forms of harm are covered by the duty to respect benefactors. The third is covered the duty to keep just agreements.

The overall structure of Socrates' argument should now be plain enough. If he escapes, he neither obeys nor persuades. That would, in turn, constitute a violation of the duty to show respect and the duty to keep just agreements, both of which would constitute doing evil to the Laws. But as we saw before the Laws began to speak, Socrates thinks one must never do what is evil and unjust, for that damages his soul and makes living well – which he values above all else – impossible. In the end, then, Socrates is offering a self-interested argument against escape. He must choose not to escape, for the harm he would do the city would be an injustice and, thus, ultimately escape would harm Socrates' most precious possession, his own soul.

The Laws are doubtless right that were Socrates to escape he would be violating one of their commands without persuading anyone. But just what would count as persuasion were Socrates to attempt it? What sort of persuasion does he have in mind and to whom must it be directed? Certainly one way to understand the Laws' point is to see them as pointing out that their rule is not a dictatorship. The citizen is invited to join in the making of laws and criticizing laws after they have been passed. According to one reading, which we might call the "strict compliance" reading, the Laws are asserting that the citizen must direct any attempt at persuasion to those who make the laws, the city's legislators, and the citizen must persuade them that some law they have created is not just and should be rescinded or otherwise appropriately altered.[17] According to this reading, the attempt at persuasion must be accomplished before the law at issue actually impinges on the citizen and obligates the citizen to do something that the citizen believes is unjust.

It is crucial to the strict compliance reading to note that the Laws do not say that the citizen who chooses not to obey and yet fails to persuade may then simply agree to take the punishment that is meted out by the court. Thus, it is not showing the proper respect and it is not in keeping with the agreement for someone who, for example, thinks that a law requiring military service is unjust but also fails to persuade the appropriate legal authorities to alter the law, then simply to agree to accept the punishment for disobedience. Of course, the Laws believe that someone who neither obeys nor persuades must accept the punishment for disobedience. But a willingness to accept the punishment does not make a refusal to obey and a failure to persuade acceptable to the Laws. To do neither fails to show the proper respect owed to the Laws and it violates the agreement struck between them and the citizen.

It is also crucial to the strict compliance reading that we distinguish between a law that is in effect but does not actually obligate a particular citizen to act and one that actually impinges on the citizen, requiring him to comply. Recall that the Laws remind Socrates that the citizen of their legal system has the opportunity to leave Athens. "If we do not please him, it is permitted for him to take his possessions and go wherever he wants. None of the laws stops him or forbids it" (51d4–6). The Laws make it clear, then, that the citizen is free to leave after the agreement between them and him has been struck. Leaving the state when one thinks the state is requiring injustice shows no disrespect to one's benefactors. However, the citizen is not free simply to leave as a way to avoid compliance with some law that the citizen finds to be unjust, which now impinges upon him. Thus, the citizen who thinks that required military service is unjust and who fails to persuade is free to leave at any time before he is ordered to begin his service. But once ordered to appear for duty, he is not free to leave. To leave then would be to disobey without having persuaded. According to the strict compliance interpretation, then, the Laws allow for and even encourage dissent. It is clear that they recognize that they can make moral mistakes and wish to avoid them by having citizens point their mistakes out to them. But the persuasion must never take the form of disobedience.

3.6.4 Problems with the strict compliance reading – is it consistent with the *Apology*?

Readers of the *Apology* and the *Crito* have often been troubled by what appears to be an obvious inconsistency between what we are calling the strict compliance interpretation of the "obey or persuade" doctrine in the *Crito* and Socrates' vow to continue engaging in philosophy in the *Apology*. As we have seen, according to the strict compliance interpretation, a citizen who fails to persuade the appropriate legal authorities to rescind a legal command is at that point morally obligated to obey that legal command. But at one point in his speech to the jury Socrates appears to be saying that he would disobey any legal order issued by the jury to cease philosophizing. Let's look at what he actually says to the jury. He begins by imagining the jury offering to release him if he will stop engaging in philosophy:

> "Socrates, this time we won't do as Anytus says. We'll let you go, but on this condition, that you stop spending your time in this inquiry of yours and philosophizing. But if you're caught still doing so, you'll die." Thus, if, as I was saying, you were to let me go on this condition, I'd tell you, "Athenians, I respect and I love you, but I'll obey the god rather than you, and as long as I breathe and am able, I won't stop philosophizing ...
>
> (29c5–d5)

It certainly appears to many readers that in this passage Socrates is stating categorically that he will disobey a legal order and that he will do so because he has a higher, a more important obligation to obey the god.[18] If so, in the *Apology*, Socrates appears to be endorsing a hierarchical view of moral obligation and thus regards some moral duties as weightier or more important than others. Because he attaches the greatest possible importance to what the god commands, whenever a legal command collides with a command issued by the god, the legal command must give way. Otherwise, one has an obligation to do whatever one has been ordered by the appropriate legal authority to do. The problem, of course, is that if Socrates really holds the strict compliance view in the *Crito*, he is telling his concerned friend, through the fiction of the personified Laws, that the citizen must *never* disobey the law. The citizen may try to persuade *before* the law actually impinges on him. But once the order applies to him and directs him to act (or to forebear), the citizen has no choice but to obey. Consider once again this passage from the Laws' first argument for the "obey or persuade" doctrine.

> You should revere your country and yield to it and cajole it when it's angry more than your father, and either persuade or to do what it

orders and you should suffer in silence if it orders you to suffer something, whether it's to be beaten or to be imprisoned, and whether it
leads you into war to be wounded or killed, you must do this, and it's
just that you do so, and you shouldn't yield, or retreat, and abandon
your post, but in war and in court and everywhere, you must do what
your city and country orders, or persuade it as to the nature of what's
just.

(51b2–c1)

It is hard to see from this passage how Socrates might be leaving
room for some sort of hierarchy of moral duties. Of course, it is
possible that Plato simply did not recognize the problem, or, if we
think that Plato was determined to be faithful to the arguments
Socrates actually used, that Socrates himself did not see the conflict
between what he said to the jury and what he said about the
wrongfulness of escape. But even if we cannot be absolutely sure
that either of these was not the case, it certainly seems unlikely on
its face that either would have failed to notice such an obvious
inconsistency about a matter of such importance. While perhaps it
is too much to expect of them to suppose that Socrates or Plato
never contradicted themselves, we should accept such a view only
if all other available interpretations prove even less plausible.

Another possibility is that the *Apology* expresses the substance
of what the historical Socrates actually said at his trial about the
categorical nature of his commitment to continue the practice of
philosophy and that "obey or persuade" doctrine found in the *Crito*
expresses *Plato*'s view of the moral duty to obey the law. Once
again, although we cannot absolutely rule out this possibility, we
do not find it very plausible. Without taking a stand here on the
question of whether we find the philosophy of the *historical*
Socrates in the early dialogues of Plato, we must point out that, setting aside this apparent conflict between the *Apology* and the *Crito*
over the citizen's duty to obey the law, the other doctrines
expressed in the two works fit quite well with each other and with
those we find in the other "Socratic" dialogues. Again, though it is
possible that Plato broke with Socrates on the issue before us, it
seems to us far more likely that what appears to be a conflict

between the *Apology* and the *Crito* is really the result of a failure to understand one or both of the seemingly contradictory passages. Thus, before we conclude that there are really different philosophical views at work in the passages we have just reviewed in the *Apology* and the *Crito*, we would do well to search for an interpretation that shows why the passages are really consistent and that does full justice to the texts.

3.6.5 The alleged internal inconsistency of the Crito

Before we begin our search for such an interpretation, we should first take note of a different but no less troublesome problem for the strict compliance reading. Many commentators have argued that the strict compliance reading makes the argument of the *Crito* itself incoherent. The problem is not difficult to generate. Let's imagine that the Assembly passes a law requiring all males between the ages of, say, twenty-one and forty, to serve in the armed services if and when called upon. And suppose also that a certain citizen who has reached the necessary age sincerely believes such a law is unjust (for whatever reason). At the time, however, no new recruits are needed and so the citizen is not yet required to serve. So, believing the law to be unjust, he sets out to do everything in his power, within the bounds of the law, to persuade the Assembly to rescind the law. The Assembly, however, is not persuaded. Of course, the citizen is still at this point free to leave the state. But if he elects to stay and make further attempts to persuade the Assembly *and then* is ordered to begin his service, he is not from that point on free to leave. Nor is he free to disobey, according to the strict compliance interpretation, for the law now applies to him. Since he has failed to persuade and did not leave, he must obey. *Ex hypothesi*, what he is obligated to obey is a law requiring that he do what he thinks is unjust. Those who press this objection will argue that requirement plainly contradicts the most basic of Socrates moral commitments, what we were earlier calling "the prohibition against injustice." If so, and because the strict compliance interpretation also conflicts with the hierarchical view

Socrates appears to endorse in the *Apology*, most commentators have argued that we should look for an alternative reading of the "obey or persuade" doctrine, one that does not require that the citizen do what he thinks he ought not do.

3.6.6 The hierarchical approach reconsidered

Perhaps we were too pessimistic about reconciling the "obey or persuade" doctrine in the *Crito* with the hierarchical view of moral obligation the *Apology* seems to endorse. Gerasimos Santas argues that Socrates does indeed endorse the view that some duties are more important than others in the *Apology* and that what gives the duty to philosophize a greater weight than the duty to obey the law is its religious origin,[19] the fact that it was issued by the god to Socrates. But, according to Santas, in the *Crito*, Socrates does not make this point, for there, since the supremely important principle that the god must be obeyed does not require that Socrates escape, it does not conflict with Socrates' legal duty to remain in prison. What does impinge on Socrates, as he sits in prison, is his obligation not to harm the Laws through disobedience. According to this interpretation, were Socrates to believe that his religious mission required escape he would have done so, since no duty is weightier than the duty to obey the command of the god. But since the god commanded no such thing, there is no conflict between civil authority and divine authority. Thus, in the *Crito* Socrates considers only what his obligation to civil authority, the personified Laws, entails.

Does the hierarchical solution really solve the interpretative problems we have been considering? At best, it only resolves the apparent conflict between the *Apology* and the *Crito*. It does nothing, however, to resolve the apparent internal inconsistency of the *Crito* itself, since in those instances where the citizen sees no conflict between duty to obey the god and duty to obey civil law, the citizen must either obey the law or persuade the appropriate authorities to change the law. But, once again, if the attempt at persuasion fails, the citizen must do what he, presumably, still thinks is unjust, in apparent violation of the prohibition against injustice principle. Quite apart from this limitation, there is good reason to think that Socrates does not even hold the hierarchical view. Recall that in the *Apology* Socrates makes much of his military service (28d6–29a1). It is only reasonable to think that during battle, and even during preparation for battle, Socrates was prevented from engaging in philosophical activity. If so, Socrates himself apparently thought that there were some duties owed to the city that required that he at least temporarily suspend his philosophical activity and indeed, that he risk having it brought to an end, for he surely realized the danger that he might be killed on the battlefield. Because the passage in which Socrates discusses his military service serves as a preface to his claim that he will not disobey the god's command that he philosophize, we have to infer that Socrates did not see himself as disobeying the god's command as he marched forth from the city to engage the enemy. Clearly Socrates did not regard the duty to philosophize as *always* overriding the commands of civil authority. But if not, we lose any reason to think that he assigned it greater importance than the duty to obey the commands of civilian authorities.

3.6.7 *Disobedience as persuasion*

One clever attempt to resolve the apparent inconsistencies we have just outlined argues that Socrates actually holds a remarkably modern view of the moral duty to obey the law. Just as certain enormously influential social reformers such Gandhi and Martin Luther King and their followers regarded nonviolent disobedience of the law as a way, indeed, the best way, to call attention to certain social injustices that afflicted their respective societies, so Socrates (through the Laws) is actually advocating disobedience of any law the citizen believes to be unjust *as a way of persuading the appropriate legal authorities to rescind the law*.[20] By disobeying a law that he regards as unjust, such as a law forbidding the practice of philosophy, Socrates would actually be persuading the appropriate legal authorities to change the law, and since persuasion is one of the options that the Laws allow the citizen to exercise, disobedience as persuasion does no harm to the city.

Whatever the philosophical attractiveness of a philosophy of law that allows for acts of civil disobedience, it is doubtful that such is Socrates' position. In the first place, there is nothing about Socrates' vow to the jury to disobey their order that he stop philosophizing that indicates that he would disobey in an attempt to persuade them (or anyone else) that such a command is unjust. Whether they would be persuaded or not appears to be irrelevant to Socrates in the *Apology*. More troubling is the fact that the attribution of this view to Socrates does nothing to solve the apparent inconsistency of the "obey or persuade" doctrine with Socrates' commitment to the prohibition against injustice. Plainly attempts at persuasion of whatever sort can fail, and even if the Laws do set down any conditions on how long one may take to persuade, as they do in the *Crito*, the relevant authorities are free to stipulate after some reasonable time has passed that they are simply not persuaded. They may then order Socrates, in the case we are imagining, to obey and cease philosophizing. If so, the same problems reappear. How can Socrates remain faithful to his vow in the *Apology* and to the doctrine he appears to endorse in the *Crito* and how can Socrates conclude, once persuasion fails, that he must do what he said he was prohibited from doing?

Nor can we salvage this approach by arguing that the "obey or persuade" doctrine does not require that the citizen actually succeed in persuading if the citizen thinks that a legal command is unjust. This is precisely the solution proposed by Richard Kraut, who argues that the Laws require only that the citizen make a good-faith effort to persuade the appropriate authorities to change the law.[21] According to Kraut, the Laws require only that the citizen *try* to persuade. Even if the citizen fails to persuade, he need not obey what he considers to be an unjust law, because by merely making a sincere attempt to persuade the authorities he will have shown the proper respect owed to the Laws as his "parents and master" and he will have fulfilled their just agreement. Kraut, of course, is well aware that the Laws do not actually say that the citizen need only make a sincere attempt. But he argues that the Greek verb (*peithein*) Socrates uses for "persuade" in the formulation of the "obey or persuade" doctrine has a conative sense. For example, the English verb "to prevent" is used in its conative sense when the general orders a subordinate "to prevent the enemy from reaching the town." If the subordinate fails to prevent the town from being taken after having done all in his or her power to block the enemy's advance, the subordinate has nonetheless carried out his superior's command. According to Kraut, then, the Laws never require a citizen to do what he thinks is unjust. If he thinks that some law requires that he carry out an injustice, the prohibition against injustice principle requires that he disobey. But if he disobeys he must be willing to go before the court and to justify his disobedience by *attempting* to persuade the appropriate authorities that disobedience was justified because of the injustice of the law.

Kraut's interpretation, if correct, would show how to reconcile the apparent conflict between the *Apology* and the *Crito*. Were the Athenians to pass a law prohibiting the practice of philosophy, Socrates would disobey just as he seems to say he would in the *Apology*. But he would nonetheless have carried out his moral obligation to respect the Laws and to fulfill his agreement with the Laws provided that he was also willing to get arrested and explain to the jury why complying with the law would, in this instance, be unjust. Moreover, Kraut's interpretation allows us to avoid concluding that the *Crito* itself is internally contradictory, for if Kraut is correct, the citizen is never required to obey an unjust law, contrary to the prohibition against injustice principle, if he fails to persuade. He need only have tried to persuade.

One important difference between Kraut's view and the strict compliance interpretation concerns who are the appropriate legal authorities to whom attempts at persuasion must be directed. Because the strict compliance interpretation holds that the Laws permit no disobedience whatever, attempts at persuasion must take place *before* the law actually obligates the citizen to act and thus must be directed at those officials who have the legal power to rescind or alter the law. For Kraut, attempts at persuasion may take place after the law believed to be unjust has been disobeyed and thus may be directed at the jury hearing the charge of illegality brought against the citizen. Now it may well be that we can find cases in which defendants in Athenian cases at about this time in

Athens' history never denied that they were guilty of breaking the law, but, in effect, asked the jury to set aside the established law on the ground that conviction would be a grave injustice.[22] The question we must ask, however, is whether *Socrates* would have approved of such a practice. Now the *Apology* gives us some reason to think that he did not. Recall that at the end of his defense he takes time to remind the jury of its specific duty. "For the member of the jury doesn't sit for this reason – to make gifts out of what's just – but to judge what's just. He's taken an oath not to make gifts to whom he wants but to judge according to the laws" (35c2–5). It is important to notice that Socrates does not say that it is the jurors' duty to take it upon themselves to see that justice is done, as Kraut's interpretation would have it. Instead, jurors are to look to only one thing: how the law requires them to judge the case before them. On this issue, then, we should prefer the strict compliance view to the alternative Kraut has proposed.

3.6.8 Does the Apology *really allow for disobedience of the law?*

As we have shown, however, the strict compliance view must face another problem, and that is Socrates' apparent willingness in the *Apology* to disobey at least one possible law – a law prohibiting the practice of philosophy. But before we conclude that consistency with the *Apology* requires that we abandon the strict compliance interpretation of the "obey or persuade" doctrine, perhaps we should take a closer look at whether Socrates' vow never to abandon the practice of philosophy really entails that it is morally permissible ever to disobey the law. The first thing to notice is that Socrates' view is hypothetical: he tells the jurors "*if* you order me to stop philosophizing, I will obey the god rather than you." Now as a matter of legal fact in Athens, the jury had no such authority to issue such an order upon conviction unless either the prosecutor had requested it as his proposed penalty or if Socrates himself had requested it as his counter-penalty offer. But, of course, neither proposal was made. Meletus has asked the jury to condemn Socrates to death and Socrates offers to pay a fine of 30 minas (*Ap.* 38b6–9),

The jury, in trials of this type, was required to choose between the two proposals. It had no authority to impose a penalty of its own design. Thus, had the jury ordered Socrates to cease the practice of philosophy on the penalty of death if he is caught in violation of the order, the jury would not have been issuing a legally valid command. Had Socrates, then, left the court and obeyed the god's command, as he understands it, and continued the practice of philosophy, he would not be in violation of any lawful command whatever and he would not be contradicting even the strict compliance interpretation of the "obey or persuade" doctrine.

We are not yet in a position to infer that the *Apology* and the *Crito* advance consistent views with respect to the citizen's duty to obey legal orders. Suppose the Assembly, the law-making body in Athens, passed a law forbidding any activity that Socrates regards as constituting his philosophical service to the god. Assume further that he tried (and failed) to persuade the Assembly that such a law would be unjust. Wouldn't defiance of *this newly enacted* law violate the natural reading of "obey or persuade"? And if he complied with the law and stopped philosophizing, would he not be disobeying the god's command that he engage in philosophy? Either way, one might think, he will be doing what he says he ought not do, which only shows that he cannot consistently hold both views.

In fact, however, we cannot draw such an inference, for the hypothetical situation we are now imagining assumes that such an enactment by the Assembly would itself be legally possible and conceivable in Athens. But exactly what such a law might be imagined to say is anything but obvious. Recall that one of the mainstays of Athenian democracy was the protection of free speech. Athenian citizens could criticize anyone and any policy in the state. Of course, in doing so, a citizen could face legal recrimination – for another freedom enjoyed by the Athenians was the right to accuse anyone at any time of any crime that the accuser himself chose to allege, and as Socrates' case shows, Athenian laws were sometimes formulated in fairly vague and general ways, and would allow broad latitude in the ways they might be applied to specific cases. But it is one thing to recognize that the practice of free speech could face such risks, and quite another to say that free speech might in some way be eliminated as a legal right in Athens' democracy. To imagine that questioning others in the way that Socrates did could be made illegal in Athens, we contend, is to imagine that the most basic practices of Athenian democracy – questioning others about the values they profess and the programs they propose – could be outlawed. It is, of course, not inconceivable that the Athenians might outlaw the kinds of "philosophizing" that Socrates' accusers claim he was guilty of – "scientific" speculation about "the things beneath the earth and in the heavens" (*Ap*. 19b4–5; see also 23d5–6). Socrates may well have actually lived in Athens when exactly this sort of law was in effect, at least for a time.[23] But Socrates quite plainly says that he does not engage in *this* sort of "philosophizing" (*Ap*. 19c8). What he *does* do is to talk with people about justice, about piety, about temperance, and wisdom, and friendship, and all of the other "most important things" (*Ap*. 22d7) about which he finds himself and others lacking in knowledge. Scholars who so confidently proclaim that Socrates would violate a legally valid law proscribing philosophizing owe us an explanation of how such a law could even conceivably be worded in a way that both makes the very idea of such a law conceivable in democratic Athens and would also force Socrates either to violate that law, or to stop philosophizing in the way that he did. We contend that the law scholars have so often imagined is, as a matter of fact, simply inconceivable in Athens.

Recall, moreover, that Socrates was prosecuted for having violated the law against impiety – a law forbidding acts of impiety, but which did not itself specify any particular actions that were to count as impious. The law left it to the accuser to spell out what the accused had done that was impious. Meletus was asserting, then, that corrupting the youth, not believing in the gods the city believed in, and introducing new divinities are instances of impiety and that Socrates had engaged in all three. Now there can be little doubt but that Socrates believes that violating the god's command is impious and a law requiring such impiety, accordingly, would be invalid. Thus, were the Assembly to order that, in effect, Socrates engage in an act of impiety by ceasing the practice of philosophy, the Assembly itself would, in Socrates' eyes, have issued contradictory legal orders, for it would have ordered citizens to violate the law forbidding impiety. Faced with such a situation, would Socrates refuse to obey the law prohibiting the practice of philosophy? Perhaps he would, in which case he would be at odds with the strict compliance interpretation. But here it is worth emphasizing that we can only come up with a case in which Socrates would willfully violate a law by straying very far from what the relevant passage in the *Apology* actually says! Moreover, the fact that the *only* law Socrates would break, namely, a law proscribing acts of impiety, is one that he would necessarily have to break in order to comply with another law is hardly evidence that Socrates holds the hierarchical view of moral obligation so often attributed to him, for either choice he made would violate one or the other of the orders binding him. If the laws themselves require contradictory actions, no theory of fidelity to the law, no matter how clever, will allow the citizen to fulfill his duty the law.[24]

But should we even assume that were a law passed forbidding the practice of philosophy, the view announced in the *Apology* requires that he disobey it? Most scholars assume that he would, given the categorical nature of Socrates' vow in the *Apology*. But perhaps we should be more circumspect about the assumption. Whatever Socrates thinks about the duty to philosophize, surely nothing he says in the *Apology,* or elsewhere, for that matter, requires that he practice philosophy *unjustly*. For example, when an interlocutor has had enough of Socrates' questioning and decides to break off the conversation, Socrates' commitment to philosophy does not entitle him to kidnap and detain the interlocutor against the interlocutor's wishes, in order to continue the discussion. Or if Socrates could have engaged some particularly bright and promising young mind only if Socrates had shirked his duty to serve in the military on behalf of the city, we can be quite certain that Socrates would not have deserted his military post (*Ap.* 28d6–10). And if the opportunity to make the young person better through philosophy were lost as a result of Socrates' bowing to military service, Socrates would surely not think that he himself was to blame. In other words, even in the *Apology* we see that Socrates' duty to philosophize was constrained by his other just commitments.

Now *if* we can show that justice, for Socrates, requires that the citizen defer to the city when disputes arise between the city and the citizen regarding what is best, then, just as it would be in accordance with justice for Socrates to abandon philosophy for service in Athens' military (even at the cost of his life), so Socrates would be prepared to abandon philosophy for other reasons that the city deems appropriate. If so, the door is open for us to argue that Socrates' claim that he will never abandon philosophy must be understood as the claim that he will never abandon philosophy *for some reason that he considers to be unjust* and that he is putting the jury on notice that he does not consider the threat of being killed for continuing to practice philosophy to be a just reason for abandoning philosophy. Seen in this light, Socrates' vow to the jury never to abandon the practice of philosophy is not the categorical claim so many scholars have taken it to be, for it is conditioned upon that practice's being *just*. Moreover, this vow to continue philosophizing is not made in defiance of the jury's authority; it is a promise that he will always do what he thinks is right.

Still, why would Socrates think that justice would ever require that he abandon philosophy if the city ordered him to do so? The obvious answer is that he thinks his debt to the Laws as his benefactors and his agreement with the Laws requires that the citizen let the city be the final arbiter of disputes between it and the citizen regarding what justice requires in particular situations. This is not to say that the city defines what is just or that if the city ordains it, it must be just. Rather, it is only to say that Socrates sees the city as having the authority over the citizen to make judgments about what is just and the citizen must yield to that authority. Recall that earlier the Laws asked rhetorically, "Is this the agreement between us and you, or was it to stand by the judgments that the city hands down?" (50b4–6). Since Socrates obviously thinks that this is indeed what he has agreed to and that the agreement is just, then were the city somehow to order him to cease philosophizing, it appears that he would have to do so. Certainly, as his argument with Crito shows, he is willing to accept and not disobey the court's order that he be executed – despite the obvious fact that by doing so he assures the end of his philosophizing in Athens.

In his own case, then, the city has made a disastrous mistake. But Socrates is convinced that he owes a duty of justice to the city to follow its order.

3.6.9 The internal contradiction problem

At this point one might well argue that even if there is no conflict between the *Apology* and the *Crito* over the issue of the citizen's duty to obey the law, we have done nothing to solve the apparent internal contradiction problem. If the citizen fails to persuade and has agreed to allow the city to adjudicate disputes between the city and the citizen, then, according to Socrates, the citizen is obligated to do what the citizen thinks is unjust. But according to "the prohibition against injustice" principle, the citizen must never do what is unjust.

Perhaps we need to look more carefully at prohibition itself. At the very least, Socrates cannot literally mean that one must never do what is unjust. Sometimes we do not know, and could not reasonably know, that we are creating an injustice. We might, for example, give someone another's property, believing mistakenly that we are returning the property to its rightful owner. But even if Socrates means that one must never do what is unjust voluntarily, the problem of the internal consistency of the *Crito* remains. To see why, let's consider the case of Socrates' own jailor, whom we meet in the *Phaedo* (116b7–d2). Socrates' jailor characterizes his prisoner as "the noblest, gentlest, and the best man who as ever come here" (116c5–6), and although this may seem faint praise under the circumstances, the jailor goes on to note that he is only "obeying orders" (116c4) and claims that Socrates will not hold the jailor responsible for what he must do, but will understand that it is others who are really responsible (116c7–8). After the jailor leaves, weeping, Socrates has kind words to say about the poor man, and notes that the two have had several occasions to converse during the time he was in prison (116d5–7). It is, as the jailor wished, quite obvious that Socrates does not blame him for carrying out his orders. Nor should we, it is clear. We may even suppose that the jailor is personally entirely convinced that Socrates was innocent and – had justice prevailed – should have been acquitted. Nonetheless, Socrates was convicted and sentenced by the jury to be executed. The jailor was then ordered to oversee and carry out the execution. Saddened by the thought that an innocent person will be killed, the jailor nonetheless did as he was ordered by the court.

It is certainly true that an injustice was committed and the jailor played a *causal* role in that injustice. (The fact that someone else would have stepped in to do his job had he refused is irrelevant.) It is also true that the jailor's role was voluntary. He participated, knowing what he was doing. He was not coerced. He believed that the state had convicted and executed an innocent person. Yet, most of us would say that only a moral fanatic would hold the jailor to account *in any way* for his role in the commission of the injustice, assuming that he too was subject to an agreement to carry out the orders of the court and that he was not morally free to decide for himself in which cases he would discharge his duty and in which cases he would not. In fact, most of us would say that in spite of the jailor's own beliefs about how the trial should have been concluded, the jailor would have been acting *unjustly* were he to have violated his duty as a servant of the state and secreted Socrates away to safety. Nor is it hard to see why we would say this. It was not the jailor's job to determine guilt or innocence at the trial. So, although there is an obvious sense in which he had a hand in the injustice, he was not in any way *responsible* for the injustice done to Socrates. If responsibility is to be placed, it lies with the prosecutors, and with the jury members who arrived at the wrong decision. *They* are the ones who have been unjust. What this shows us is that willful, fully voluntary participation in an unjust act is not sufficient for saying that the agent has acted unjustly.

We can now see that if we take Socrates' admonition to avoid injustice to mean that one must never do what is morally forbidden, it is does not follow that one is, in the morally relevant sense, doing anything unjust when one complies with an unjust law and so participates in an injustice. Before we can derive a contradiction in his view, we need to show that Socrates thinks the individual agent is always morally responsible for any participation in any injustice whatever. But it is doubtful that Socrates has anything so extreme in mind, as his very amiable relationship with his jailor seems to show. In a passage in the *Apology* Socrates says that he "know[s] that it's evil and disgraceful to do what's wrong and to disobey one's superior, whether god or man" (29b6–7). The point he is making, of course, is that it would be wrong for him to give up the practice of philosophy because he has been commanded to practice it by the god, who is his superior. That he would think that the god is his superior is not hard to understand. But in what sense could another human being be his superior? Socrates gives us an example when he reminds the jury that he stayed where his officers stationed him during various campaigns (28e2–29a1). Now Socrates surely did not regard those officers as his moral superiors in the sense that they better understand how one ought to act. Nor, surely, did he mean that they were more resolute in doing what they think is best than he is. They were his superiors in the sense that they had *legal* authority over him.

One way of thinking about authority is to think about how one can be criticized for what one does. The person who has authority can be criticized if he or she exercises poor judgment or issues commands that lead to avoidable harm. The person who is answerable to an authority can be criticized for not having shown reasonable diligence in carrying out the orders of the authority whose function it is to issue the orders. It is noteworthy that Socrates does not say that he was obligated to obey his officers when but only when he thought that their commands were just. What this passage shows, then, is that Socrates thinks that the citizen can be in situations in which morality requires that one do what one is told. If the action one is told to perform turns out badly, it is not the fault of the person who carried out the action, but instead that of the person or persons who ordered the action in the first place. This is not to say that, for Socrates, the individual citizen who is in an inferior position with respect to some authority can never be criticized for anything he has done. Perhaps the individual should never have agreed to be in an inferior position with respect to some authority in the first place. What the *Apology* passage implies, however, is that blame cannot appropriately be placed on someone who plays a causal role in the commission of an injustice that he or she has been ordered to perform by an appropriate legal authority. Blame is properly placed, not on the inferior, but on the authority who issued the unjust command. When the individual is not in an inferior position, the individual is responsible for his actions. If this is correct, when Socrates reminds Crito that they have long held that one ought never do what is unjust, he really means that one ought never be responsible for an injustice. Put this way, there is no contradiction between Socrates' commitment to justice and his agreement, which he also says is just, to obey a command that he thinks is unjust if he fails to persuade the appropriate authorities to rescind the command. If, having failed to persuade, he participates in an activity that he considers to be unjust, the responsibility for the action rests with the appropriate legal authorities, not with Socrates. According to this line of reasoning, were the Assembly to have passed a law prohibiting the practice of philosophy, Socrates would have urged them to rescind it immediately on the ground that it is impious and unjust and in conflict with the existing law prohibiting impiety. And were the Assembly to have responded not by rescinding the prohibition against philosophy but by rescinding the law forbidding impiety, Socrates would have failed to persuade. Of course, he may well have elected at that point to leave the city. But if he chose to stay, he would have to forgo philosophy. He would do so, however, in the belief that the impiety was not his but that of the members of the Assembly who voted for the prohibition.

3.6.10   Is Socrates' position too authoritarian?

At this point, one might well object that this interpretation of what Socrates means by the prohibition against injustice blocks the conclusion that Socrates' views are contradictory but only at the cost of saddling Socrates with an unacceptably authoritarian view of obedience to the law. According to the interpretation we have just considered, one might argue, Socrates thinks that the citizen is always permitted to excuse himself for having engaged in even the most horrific acts merely by saying, "Well, of course, I thought that what I had done was horrific, too. But I tried to persuade the authorities not to order this, but they would not accept my argument. At that point I had no choice but to obey and to do as I was ordered." Indeed, there is, in principle, *nothing* that the citizen would not think he is morally obligated to do if commanded and if his attempt at persuasion fails. But surely, the objection concludes, it is unacceptable to say that a citizen can *always* excuse himself by saying, "After persuasion fails, I was just following orders." We, quite properly, executed German officers after World War II despite their offering the very same argument.

This objection is not entirely fair to the interpretation we are considering. First, recall that the Laws are trying to do what is just and that they invite attempts to persuade them if they are ordering anything unjust (51e7). Because this is a condition of the citizen's obligation to obey or persuade, if the appropriate authorities simply refuse to consider persuasion from the citizen, then the authorities have nullified their own agreement with the citizen, in which case the citizen is not morally required to obey if he fails to persuade. Socrates does not tell us what the citizen ought to do in such a case. One option, of course, is to leave the state. But the citizen is not even obligated to do that if the Laws actually refuse to consider persuasion as opposed merely not to be persuaded by argument. When the state will not "listen to reason," Socrates' "obey or persuade" doctrine leaves the citizen morally free to disobey. Although Socrates does not say that the citizen is actually obligated to *disobey* a legal order issued by irrational authorities, such is consistent with the interpretation we are now considering. Thus, the charge that Socrates' position is identical to that advanced by certain Nazis when tried for their moral crimes is incorrect.

Second, even though the individual did go through a formal process by which he entered into citizenship, his commitment to obey or persuade was not sealed for all time at that point. The citizen is free to change his mind about whether he wishes to live in the state of which he is a citizen. As we have seen, the Laws emphatically declare that the citizen may leave and "emigrate to a colony or to go somewhere else and live as an alien, if we and the city should fail to please him, no law stands in his way or forbids him to go where he desires and keep his things" (51d6–e1). Thus, even if the appropriate authorities are open to persuasion, the citizen is free to leave if he believes that the city is adopting goals with which he disagrees. To those Germans who chose to stay in a violent and egregiously unjust society, Socrates can say, "Once you saw the path your leaders were taking your country down, you should have left before you were ordered to do anything you considered to be wrong."

Still, to press the objection a bit further, even if the interpretation we are considering does not let Nazis who were "just carrying out orders" off the moral hook, does not the point remain that, in principle, Socrates would require that when all of the conditions governing the agreement are met, the citizen who fails to persuade is morally obligated to do something he finds thoroughly unjust? For example, would not the individual soldier be obligated to kill civilians he believes to be innocent provided that he tried and failed to persuade his commanding officer (who is rational, open to persuasion, and so forth) to rescind the order?

It is important to distinguish between an order that is part of a discernible pattern of injustice – and so one which could have been anticipated – and one that is not part of such a pattern. Doubtless, all states fall somewhere on a spectrum of just laws and institutions, and reasonable people can be expected sometimes to disagree about whether a particular state requires that injustices constitute a pattern. But where the individual citizen is satisfied that a pattern of injustice can be discerned, one in which there is a substantial likelihood that he or she will be called upon to engage in unjust activity, the citizen should be "displeased" with the Laws and leave the state. But when the unjust order is unexpected and the citizen fails to persuade, the citizen might reasonably wonder whether in fact all of the conditions required for it to be binding have been met. To return to our earlier point, was the officer who orders an atrocity really able to entertain arguments to dissuade or was his mind so clouded with anger or fear or both that he could not entertain them? Again, as we showed above, if the officer does not or cannot, in fact, consider persuasion, Socrates' "obey or persuade" doctrine does not require the citizen to obey. In the end, however, if the conditions have been met and when the appropriate representative of the laws is confronted with the citizen's attempts to persuade otherwise has reached a different, even disastrously wrong conclusion, unless we are to convict Socrates of internal inconsistency, Socrates believes that the citizen must do as he is ordered. The same, we must suppose, will be the case if the situation is such that it would not be reasonable to expect the appropriate representative of the laws to take the time to consider the citizen's attempts to persuade – as might often occur during a military battle or some other immediate emergency. The obedient citizen will have been an instrument in the commission of an injustice, in such cases, but the citizen himself will not have been unjust. When blame is placed, it belongs with the appropriate authorities.

3.7 THE CONCLUSION OF THE LAWS' ARGUMENT

3.7.1 Will Socrates benefit anyone by escaping? (53a9–54b2)

To this point the argument of the Laws has been directed at showing how Socrates will harm them and the city if he "leaves without the permission of the Athenians." At the end of their speech, they ask whether there is anyone who would be benefited if he were to escape. Crito, we will recall, had argued that Socrates would benefit his friends, his children, and himself. The Laws are not persuaded. First, the Laws briefly inform Socrates that Crito was right when he earlier said that Socrates' companions will probably face legal penalties if they aided in his escape (53a8–b3). The Laws do not deny that "the many" will slander his friends by saying that they cared more about their money than their friendship with Socrates. But presumably the Laws think that Socrates has already made the point that one ought not care about what the many, "who lack understanding," say about anything.

The Laws then turn to Crito's claim that Socrates could still live a worthwhile life if he escapes and goes to another city. He could go, for example, to a nearby city, such as Thebes or Megara, both of which the Laws say that Socrates himself says are well governed. But because they are well governed, the Laws offer Socrates the following argument:

> You will be viewed as someone who destroys laws, and you'll confirm for the members of the jury their opinion, so they'll think they decided the case correctly. For whoever destroys the laws would probably seem to be someone who corrupts the young and who corrupts people who don't know any better.
>
> (53b7–c3)

The implication is that Socrates certainly would not last long in a city governed by just laws. Of course, if Socrates avoids well-governed cities and civilized persons, the Laws say, he may well be allowed to carry on his customary conversations with those who will listen. The Laws' suggestion that Socrates would find it shameful to carry on philosophical discussion with the uncultured and licentious (53c5–6) might at first seem puzzling. After all, in the *Apology*, Socrates says that it is his mission to speak to "young and old, citizen and stranger" – that is, to everyone. And if Plato's reporting is at all accurate, Socrates was eager to speak to those who aspired to the most intemperate lives. But presumably the Laws clarify their position when they suggest that in poorly governed cities no one will take him seriously, since he has always professed "virtue and justice and laws and customs are the most valuable things for people" (53c7–8). Among the uncultured and licentious, such claims will surely be dismissed peremptorily, especially when made by one who has been shown to profess one thing and do the opposite when it meant clinging to life for but a little longer. Socrates' hypocrisy, then, will actually prove to the uncultured and licentious that their unscrupulous ways are preferable to those Socrates was known to advocate.

The Laws clearly regard Thessaly, the region where Crito suggested Socrates go to live in safety among Crito's friends, is among the most lawless and disorderly places. Maybe, if Socrates avoids offending anyone, he could live out his last few years without anyone bringing up his rank hypocrisy for having violated the most important laws (53d7–e3). But what will he do in Thessaly? Such licentious people only want to feast, not engage in philosophy. Once again, if philosophy really is important to Socrates, he surely will not find willing practitioners in Thessaly. On the contrary, he will be at the beck and call of his Thessalian hosts (53e4–5).

The Laws next turn to what many readers take to be Crito's most compelling reason in favor of escape (54a1–b1). Socrates has an obligation to raise and educate the children he chose to bring into the world. The Laws do not deny, of course, that Socrates has an obligation to his children, but they take his obligation to be for him to see to it that his children receive the best upbringing and education they can, from which it does not follow that Socrates himself must be the one to provide for their well-being directly. Thus, the Laws ask Socrates whether he really thinks that his children would be better off raised in Thessaly, where they will inevitably become "strangers" to the ways of Athenian living. Or, will they be better off being raised in Athens by Socrates' friends, who can be counted on to look after them? Since the answer is clearly that they will be better off remaining in Athens, then they will receive what is best for them without Socrates. But since his children will be better off whether Socrates escapes and travels to Thessaly without them or dies and travels to Hades, ensuring that his children are properly raised and educated ceases to be a reason to escape. This argument turns, of course, on Socrates' assessment of the value of growing up in Athens, rather than in wild and lawless Thessaly.

3.7.2 The Laws of Hades (54b3–d2)

The Laws' final appeal concerns the fate that awaits Socrates when he dies (54b2–c9). As we have noted, the Laws concede that Socrates was unjustly convicted. But if he accepts the decision of the court, he can go to his death confident that he can truly say in the afterlife that he valued goodness more than anything else. If, on the other hand, he escapes, he may well be able to eke out a few enjoyable years in Thessaly. But he will have incurred not only the enmity of the Laws that exist on this earth, but also that of their brothers, the Laws of Hades, and they will judge him and those who aided his escape harshly. The Laws state their case as follows:

> [By awaiting execution] you'll leave – if you do leave – having been unjustly treated not by us, the Laws, but by men. If you escape after so disgracefully retaliating and returning wrong for wrong, and having broken the agreements and compacts with us, and having mistreated those whom you ought least of all to harm – yourself, your friends, your country, and us – we'll deal harshly with you while you're alive, and our brothers, the laws of Hades, won't receive you kindly there, knowing that, for your part, you tried to destroy us.
>
> (54b9–c9)

The Laws do not need to make the obvious point that whatever time Socrates has left to live in Thessaly is trivial compared with the time he will spend in Hades.

Now some[25] have argued that Socrates cannot really mean what he says here, and that at least in these lines, the Laws do not speak for Socrates. The reason for thinking this is that Socrates seemed to be entirely agnostic about the existence of an afterlife in the *Apology*, where he says that no one really knows what happens after death (29a4–b1) and seems to consider the possibility that death is the true termination of a human life as a genuine possibility (40c5–e3). But here in the *Crito*, we find him claiming there to be life after death, in which some "laws of Hades" might judge him harshly if he behaves badly in this life.

We are not much impressed by this argument. For one thing, for Socrates to say that no one knows what death might be like, it does not follow that he has no opinion on the matter. What he says about this in the *Apology* is only that one should never act on the basis of what one does *not* know, when what one *does* know clearly compels one to do something else (29b2–7). And when Socrates tells the jurors that death might be "one of two things" (40b5), there is no reason to suppose that he regards each one as equally probable or that he regards himself as having no reason to believe one over the other. He explicitly characterizes his argument as providing grounds for his jurors to have "good hope" about death

(40b4), and formulates it as what is called a constructive dilemma: either death is X, or death is not-X; if it is X, there is reason for "good hope," and if it is not-X, there is reason for "good hope." So, no matter what death might turn out to be, there is reason for "good hope" with regard to death. Those who employ such arguments are not logically required to regard each of the options as equally probable; nor must those who are asked to consider such arguments suppose that each of the options is equally probable. The point is that on *either* option (regardless of how probable we might find it) we get the same result. Accordingly, we find nothing in Socrates' argument about what death might be like in the *Apology* to suggest that he could not believe in the picture of the afterlife he puts into the mouth of the personified Laws in the *Crito*. The same picture (or at least one entirely compatible with it) is represented as accepted by Socrates in Plato's *Gorgias*, as well (523a1 ff.).

3.7.3 The end of the dialogue (54d3–e2)

In the final lines of the *Crito* the august Laws fall silent and Socrates once again speaks *in propria persona*, though just what he means is not at all obvious.

> Rest assured, dear friend Crito, that I think I hear this, just like the Corybantic revelers think they hear flutes, and the same sound of these arguments buzzes in me, and keeps me from hearing anything else. And know that if you say anything contrary to what seems now to be true, you'll be speaking in vain. Nonetheless, if you think it'll do you some good, say it.
>
> (54d2–d7)

When Crito declares that he has "nothing to say," Socrates ends the discussion with this final remark: "Let it be so then, Crito, and let's act in this way, since this is the way the god is leading" (54e1–2).

The comparison Socrates draws between himself and a "Corybantic reveler" may well strike us as puzzling. These "revelers," who may have participated in rites celebrating the goddess Cybele, were well known for the frenzied, irrational states into which they would work themselves by listening to drums and flutes played with great intensity. How can Socrates, the champion of the "examined life," say that the arguments they have just heard have so excited him that he can "hear nothing else" and that if Crito tries to oppose them, he will "be speaking in vain"? Is he suggesting that the foregoing arguments have somehow made him irrational or in some way unable to evaluate opposing arguments?[26]

It is doubtful that Plato has anything nearly so extreme in mind. We should notice that he does invite Crito to try to counter the foregoing arguments if he can. When Socrates says that the arguments "keep [him] from hearing anything else," he may simply mean that he finds the arguments utterly convincing, so much so that try as *he* might he can think of nothing that will refute them. And when he tells Crito that he, Crito, will be speaking in vain if he attempts to undo them, Socrates is probably just *predicting*, not assuring, that his friend will not be able to succeed if he offers additional arguments. If he were assuring that Crito could not succeed, his offer to Crito even to make an attempt would be pointless. Now it is not out of character or "unsocratic" for Socrates to say that there are some things that he is convinced are true and which he doubts anyone could ever prove otherwise.[27] What would be "unsocratic" is an assertion that Socrates will not even listen to counter-arguments. But there is no reason to think that this is what he means here.

We might also be puzzled by Socrates' reference to the god at the very end of the dialogue. Why does he refer to just one god and who is this god? We might be tempted to think that the god is the same divinity who communicated with him through the *daimonion*. But counting against this suggestion is the fact that in the *Apology* Socrates says that the god, through the *daimonion*, always turns him away and never towards anything. It is possible that Socrates is thinking about Zeus either in Zeus' capacity as protector of friendships (see *Euthyphro* 6b4) or, more likely, as the god overseeing the oath Socrates took upon becoming a citizen of Athens. It is more likely, however, that Socrates is not thinking about any particular god but instead is engaging in the not uncommon practice of referring to the collective divine will as "the god." Indeed, if Socrates believes that each of the gods is wise, and hence that they agree on matters pertaining to justice and injustice (see *Euthyphro* 6a6–8e8), he would indeed think that they would be of one mind that it is for the best that he remain in prison and await his execution. By following "the way the god is leading," Socrates is merely doing what he is convinced is the best thing. In the end, then, he concludes that it is better for him to remain in prison to await his execution than to escape and to live on outside the city in which he spent virtually his entire life.

3.7.4 Conclusion

In this chapter, we have reviewed Plato's *Crito* and provided an interpretation of its arguments that allows us to understand Socrates' arguments and positions in a way that makes them entirely consistent with those we find him advancing in the *Euthyphro* and the *Apology*. Not all scholars have shared our perception of this matter, and have instead proposed interpretations that required us to understand the arguments of the *Crito* as in some ways starkly contrasted to those we find in the *Apology*.[28] In doing so, however, in our view such scholars underestimate either Socrates' profound dedication to philosophical argumentation, which values consistency and truth above all, or else underestimate the intellectual capacities of Socrates' lifelong friend, Crito – in effect, leaving the very fact that Socrates has maintained such a friendship for so long inexplicable.[29] Scholars have been driven to interpretations that so subvert the natural sense of Socrates' arguments, we contend, because they start out with incorrect understandings of the views Socrates provides elsewhere. The *Crito* reveals a Socrates who, though not always agreeing with what his state does or requires, believes that the citizen has agreed to abide by the laws of the state if he makes a just agreement to do so, and then elects to remain in the state. This, we claim, is the same Socrates who tells us, in the *Apology*, that he felt duty bound to abide by the commands of his military superiors at Potidaea,

Amphipolis, and Delium (28e1-3), risking death (and thus the end of his philosophic mission in Athens) by so doing, without suggesting, in addition, that his obedience needed always to be conditioned upon his own individual agreement with the justice of whatever they happened to command. It is the same Socrates as the one who again risked death and the premature end to his mission when he refused to support the illegal trial of the Arginusae generals (*Ap*. 32a4–c3) and disobeyed the command of those who overthrew Athens' democracy (*Ap*. 32c2–e2) when they commanded evil, because his duty to obey the laws of Athens required him to disobey, in the first instance, and compelled no obedience to those who overthrew those laws, in the second. To suppose that Socrates did not accept the arguments he makes (in his own voice or in that of the personified Laws) is to make him simply a liar when he announces (in his own voice) at the end of the dialogue that he strongly believes the arguments that his old friend, Crito, is at a loss to refute (54b5–6).

Rightly understood, Socrates' doctrine that we must obey the laws or persuade them allows one who has made a just agreement to be a citizen of a given state to maintain an entirely independent critical stance about the justice or injustice of any specific law enacted within the state, while relieving the citizen of personal moral responsibility for actions he performs under legal command by the state. This, as we have argued, is neither an unacceptably authoritarian doctrine, nor does it entail the sort of "blind obedience" that scholars have been unwilling to attribute to Socrates. Instead, Socrates articulates a doctrine of the duties of the citizen that is well designed to preserve the social order, when that social order is the product of a just and reasonable agreement between a state and its citizens. One feature of this agreement, we claim, articulates wherein final authority within the state resides: at the end of the day, if and when differences of opinion cannot be reconciled through persuasion, the state is provided with the authority to make final judgments. With final authority goes final responsibility, however, which is why we should not fault individual citizens for judgments their state has made, and to which their state requires obedience. But the decision to obey the commands of one's state,

when made (however reluctantly) within the context of a just agreement to *be* a citizen of that state, cannot be one we should ever fault.
Not finding this doctrine implausible or reprehensible in any way,
and detecting no conflict between it and anything else we find in
Plato's early or Socratic dialogues, we see no reason to flinch at the
fact that the *Crito* quite obviously portrays Socrates as arguing for it.

In accordance with this doctrine, then, Socrates persuades his old
friend Crito that it would not be right for him (or for his friend to
persuade him) to escape, having neither persuaded his state that he
should leave, nor obeyed what his state has commanded. Our own
reverence for Socrates, and the grief we share with Crito at the dramatic prospect of his execution, should not blind us to the fact that,
in reaching the conclusion that it does, the *Crito* ends tragically, but
not badly.

NOTES

1 In what follows we follow the traditional practice of referring to the personified laws of Athens simply as "the Laws."
2 Not all interpreters think the assumption is warranted. See, for example, Weiss 1998, esp. 80 ff.
3 As Burnet 1924 notes (note on 43a8, 255), there is no reason to think
   that Crito has done anything more than been of assistance to the guard
   in some undisclosed way in the past. There is no reason to think that
   this is a reference to bribery.
4 In the *Crito* (44a4), Crito says only that the authorities (*hoi kurioi*) say
   that Socrates must die on the day after the sacred ship arrives. The
   Phaedo (58b5–6) refers to the law (*nomos*) that forbids executions during the time that the ship is away from Athens.
5 Burnet notes that, according to Plutarch, the Athenians continued to
   celebrate the Delia until the reign of Demetrius Phalerum. See Burnet's
   (1911) note on *Phaedo* 58a10, note 58.
6 That Plato includes the dream at all in the *Crito* suggests that Socrates
   actually did have some such dream in prison. Diogenes Laertius (2.35)
   reports the dream also, although he says that Socrates related the
   dream to Aeschines, not Crito.
7 See, for example, Burnet 1924, note on 44b2, 257–58.
8 Simmias and Cebes are Socrates' principal interlocutors in the *Phaedo*.
   Although they are there described as Pythagoreans (*Phd.* 61d7) and so,

presumably, engaged in metaphysical speculations that were quite foreign to the philosophical concerns of Socrates, Xenophon lists them as among the true followers of Socrates (*Mem*. 1.2.48).

9   How Socrates arrived at his principles, some of which are highly counterintuitive, is a long and controversial story, and is not something we can adequately take up here. For an extended discussion of this question, we refer readers to Brickhouse and Smith 1994, 10–29.

10 Socrates does make this point explicitly in the *Gorgias* at 477a5 ff.

11 This is the view taken by Weiss 1998, 80–83.

12 The word Plato uses to refer to laws is a very common one, "*nomoi*." We are using "state" to translate the difficult and usual phrase "*to koinon tês poleôs*." Aristotle uses it to refer to public or common interests as opposed to private interests (*Pol*. III.13.1283b40–42). See also Burnet's (1924) note on 50a8, 200.

13 See McPherran 1996, 265–66; Weiss 1998, 3 and *passim*; Colaiaco 2001, 201–10.

14 Music and physical training were standard forms of education expected of all free male children in Athens. For an excellent discussion of what that education consisted in, see Roberts 1984, 94–108.

15 This is a somewhat misleading way to state the point that Socrates made in the *Apology*. There he says that he could not offer exile as a counter-penalty because he was convinced that he would not be allowed to practice philosophy in other cities and so, given that fact, he implies that death would be preferable to living in disobedience to the god's command that he spend his life examining others. This passage in the *Crito* is good evidence that Plato believes that had Socrates proposed exile as his counter-penalty, the jury would have accepted it.

16 Kraut 1984, 154–55. See also MacDowell 1978, 69.

17 For an example of a defender of the strict compliance reading, see Grote 1865, vol. I, 303.

18 See, for example, Santas 1979. We discuss Santas's view in section 3.6.6.

19 Santas 1979, 208.

20 Woozley 1979, esp. 30 ff.

21 Kraut 1984, 55–90, esp. 69–80.

22 Kraut (1984, 80) admits that he knows of no such cases, but cites Kenneth Dover's (1974, 292) authority that the Athenian court was the appropriate place for the disobedient citizen to show that compliance with the law would have led to an injustice. Again, we accept that

some might well have thought that the Athenian jury had the power to nullify the law. We deny, however, that such was Socrates' view.

23 The psephism of Diopeithes, under which Anaxagoras was prosecuted in 430 B.C.E., apparently made such activities illegal. Some scholars, however, have doubted that reports of this – and of the trial of Anaxagoras – were historically reliable. For discussion, see Brickhouse and Smith 1989, 32–33.

24 We have defended this interpretation of the vow to practice philosophy made in the *Apology* in Brickhouse and Smith 2000B, 210–12.

25 See McPherran 1996, 265–66.

26 A scholar who has recently understood these lines in this way is Weiss 1998, 134–43.

27 For examples of Socrates claiming to know particular things of moral significance, see *Ap.* 29b6–7, 37b2–8 and *Euthyd.* 286e8–291a1.

28 See, for examples, Weiss 1998 and Colaiaco 2001, esp. 199 ff.

29 It is commonly claimed that the reason Socrates would offer arguments to Crito that he did not himself truly accept is because Crito is somehow too stupid or too emotional to comprehend good reasoning. Colaiaco, for example, speaks of Crito as being "intellectually incapacitated" by the nearness of Socrates' demise (Colaiaco 2001, 199), and as a result failing "to grasp the irony of the speech of the Laws" (Ibid., 212; see also Weiss 1998, 4). But such an assessment of Crito's capacities makes Socrates' insistence, at the beginning of the dialogue, that he and his friend must follow correct reasoning and not allow themselves to be swayed by anything else (*Crito* 46c6–47a5) into a mockery, for it requires us to suppose that by the end of the dialogue, good reasons have become unimportant to what Socrates is doing with his friend.

4

THE DEATH SCENE FROM
THE *PHAEDO*

4.1 INTRODUCTION TO THE *PHAEDO*

4.1.1 *Plato and Socrates*

As we said in the Introduction to this book, the *Phaedo* almost certainly does not provide an accurate account of Socratic doctrines. There are several reasons behind this claim. First, in his first speech in Plato's *Apology*, Socrates plainly says that it is "the most shameful kind" of ignorance to think one knows what one does not know:

> In truth, the fear of death, men, is nothing but thinking you're wise when you're not, for you think you know what you don't. For no one knows whether death happens to be the greatest of all goods for humanity, but people fear it because they're completely convinced that it's the greatest of evils. And isn't this ignorance, after all, the most shameful kind: thinking you know what you don't? But in this respect, too, men, I'm probably different from most people. If, then, I'd say that I'm wiser than someone in some way, it would be in this way: while I don't really know about the things in Hades, I don't think I know.
>
> (*Ap.* 29a5–b6)

Later, in his third speech in the *Apology* Socrates declares that death might be one of two things – either complete annihilation, or else a migration to another place, where all of the dead are (*Ap.* 40c6–41c7). In the *Crito*, Socrates characterizes death as "going away to Hades" (*Crito* 54a9–10, 54b5) and imagines the personified laws of Athens warning him that if he is a law-breaker in this life, the laws in Hades will not receive him kindly there (*Crito* 54c7–8).

Much of the *Phaedo*, however, is devoted to arguments Socrates makes, intended to prove that there is an afterlife. Death, Socrates declares at *Phaedo* 64c4–8, is the separation of the soul from the body. But Socrates in the *Phaedo* argues that death is neither annihilation nor simply a migration of the soul to Hades; it is, instead, part of a cycle of reincarnation (*Phd.* 70c4–d4, 71d5–72d10). The best of ordinary human beings, Socrates claims, come back in their next lives as bees or wasps or ants, or as a moderate human being (*Phd.* 82b5–8); the true philosopher, however, can hope to escape reincarnation altogether, never again to be "imprisoned" in a body (*Phd.* 82b10–84b3).[1]

Plainly, what Socrates has to say about death and the afterlife does not fit at all well with what he had to say about these subjects in the *Apology* and *Crito*. Moreover, one of Socrates' arguments for the cycle of reincarnation involves the notion that all knowledge is recollection (72e1–77a5), and in this and other arguments, we find Socrates introducing what has come to be known as the "theory of Forms." In this metaphysical theory – one of the best-known aspects of Plato's own philosophy – every particular thing has certain characteristics it has in virtue of "partaking of" or "participating in" the Forms. A beautiful work of art is beautiful because it partakes of the Form of Beauty; two equal things are equal because they partake of the Form of Equality, and so on. Particular sensible things are never complete, or perfect exemplars of any of their qualities or characteristics. Particular sticks and stones, for example, are never absolutely equal in size or weight or in any other way. The Forms, on the contrary, are all and always completely, purely, perfectly, timelessly, and changelessly what they are: the Form of Beauty (or, as Plato sometimes has Socrates express it, The Beautiful Itself) is completely, purely, perfectly, everlastingly beautiful. Unlike anything else that it is beautiful, Beauty itself never appears to be less than perfectly beautiful. All knowledge, then, is knowledge of Forms, since only Forms can sustain unequivocal judgments of what is.

None of these theories – about reincarnation, about knowledge as recollection, or about the Forms (as perfections existing in some separate supra-sensible realm) – can be found in any of Plato's early or Socratic dialogues, and their appearance in the *Phaedo* has persuaded developmentalists – those scholars who believe that early in his career Plato portrayed Socrates accurately, but later used Socrates as a mouthpiece for his own philosophical views – that we cannot look to the *Phaedo* for accurate representations of the historical Socrates or his views.

Even if we grant this reasoning, however, it is entirely possible that Plato might still have decided not to change any of the specific facts about the historical event of Socrates' death and last words. So even if we are persuaded that the arguments of the *Phaedo* should not be attributed to Socrates or regarded as Socratic, it may still be that the actual description of Socrates' death is essentially accurate in its details. As we will see in this chapter, there has been lively debate about this very question, and only recently has evidence been presented that appears to settle one element of this debate. But before we get to that debate, let us consider the way in which Plato sets the final scene for Socrates' death.

4.2 PREPARING FOR DEATH

4.2.1 Making his final preparations (115a5–116a1)

At the beginning of the *Phaedo*, we are told that on the day of his execution, Socrates' wife, Xanthippe, was with Socrates very early in the morning, holding their youngest child, and obviously already grieving the imminent loss of her husband. Socrates instructs his friend Crito to have someone take her home, and she exits the scene (and Socrates' life) "lamenting and beating her breast" (60a1–b1). History has not been kind to Xanthippe, whose name has come to be associated with her characterization by other ancient writers as a violent and angry woman with little love for or patience with Socrates. None of this sort of nasty gossip can be found in Plato, and certainly none of it is evident in his brief description here in the *Phaedo*. Moreover, later, at 115a6, Socrates seems to express in a small way his care for her: after completing his discussions with his friends, Socrates suggests that it is time for him to take a bath. Were he not to take a bath before drinking the poison, he explains, the women (including presumably Xanthippe and her servants) would have to wash his corpse (115a7–9). Socrates then chides Crito for asking how Socrates would like to be buried: it will not be *Socrates* who is buried, he insists, but only *Socrates' body*, which will be of no concern to Socrates at all after he is dead (115c4–116a1).

4.2.2 Socrates' jailor (116a2–d9)

After his bath, his three children were brought to him as well as the women of his household, and Socrates said his goodbyes to them and then had them led away before his actual execution (116a8–b5). When he returned to his friends, the jailor comes in and bids Socrates goodbye, and Plato has his narrator (Phaedo) recall the man's short speech to Socrates:

> Socrates, I won't think of you the way I think of others, because they made it difficult for me and cursed at me when I gave the order to drink the poison when the officers required it. But I know you to be the noblest and gentlest man who's ever come here. And now especially I know that you're not going to be upset with me – for you know who's responsible – but at them. So now you know what I came to tell you: farewell and try to bear what you must endure as easily as possible.
>
> (116c1–d2)

As he departed, Phaedo recalls, the man was weeping. Socrates calls out a farewell to the jailor, and then turns to his friends and exclaims:

> How kind this man is. Throughout my whole time here, he put up with me and talked with me sometimes, and couldn't have been better. And now how genuinely he's weeping for me!
>
> (116d5–7)

It may seem unremarkable that Socrates – who is characterized throughout Plato's account of his trial and death as caring only to do what is right and unconcerned about his own death – would be on such good terms with his jailor. We can well imagine, as the jailor himself suggests, that not all prisoners scheduled for execution would enjoy such calm and friendly relations with the jailor. But, as the jailor says, Socrates is not a man to berate or struggle against the jailor, who is only following the orders of his legal superiors. Indeed, the scene appears so unremarkable and typical of Socrates that it has received little attention in the scholarly literature. But in fact, this scene is pertinent to at least one very interesting question, which we considered at length in Chapter 3 of this book.[2]

Those who have read our discussion of the "obey or persuade" doctrine in the *Crito* (section 3.6) will recall that the main debate over the proper interpretation of that doctrine centers on whether or not Socrates thinks that one should obey a command one recognizes as *unjust*, if the command is given by an authentic legal authority. In our chapter on the *Crito*, we argued that Socrates' position should be understood in such a way as to disallow disobedience to authentic legal authority – even when that authority commands what the one so commanded regards as an injustice. This view, we acknowledged in that chapter, has not persuaded many other scholars, who have held that Socrates' universal prohibition against doing injustice would require one to disobey even an authentic legal command that one regarded as unjust, or as requiring an injustice to be done.

Now, as we have said, the *Phaedo* is generally regarded as having been written later in Plato's career as a philosophical writer, and most of the theories developed in this dialogue should probably be regarded as Plato's rather than as Socrates' – even if we accept that the theories given in the earlier dialogues, including the *Crito*, may be regarded as Socratic. Granting this, it may be that the picture Plato gives us of the relationship between Socrates and his jailor is not at all historically accurate. But if we are inclined to find this relationship in keeping with the character of Socrates we find in the *Euthyphro, Apology, Crito,* and the other early or Socratic dialogues, then it is worth noting that the very characteristics of the relationship the jailor himself mentions are incompatible with the view, sometimes attributed to Socrates, that any performance of injustice – even if it is performed under the command of an authentic legal authority – is shameful and blameworthy.

The jailor, notice, credits Socrates for not holding it against him (the jailor) that he is the one who must direct the execution. The jailor himself plainly has nothing but high regard for Socrates, but he also allows that Socrates may well be "upset" with the ones who actually ordered the execution – and there is certainly no hint in what anyone says in the *Phaedo* (or, indeed, in any of Plato's dialogues) that Socrates actually *deserves* to be executed. Socrates is calm in the face of death and by the time he is executed, he even welcomes it. But he does not welcome it as a death rightly or justly imposed upon him. The prosecution, the jurors' decision, and this execution, we may be sure, were all unjust. Accordingly, in overseeing and assuring that the execution is completed, the jailor is in the exact situation we discussed in the chapter on the *Crito*: he has been commanded by those who have legal authority over him to complete the execution of Socrates. The execution is an injustice and those responsible for it are implicated in that injustice. If one acting under the authentic legal command of a proper legal authority is also implicated in the injustice, if the legal authority's command is unjust, then the jailor is not blameless in his role in this execution, and there is no reason for Socrates *not* to berate the jailor for his participation in the injustice. Yet, as much as Socrates has harsh things to say about his prosecutors (see *Ap*. 39b1–6), and to those jurors who voted against him (see *Ap*. 38d3–39a7, 39c1–d5), his jailor plainly thinks well of Socrates for *not* blaming him for ending Socrates' life.

If the view we have opposed (in Chapter 3 and elsewhere) were right, the relationship between Socrates and his jailor should *not* have been the way his jailor says it was. Unless Socrates was simply behaving in a way that was inconsistent with his philosophical views, those views must have included the provision for which we have argued, namely, that one is blameless in enacting an injustice if that injustice is performed under command of an authentic legal authority. At least one advantage of this view is that it allows Socrates not to violate his own philosophy in enjoying such a cordial relationship with his jailor. It explains why the jailor recognizes Socrates' preeminence among men and why he will grieve the philosopher's passing. So, too, our account authorizes us to regard the jailor as an innocent party, required by duty to do what he himself would rather not at all do – a sympathetic character whose judgments of Socrates Plato plainly intends to be understood as the right ones.

4.3   DEATH BY HEMLOCK

4.3.1   *Drinking the poison (116e1–118a17)*

When the jailor leaves, Socrates suggests that the poison be prepared and brought to him. Crito at first objects, for he wants Socrates to wait until the sun is fully set (which is when the law requires the execution to be completed), but Socrates refuses to "hang on to life" as if some little more of it were something precious, and he repeats his request and Crito sends a slave to fetch the assistant who will actually administer the poison (a public slave – not the jailor himself). The slave returns with the assistant, who has the poison ready in a cup (116d7–117a8). Socrates receives his instructions, takes the cup, and then jokes with the assistant about giving a small portion to the gods (as if the contents of the cup were wine or some other delicacy). The assistant responds that they only mix as much as they think will be necessary (117a8–b9). Socrates offers a prayer to the gods, and then drinks the poison (117c1–5).

4.3.2   *Could Socrates really have died so peacefully?*

The way in which Plato depicts the death of Socrates has been a matter of controversy for centuries. Is Plato's account historically accurate, or should we suppose that Socrates' death was, in fact, very different from the way it is depicted in the *Phaedo*? Until very recently, scholars have almost universally accepted that Plato's depiction of the death of Socrates could *not* be truthful, on the ground that the death Plato gives to Socrates in the *Phaedo* does not accord with what some toxicologists have said about the symptoms of hemlock poisoning.

The contrast between the death scene in the *Phaedo* and the supposed symptoms of hemlock poisoning can actually be found first implied by a work on poisons by Nicander, a Roman army physician of the second century B.C.E. Nicander provides a frightening list of symptoms that includes loss of motor control, eyes rolling back in the head, and a "terrible choking" in the throat and windpipe.[3] Scholars doubtful about Plato's reliability have also noted that Nicander's report also accords with what we find in several modern toxicology texts:

> Accounts of hemlock-poisoning in modern medical authorities recount more effects of this kind. They speak of salivation, nausea, vomiting, as well as dryness and choking in the lower throat; the pupils are dilated, the vision and hearing become imperfect, and the speech is thick. Paralysis occurs in the arms as well as the legs, and is often accompanied by spasms and convulsions.[4]

Contrast these symptoms with the account of Socrates' death given by Plato:

> He walked around and when he said that his legs were heavy, he lay down on his back, for that's what the man told him to do. And then the one who administered the poison touched him, and after a time examined his feet and legs and after pressing hard on his foot, he asked him if he could feel anything. And he said that he couldn't. Next he touched his calves and going up in this way he demonstrated to us that they were cold and stiff. And then he touched him and said that when it, the coldness, reaches his heart, he'll be gone. And then the coldness was almost to his abdomen, and he uncovered his head — for he had covered it and he said his last words, "Crito, we owe a cock to Asclepius. Pay it and don't neglect it." Crito said, "It will be done. Tell us if you want anything else." And after Crito said this, Socrates didn't answer, and after a little while he moved and the man uncovered him and his eyes were fixed. When Crito saw this, he closed his mouth and eyes. Such was the end of our companion.
>
> (117e4–118a16)

Socrates' end in the *Phaedo* could hardly have been more peaceful – no vomiting, no choking, no convulsions. This description of Socrates, with his consciousness and clarity of thought remained undisturbed even to the end, is clearly at odds with the symptoms of hemlock poisoning we find in Nicander or in many of the toxicology texts written in the early and middle twentieth century. Accordingly, scholars have dismissed Plato's depiction of Socrates' death as purely fictional, claiming that instead of reporting the ugly and unpleasant truth about Socrates' death, Plato chose to provide his readers with a happier picture:

> The quietness, the calmness, the regularity of the effects of the penetration of poison into Socrates' body (so different from the chaos, squalor, and collapse described by Nicander and modern toxicologists) is the quietness of a ritual, the *katharmos* or purification of the soul from the prison of the body. The vivid and detailed picture of this death that Plato gives is not that of a man reproducing an actual event in every particular, but of an author selecting and embellishing those features which will illuminate, in visual form, the intelligible meaning of his argument.[5]

Given the apparently incontrovertible authority of medical experts, scholars have until very recently not questioned this appraisal of Plato's account. The problem this appraisal raises, however, is a very serious one:

> This instance, in which a historical event is transformed into a representation of a philosophical idea, should alert us to the possibility that many of what seem to be authentic glimpses into the life, or death, of the historical Socrates may in fact be illustrative pictures, attached or inset ... into Plato's arguments.[6]

In other words, to put it somewhat starkly, having here caught Plato in a patent lie about one historical event involving Socrates, we can no longer trust any of Plato's other depictions of Socrates (including, most importantly for readers of this book, those we get in the *Euthyphro*, *Apology*, and *Crito*, all of which may be just as

far from the historical truth as scholars have claimed Socrates'
death in the *Phaedo* to have been).

4.3.3   Defending the accuracy of Plato's account

A recent and admirably thorough examination by Enid Bloch, who
reviewed and analyzed all of the ancient and modern evidence,
however, has completely overturned this negative appraisal of
Plato's account.[7] Bloch begins by questioning the authority (which
is granted uncritically by those who dispute Plato's accuracy) of
Nicander's account.

> Why should Nicander's account be credited above that of Plato? Not
> only was Nicander writing a good two centuries after Socrates' death,
> he was describing illness, not execution. The victim in Nicander's
> poem is not a prisoner, forced to ingest a toxin known at the very least
> to his executioner, but a man free to wander about and "totter"
> through the streets. We are not told how he came to be poisoned.
> Would an observer have been able to say which substance, if any, had
> been responsible for his condition? Nicander was writing at a time of
> high anxiety about poisons, when any acute episode of appendicitis,
> or asthma, or choking, in the absence of other explanation, was likely
> to be deemed a surreptitious murder.[8]

The editors and translators of Nicander's work on whom Plato's
detractors rely actually express doubt as to how much authority
he brought to his subject. "His descriptions," they note, "do not
always tally with the known habits of the plants of which he is supposed to be speaking."[9] Bloch, in fact, strongly doubts that Plato
and Nicander are even speaking about the same plant. She notes
that in Greek-speaking communities in Italy, variants of the same
term were used to identify several different poisonous plants,
including hemlock.[10] And one of the *other* plants to which this
term was applied – aconite – is the source of a poison whose toxic
symptoms *exactly* match those given by Nicander for hemlock.[11]
    Plato only refers to the contents of Socrates' final cup as "the poi-
son," but the ancient sources all agree that the specific poison used

for executions in this period was *Conium maculatum*. So why can't we simply consult with toxicology textbooks about what the symptoms of poisoning by *Conium maculatum* are, and get our answer?

Bloch herself undertook exactly this project and discovered that a profusion of different "hemlocks" were known in the ancient world. After exhaustive research, Bloch discovered that the toxin in *Conium maculatum* is unique among all of the other poisonous members of the "hemlock" group. Bloch's study concludes that the symptoms of poisoning by *Conium maculatum* are an "ascending paralysis as a peripheral neuropathy of the Guillain–Barré type."[12] Although not strictly what is known as "Guillain–Barré Syndrome," which is generally assumed to be caused by a virus, Bloch argues that the symptoms are enough alike that, as with Guillain–Barré Syndrome, the main threat is temporary paralysis of the muscles of respiration. In effect, then, the poison killed Socrates by suffocation. This would explain the small seizure Plato describes as Socrates' last movement (118a12).

In fact, were it not for Nicander's original mistake, we might have been in a much better position to assess Plato's account, for all of the other descriptions of hemlock poisoning from around the same period are entirely in accord with Plato's description of the workings of the poison on Socrates. Aristophanes' *Frogs*, written at least five years before the death of Socrates, includes a joke about hemlock poisoning making its victim "cold and wintry." (Just thinking about it makes one of the characters in *Frogs* feel numbness in his lower legs [*Frogs* 125–6].) Theophrastus, one of Aristotle's students, a few generations later, describes death by hemlock poisoning as "swift and easy," and Plato's contemporary, Xenophon, has Socrates describe his lack of concern about his possible condemnation by the jury in this way:

> "Perhaps," he explained, "the god, out of good will, is protecting me by ending my life not only at an opportune age but also in the way that is easiest. For if I am condemned now, it is clear that I would suffer a death which is judged, by those who consider these things, easiest, least troublesome to loved ones, and productive of the most regret"
>
> (Xenophon, *Ap.* 7).

Xenophon has Socrates again claim that the death at the hands of the state will be "the easiest sort of death" at *Apology* 33. It is difficult to imagine what Xenophon could have in mind in having Socrates characterize his prospective death by hemlock poisoning as such an *easy* one, if (what would have been common knowledge among the Greeks, if true) condemned criminals were known to suffer delirium and to convulse, choke, and vomit their way into death.

One interesting result of Bloch's study is that it actually permits us to take another look at Plato's description of Socrates' final moments. What is striking, if we do, is how very inadequate the earlier scholarly explanations actually are. Scholars seem somewhat at a loss to explain exactly *why* Plato would so distort what they supposed was the ugly historical reality of Socrates' actual death. Some imagine that Plato just couldn't bear to represent the convulsions, choking, and vomiting they supposed he must have suffered, on the ground that Plato "wanted to preserve the noble image of his friend and teacher" with "no undignified details to obscure the heroic manner of his death."[13]

According to this hypothesis, Plato simply suppresses the more gruesome aspects of Socrates' death. But scholars have gone further than this, suggesting that Plato's description may actually have taken what they supposed were the common reactions to hemlock poisoning into account, and gave Socrates a very peaceful death in order to reveal some special strength of character in the philosopher. So Graves *et al.* speculate that Plato shows Socrates' mastery over himself in this final scene: such stoicism represents a most impressive example of "mind over matter," and serves to prove another point. In *Phaedo*, Socrates states his belief that the true philosopher "as much as possible sets free the soul from communion with the body, more than other men." Is he not, by demonstrating such control over the physical signs and symptoms of the poison, proving himself the true philosopher?[14]

If we look at the way Plato actually describes Socrates' last moments, however, it is plain that these speculations apply very poorly to the scene. If Plato's point was to ascribe to Socrates a miraculous and unusually calm reaction to a poison well known to cause violent seizures and other terrible effects, why would he make the assistant who prepares the poison (and who would surely know better) explain what would happen to Socrates is such a patently incorrect way? It seems that Plato would do a far better job of emphasizing Socrates' heroic strength by having the assistant warn Socrates and his friends of the predictable and ghastly effects of the poison, only to be contradicted by Socrates' noble restraint as he practiced his mastery of "mind over matter." By having the *assistant* describe what would happen to Socrates in the way he does, and then showing Socrates to go through the predicted effects of the poison exactly as the assistant described them, Plato cannot possibly be emphasizing how extraordinary Socrates' death was, relative to what are described as the predictable symptoms. In fact, the reverse is true: Socrates' death goes exactly the way the assistant predicted it would – his reactions to the poison are made out to be perfectly ordinary ones. Had Plato's motives included a wish simply to suppress the well-known effects of the poison, it would be senseless to write into the final scene all of the details given by the assistant about how the poison will work, since these add nothing to the drama of the scene, and suggest only that Socrates' actual reactions to the poison were unremarkable.

The effect of Bloch's study, then, is to assert that the description of hemlock poisoning we find in Plato is entirely factual. "The calm, peaceful death of the *Phaedo* was an historical reality."[15] Bloch's conclusion, accordingly, allows us to avoid the more speculative interpretations of Plato's depictions of Socrates' final days and hours. We can never know if any specific detail in any of the works we discuss in this book actually happened in exactly the way Plato records it. But it turns out that what has been regarded as the best-known and most obvious example of Platonic fictionalizing is probably nothing of the kind. As far as anything medical science or scholarly study has to show, Plato's account of Socrates' death may simply be the truth. If so, the upshot of Bloch's study may be even more remarkable than all of the literary ingenuity scholars have been imagining: perhaps, after all, the moving scene at the end of the *Phaedo* records the way the death of Socrates actually occurred.

4.4 SOCRATES' FAMOUS LAST WORDS

4.4.1 "We owe a cock to Asclepius" (118a7–8)

One final issue remains for us to consider. Socrates' last words are, "Crito, we owe a cock to Asclepius. Pay it and don't neglect it." Asclepius is the ancient Greek god who healed the sick and protected his worshipers' health. Crito seems to understand, and without any apparent puzzlement as to the meaning of Socrates' famous last words, immediately promises to fulfill Socrates' request, and asks the dying man if there is anything else he wishes. But Socrates says nothing more, and soon after, he is dead.

4.4.2 Sorting the options

Socrates' last words have been the source of the most intense (and occasionally the most fanciful) speculation by scholars. Indeed, in a beautifully written and elegantly argued recent paper on this very subject, Sandra Peterson has counted as many as twenty-three different interpretations of Socrates' famous last words.[16] In this section we will refer only to those that help shed light on this question about which Plato himself offers so little help.

It really seems like this *should* be an easier task: Socrates' words seem simple enough. His final message may be broken into two parts: (A) he tells Crito that they owe a cock to Asclepius, and (B) he enjoins Crito to discharge the debt and not to neglect it. As simple as this two-part statement is, scholars have not unreasonably focused entirely upon the first part (A): no one, to our knowledge, has found anything difficult to understand about the second part (B) – if a debt is owed to a god, the debt must be discharged, and Socrates is asking Crito to be the one to discharge it.[17] So the only controversy about Socrates' last words is about how we should understand the first part (A).

So let us break this part down into its relevant parts and consider how each part might affect our interpretation of Socrates' words. First, it may be significant that the last words are addressed to Crito and not to anyone else in the room at that time. Why to Crito?

The answer is that we cannot know for sure, but it seems clear that most scholars have assumed that Socrates speaks to Crito in his final words for the same reason that he gets Crito to do so many other of the final tasks during Socrates' final hours – Crito is the oldest friend Socrates has at his side in his final hours, and so it is simply natural that he would ask this friend to discharge his final duty.

Why, then, does Socrates say, "*we* owe a cock ..."? Whom does Socrates intend to include in the plural? On this issue, scholars seem to be divided. Most who have hazarded an opinion seem to take Socrates' plural to refer only to himself, perhaps because it is not altogether obvious why Socrates would think that anyone else in the room but he was in any imminent need to make an offering to the god. Although it is not impossible (in Greek, as in English) that Socrates is using the plural mainly to refer to himself – perhaps to include the others insofar as they are plainly taking what happens to Socrates so personally themselves – we contend that the plural "we" in his final words indicates that he regarded the debt to which he refers to be one that is shared with at least Crito.

If so, the next question is whether anyone in addition to Crito is included in the debt to Asclepius. Many interpreters seem to think so, though they differ about just who is being referred to as having the debt. Some include those with whom Socrates speaks in the final scene.[18] Others include perhaps absolutely everyone who has come into contact with Socrates (including even us, the readers of Plato's dialogues) for the psychic healing his philosophizing performs.[19] It would appear that there is no clear limit we can place on the scope of Socrates' plural, accordingly. But it would at least appear that any adequate interpretation must account for it.

Socrates says that he (and, it seems, one or more others) share a debt to Asclepius. But on the basis of what is this debt owed? In some interpretations, the very idea that a *debt* is involved gets lost, and the point of Socrates' remarks is understood either as attempting something like a bribe or at least making some petition to Asclepius, rather than instructing Crito to pay a debt. In other cases, the debt Socrates is seeking to repay is a result of the "benefit" of his own death – for example, for being relieved of the "disease" of embodiment, or life. It is at least awkward for such views, however, that this makes his "debt" a result of something that has not happened yet (or, at any rate, is not yet completed), in which case it would appear to be true that strictly speaking Socrates (and perhaps others) do not actually owe anything *yet*. Perhaps Socrates' reference to a debt, then, is supposed to be seen as anticipatory. But this seems to us to be unnatural as a reading of what Socrates says. One does not owe a debt for what has not yet happened; at most, one might say that one *will* owe such a debt at some time in the future (no matter how near in the future that will be). So, Socrates' use of the present tense in "owe" seems to not to be explained well in such views. It seems more reasonable, we think, to suppose that Socrates regards himself (and Crito, and perhaps the others present, and so on) as having already incurred the relevant debt – even if we go on to suppose that the relevant debt may be continuing to increase as each moment passes, or suppose that some further addition to that debt is being anticipated in the future. So, interpretation of Socrates' last words, we contend, seems to require an explanation of what the *chronologically prior* source of Socrates' and Crito's (and perhaps others') debt to Asclepius might be (or have been).

The next question we must confront is: why a cock? Is there significance in the specific sacrificial animal Socrates selects? On this point scholars are also divided. We suspect, however, that the offering of a cock was the customary one for the purpose Socrates has in mind.

Why, then, is Socrates' debt owed to *Asclepius*? Mark McPherran argues that there must be some special significance in this association, noting that there must be more to this than the idea that Socrates is in debt for some cure or preservation, since "Apollo is very much a god of healing and medicine, and so could have done just as well" at such tasks (citing *Cratylus* 404e and *Laws* 2.664c).[20] Accordingly, McPherran notes that Asclepius' special attributes must be significant. Whereas some interpretations contend that Asclepius' special power over death is what is significant here,[21] McPherran claims that it is Asclepius' association with dreams that is the source of Socrates' debt. It was common for those afflicted with some illness to sleep at a temple dedicated to Asclepius, in the hope that they might be cured by what is called "dream induction." As McPherran explains it, dream induction is "the practice of spending a night in the god's temple with the hope of being visited by the god in a dream who then offers instruction on how to be cured, or even grants the cure itself."[22] This is why McPherran proposes that Socrates' debt is the result of the dreams he reports having at the beginnings of the *Crito* and the *Phaedo*. But this interpretation would seem to encounter at least three problems. First, Socrates' dreams did not take place in an Asclepeion (a temple dedicated to Asclepius) – they took place in an Athenian jail. Greek religion provides no special reason to suppose that dreams had in jails are sent by Asclepius. Second, the value of these dreams that McPherran alleges is that they have lent divine support to Socrates' practice of his mission. The problem here is that Socrates seems to give the major credit for the origin and support of this practice not to Asclepius, but to Apollo (as the god of Delphi), in Plato's *Apology*. Finally, as McPherran himself admits, Apollo also had temples that employed induction, and though he immediately goes on to insist that "the method was most famously tied to Asclepius,"[23] the special connection between Asclepius and beneficial dreams does not seem special or secure enough to make so much of it – especially since one of the dreams Socrates reports (in the *Phaedo*) includes the injunction to compose a hymn to Apollo (60d1–2, 61b2–3). None of these problems is decisive against McPherran's interpretation, of course – there is no reason to think that Asclepius *couldn't* send someone a dream in a jail, or that Asclepius (as Apollo's son with such overlapping interests) wouldn't have been active in supporting the same mission his father seems to have originated. And certainly Asclepius is prominently included among those divinities who work at least in part through dream induction.

The one interpretation that seems entirely and readily to fit all of the considerations we have so far listed is perhaps the interpretation McPherran mentions as an alternative to the one he claims to favor, according to which Socrates is reminding Crito of the debt they owe to Asclepius for preserving them from the outbreaks of plague that devastated Athens during the Peloponnesian War, on the basis of which the ritual mission to Delos (whose end also marked the end of the temporary stay of executions Socrates and his friends had recently taken advantage of) had been reinstituted in Athens.[24] It has been noted before that Asclepius is particularly associated with health,[25] and Socrates has reached the relatively ripe old age of seventy years. But McPherran takes this line of interpretation a further step when he finds significance in the fact that Socrates' execution was delayed because of the quinquennial mission to Delos,[26] a ancient festival that had been revived "entirely due to the plague of 430 ... [and] given Asclepius' own quite visible role in ending the plague, it would be natural for all Athenians who had survived its depredations to feel the need to give sacrificial thanks to the father–son team of Apollo and Asclepius following the safe arrival home of their Delian emissaries."[27] Socrates (and his age-mate, Crito – see *Ap.* 33d10 – and any others who lived through that terrible plague) *always* owed a cock to Asclepius on the day the ship returned from Delos, in this interpretation. On this particular day, however, Socrates must both pay his festival-related debt to Asclepius, and also pay the "debt to society" assessed to him by the state, by drinking the poison.

Now it might be objected that this view fails to explain Socrates' use of the plural, "we." If it is simply the festival-related debt to Asclepius that Socrates must pay, as a survivor of the plague, then that debt is not so much shared by Crito (and others), as it would be *duplicated* by one that Crito (and others) would owe to the god independently, because they, too, were plague survivors. If Socrates is referring simply to this debt, then why he does not say, "I owe a cock to Asclepius, Crito ... and so do you." In other words, it would appear, in this case, that Socrates should be instructing Crito to sacrifice at least two cocks and not just one.

So, to our list of considerations, we may now add one further one: why does Socrates say that he (and Crito, and perhaps others) owes *a* cock to Asclepius, rather than, say, *two* or more? Don't Socrates' last words imply that the cock Socrates and Crito (and perhaps others) owe is a *shared* debt? But perhaps this concern is not decisive. Although shared sacrifices or sacrificial debts were neither impossible nor even uncommon among the Greeks, we are not convinced that an individual debt that was generally shared could not also be referred to in the way Socrates speaks of this particular debt. Imagine a group of diners getting ready to leave a restaurant. The first to look over the bill announces, "The total is one hundred dollars, including tip." Another diner, quickly doing the arithmetic of dividing the bill among the five of them then says, "So we owe twenty dollars, then?" "Right," says the one holding the bill. In this example, the diner who says "we owe twenty dollars" does not need to be corrected – as if the other must respond, "No, *we* owe one hundred dollars; *each of us* owes twenty." Instead, the sense of "we owe twenty dollars" is plain enough.[28]

Perhaps. As we have said, it is unlikely that we can ever really know for sure what Socrates' last words mean. This is not at all to endorse the view that Socrates was being "deliberately enigmatic."[29] Crito, after all, shows no hesitation or puzzlement of any kind at Socrates' request, as if he accepts and understands completely what Socrates has told him, whereas if we were supposed to regard Socrates' words as "deliberately enigmatic," we would expect Plato's characters to react to them in the predictable way. They do not; and yet, we are certainly faced with an enigma nonetheless, an enigma that is actually increased by Crito's straightforward acceptance of Socrates' request. In fact, we regard Crito's response to Socrates' request significant evidence for the interpretation we have proposed here – most of the others, we contend, require much more subtlety of reasoning than Crito would likely have been in a position to muster at the time. Only if the ground for the debt were something Crito could be expected already to recognize would we expect him not to respond with puzzlement to Socrates' instructions.

Our readers may not find our proposed understanding very satisfying, for it makes Socrates' dying words much less interesting or subtle than they are in many other interpretations. But we find our view of them quietly appropriate to the scene. As Socrates dies, he tells his old friend to fulfill a regular religious debt of traditional sacrifice – thus making his last words yet another reaffirmation of his innocence of the charge of impiety. Moreover, by reminding his friends of this debt, he gently encourages them to go back to, to get on with, their lives. So much of their attention has been given to their anxieties about *his* (Socrates') situation. But in a moment, he will be gone, and Crito and the others will have to take care that they do not simply get lost in their grief. They must take care to get back to what they need to do: "Pay it and don't neglect it."

Plato's readers will no doubt never cease to ask questions of his texts, and especially of this one. But neither Socrates nor Plato will give us the final answer we crave. And maybe, in a way, that is something very like what we get everywhere else we look in these works: they raise lots and lots of questions, and tantalize with answers that do not quite end up being complete or final ones, and so the questions never cease, and never seem quite to go away. If there is frustration in this, there is also a particularly human kind of happiness: the happiness of knowing that our enjoyment of a very enjoyable activity will never need to come to an end. Even now, so long after Socrates' death, we still enjoy asking – and still enjoy trying to answer – the questions he raised so long ago.

NOTES

1 Another reincarnation myth is told at the end of the *Republic* (614b2 ff.). Though it differs in important ways from the discussion of reincarnation in the *Phaedo*, it provides additional evidence that Plato took the reincarnation of souls quite seriously at this stage in his career.
2 We owe this observation, and much of the argument that follows, to Chris DeMarco.
3 Gow and Scholfield 1953, 106–7.
4 Gill 1973, 25. Others who have recently characterized Plato's account of Socrates' death as historically inaccurate include Ober 1977 and Graves *et al.* 1991.
5 Gill 1973, 28. Ober says that Plato "tampers with the facts" because "he wanted to preserve the noble image of his friend and teacher" with "no undignified details to obscure the heroic manner of his death. He was writing literature, not historical annal" (Ober 1977, 257).
6 Gill 1973, 28.
7 Bloch 2002.
8 Ibid., 260.
9 Gow and Scholfield 1953, 24; cited in Bloch 2002, 260.

10 Bloch 2002, 261.

11 Ibid., 261.

12 Ibid., 269.

13 Ober 1977, 257. Graves et al. put the same point this way: "It therefore seems that Plato, relating the event some years later, chose to omit such details that were unpleasant, undignified, or that might detract from the image of Socrates" (Graves et al. 1991, 167). Gill suggests that one reason for Plato's alleged fictionalizing "may have been his desire to eliminate the more unattractive results of hemlock poisoning from his picture of Socrates' end" (Gill 1973, 27).

14 Graves et al. 1991, 166–167. Gill makes the same point this way: "Plato may have wished to show Socrates' physical toughness and stoicism, the control of his mind over his body which is also stressed in Alcibiades' speech in the Symposium (220a ff.). Other men exhibited various features of physical collapse: Socrates merely covered his face except for one final ironic remark" (Gill 1973, 27).

15 Bloch 2002, 257.

16 The following quotes and most of the accompanying citations are from Peterson 2003.

17 Now, in fact, there could be worries in this second part: if Crito accepts the first part (A), then all Socrates should have to do is to ask Crito to be the one to discharge it—the further injunction, "don't neglect it" seems superfluous, unless Socrates somehow supposes that Crito might either fail to recognize the debt, or might recognize it but nonetheless ignore it. We are not inclined to understand (B) as genuinely raising this issue, however. In our view, the superfluousness of the added injunction, "and don't neglect it" is innocuous; in other words, we are inclined to read, "pay it and don't neglect it" as a formulaic way to make the single injunction, "pay it."

18 See, e.g., D. White 1989, 280; S. White 2000, 159; Most 1993, 104–6; Spitzer 1976.

19 See, e.g., Stewart 1972, 258; Santilli 1990, 31–32; or, if extended in the way we considered above, Peterson 2003, and McPherran 2003, 8–9.

20 McPherran 2003, 77.

21 See, e.g., Eckstein 1981, 200 and Ranasinghe 2000, 95.

22 McPherran 2003, 79.

23 Ibid., n. 23.

24 Ibid., 85–87.

25 See Minadeo 1970–1971, 296.

26 Plato characterizes it as an annual celebration at *Phaedo* 58b2. It is unclear what to make of this discrepancy. See Parker 1996, 150; McPherran 2003, 85.

27 McPherran 2003, 86.

28 We owe this example to Julia Annas, who supplied it in conversation about this issue.

29 Nock 1950, 49.

BIBLIOGRAPHY

Allen, R. E. 1970. *Plato's Euthyphro and the Early Theory of Forms.* London: Routledge & Kegan Paul.

Andrewes, Antony. 1974. "The Arginousai Trial." *Phoenix* 28, 112–22.

Archer-Hind, R. D. 1883. *The 'Phaedo' of Plato.* London: Macmillan.

Beckman, James. 1979. *The Religious Dimension of Socrates' Thought.* Waterloo, Ontario: Wilfrid Laurier University Press.

Bloch, Enid. "Hemlock Poisoning and the Death of Socrates: Did Plato Tell the Truth?" In Brickhouse and Smith 2002, 255–78.

Bluck, R. S. 1955. *Plato's Phaedo.* New York: Bobbs-Merrill.

Boardman, John. 1985. *Greek Art* (second edition). London: Thames and Hudson.

Brickhouse, Thomas C. and Smith, Nicholas D. 1982. "Socrates' Proposed Penalty in Plato's *Apology*." *Archiv für Geschichte der Philosophie* 64, 1–18.

_____.1989. *Socrates on Trial.* Oxford: Clarendon Press, and Princeton, NJ: Princeton University Press.

_____.1990. Letter to the Editor. *Times Literary Supplement* Jan. 26–Feb. 1, 89.

_____.1994. *Plato's Socrates.* New York: Oxford University Press.

_____.2000A. "Making Things Good and Making Good Things in Socratic Philosophy." In T. M. Robinson and L. Brisson, eds.,

Plato: Euthydemus, Lysis, Charmides: Proceedings of the V Symposium Platonicum Selected Papers. Sankt Augustin: Academia Verlag.

_____.2000B. *The Philosophy of Socrates.* Boulder, CO: Westview Press.

_____ eds. 2002. *The Trial and Execution of Socrates.* New York: Oxford University Press.

_____.2002. "Incurable Souls in Socratic Philosophy." *Ancient Philosophy* 22, 21–36.

Burger, Ronna. 1984. *The 'Phaedo': A Platonic Labyrinth.* New Haven, CT: Yale University Press.

Burnet, John. 1911. *Plato's Phaedo.* Oxford: Clarendon Press.

_____.1924. *Plato's Euthyphro, Apology of Socrates, and Crito.* Oxford: Clarendon Press.

Burnyeat, M. F. 1971. "Virtues in Action." In Vlastos 1971, 209–34.

_____.1997. "The Impiety of Socrates." *Ancient Philosophy* 7, 1–12.

Calder, William M. 1999. "Socrates' Rooster Once More." *Mnemosyne* 52, 562.

Camp, John M. 1992. *The Athenian Agora: Excavations in the Heart of Classical Athens.* London: Thames and Hudson.

Carafides, J. L. 1971. "The Last Words of Socrates." *Platon* 23, 229–32.

Chroust, Anton-Hermann. 1957. *Socrates: Man and Myth.* Notre Dame: University of Notre Dame Press.

Colaiaco, James A. 2001. *Socrates against Athens.* New York and London: Routledge.

Cooper, John M., ed. 1997. *Plato: Complete Works.* Indianapolis, IN: Hackett Publishing Company.

Cornford, Francis M. 1952. *Principium Sapientiae,* Cambridge: Cambridge University Press.

Crooks, J. 1998. 'Socrates' Last Words: Another Look at an Ancient Riddle." *Classical Quarterly* 48, 117–25.

Cropsey, Joseph. 1986. "The Dramatic End of Plato's Socrates." *Interpretation* 14, 155–75.

Devereux, Daniel T. 1992. "The Unity of the Virtues in Plato's *Protagoras* and *Laches.*" *Philosophical Review* 101, 765–89.

_____.1995. "Socrates' Kantian Conception of Virtue," *Journal of the History of Philosophy* 33, 381–408.

Dixsaut, Monique. 1991. *Platon: 'Phædon.'* Paris: Flammarion.

Dover, K. J. 1974. *Greek Popular Morality in the Time of Plato and Aristotle.* Oxford: Basil Blackwell.

Driver, Julia. 1989. "The Virtues of Ignorance," *The Journal of Philosophy* 86, 373–84.

Dumézil, Georges. 1984. "… Le moyne noir en gris dedans Varennes" sortie Nostradamique suivie d'un Divertissement sur les dernière paroles de Socrate. Paris: Gallimard.

Eckstein, Jerome. 1981. The Deathday of Socrates. Frenchtown, NJ: Columbia Publishing Company.

Edelstein, Emma, and Edelstein, Ludwig. 1945. Asclepius: A Collection and Interpretation of the Testimonies. Baltimore, MD: Johns Hopkins University Press.

Ferejohn, Michael. 1982. "The Unity of Virtue and the Objects of Socratic Inquiry," Journal of the History of Philosophy 20, 1–21.

_____.1983–1984. "Socratic Virtue as the Parts of Itself," Philosophy and Phenomenological Research 43, 377–88.

Fox, Marvin. 1956. "The Trials of Socrates." Archiv für Philosophie 6, 226–61.

Furley, W. D. 1985. "The Figure of Euthyphro in Plato's Dialogue." Phronesis 30, 201–8.

Gallop, David. 1975. Plato: Phaedo. Oxford: Clarendon Press.

Gargarin, Michael. 1979. "The Prosecution of Homicide in Athens." Greek, Roman, and Byzantine Studies 20, 301–23.

Garland, R. 1992. Introducing New Gods. Ithaca, NY: Cornell University Press.

Gautier, R. 1955. "Les Dernières Paroles de Socrate." Revue Universitaire 64, 274–75.

Gilead, Amihud. 1994. The Platonic Odyssey: A Philosophical–Literary Inquiry into the 'Phaedo'. Atlanta, GA: Rodopi.

Gill, Christopher. 1973. "The Death of Socrates." Classical Quarterly NS 23, 25–28.

Gocer, Asli. 2000. "A New Assessment of Socratic Philosophy of Religion." In Smith and Woodruff 2000, 115–29.

Gow, A. S. F. and Scholfield, A. F. 1953. Nicander: Poems and Poetical Fragments. Cambridge: Cambridge University Press.

Graves, Bonita M., Graves, G. M., Tsakopoulos, A. K., and Anton, J. P. 1991. "Hemlock Poisoning: Twentieth Century Scientific Light Shed on the Death of Socrates." In The Philosophy of Socrates, K. J. Boudouris, ed. Athens: Kardamitsa Publishing Company, 156–68.

Grote, George. 1865. Plato and the Other Companions of Sokrates. London: J. Murray.

Grube, G. M. A. 1975. The Trial and Death of Socrates. Indianapolis, IN: Hackett Publishing Company.

_____.2000. The Trial and Death of Socrates (third edition). Revised by John M. Cooper. Indianapolis, IN: Hackett Publishing Company.

Guardini, Roman. 1948. *The Death of Socrates*. Trans. Basil Wrighton. New York: Sheed and Ward.

Guthrie, W. K. C. 1971. *Socrates*. Cambridge: Cambridge University Press.

Hamilton, Edith and Cairns, Huntington, eds. 1941. *Plato: The Collected Dialogues*. Princeton, NJ: Princeton University Press.

Harrison, A. W. R. 1971. *The Law in Athens*. 2 vols. Oxford: Clarendon Press.

Heidel, W. A. 1900. "On Plato's *Euthyphro*." *Transactions of the American Philological Association* 31, 164–81.

Hoerber, Robert G. 1958. "Plato's *Euthyphro*." *Phronesis* 3, 95–107.

Hoopes, J. P. 1970. "Euthyphro's Case." *The Classical Bulletin* 47, 1–6.

Hutchinson, D. S. 1999. Review of McPherran 1996. *Ancient Philosophy* 19, 601–6.

Irwin, T. H. 1977. *Plato's Moral Theory*. Oxford: Clarendon Press.

_____.1986. "Socrates the Epicurean?" *Illinois Classical Studies* 11, 85–112.

_____ 1995. *Plato's Ethics*. Oxford: Oxford University Press.

Jackson, B. Darrell. 1971. "The Prayers of Socrates." *Phronesis* 16, 14–37.

Jowett, Benjamin. 1953. *The Dialogues of Plato*. 4 vols. Oxford: Clarendon Press.

Kahn, Charles 1996. *Plato and the Socratic Dialogue*. Cambridge: Cambridge University Press.

Keuls, Eva. 1993. *The Reign of the Phallus: Sexual Politics in Ancient Athens* (second edition). Berkeley: University of California Press.

Klonoski, R. 1984. "Setting and Characterization in Plato's *Euthyphro*." *Diálogos* 44, 123–39.

Kraut, Richard. 1984. *Socrates and the State*. Princeton, NJ: Princeton University Press.

Liddell, H. G., Scott, R., and Jones, H. S. 1996. *A Greek–English Lexicon* (ninth edition). Oxford: Clarendon Press.

MacDowell, Douglas M. 1963. *Athenian Homicide Law in the Age of the Orators*. Manchester: Manchester University Press.

_____.1978. *The Law in Classical Athens*. Ithaca, NY: Cornell University Press.

McPherran, Mark L. 1996. *The Religion of Socrates*. University Park, PA: The Pennsylvania State University Press.

_____.2000. "Does Piety Pay? Socrates and Plato on Prayer and Sacrifice." In Smith and Woodruff 2000, 89–114.

_____.2002. "Elenctic Interpretation and the Delphic Oracle." In Gary Allen Scott, ed., *Does Socrates Have a Method?* University Park, PA: The Pennsylvania State University Press, 114–44.

_____.2003. "Socrates, Crito, and a Debt to Asclepius." *Ancient Philosophy* 22, 71–92.

Minadeo, Richard. 1970–1971. "Socrates' Debt to Asclepius." *Classical Journal* 66, 294–97.

Most, Glenn. 1993. "A Cock for Asclepius." *Classical Quarterly* 43, 96–111.

Nehamas, Alexander. 1998. *The Art of Living: Socratic Reflections from Plato to Foucault*. Berkeley: University of California Press.

Nietzsche, Friedrich. 1974. *The Gay Science: With a Prelude in Rhymes and an Appendix of Songs* trans. Walter Kaufmann. New York: Vintage Books.

Nilsson, Martin P. 1964. *A History of Greek Religion* (second edition). New York: Oxford University Press.

Nock, Arthur Darby. 1950. Review of Edelstein and Edelstein 1945, *Classical Philology* 45, 45–50.

Nussbaum, Martha C. 1980. "Aristophanes and Socrates on Learning Practical Wisdom." *Yale Classical Studies* 26, 43–97.

_____.1985. "Commentary on Edmunds." *Proceedings of the Boston Area Colloquium in Ancient Philosophy*, vol. 1. J. Cleary, ed. Lanham, MD: University Press of America.

Ober, W. B. 1977. "Did Socrates Die of Hemlock Poisoning?" *New York State Journal of Medicine* 77, 254–58.

Panagiotou, Spiro. 1974. "Plato's *Euthyphro* and the Attic Code on Homicide." *Hermes* 102, 419–37.

Parker, Robert. 1996. *Athenian Religion: A History*. Oxford: Clarendon Press.

Penner, Terry. 1973. "The Unity of Virtue." *Philosophical Review* 82, 35–68.

_____.1992. "What Laches and Socrates Miss – and Whether Socrates Thinks Courage is Merely a Part of Virtue." *Ancient Philosophy* 12, 1–27.

Peterson, Sandra. 2003. "An Authentically Socratic Conclusion in Plato's *Phaedo*: Socrates' Debt to Asclepius." In Naomi Reshotko, ed., *Socrates and Plato: Desire, Identity, and Existence: A Collection of Essays Written in Honor of Terry Penner's 65th Birthday*. Edmonton, Alberta: Academic Printing and Publishing, 33–52.

Ranasinghe, Nalin. 2000. *The Soul of Socrates*. Ithaca, NY: Cornell University Press.

Reeve, C. D. C. 1989. *Socrates in the Apology*. Indianapolis, IN: Hackett Publishing Company.

Rice, David G. and Stambaugh, John E. 1979. *Sources for the Study of Greek Religion*. Atlanta, GA: Scholars Press.

Riddell, James. 1877. *The Apology of Socrates*. Reprint. New York: Arno Press, 1973.

Roberts, J. W. 1984. *City of Sokrates: An Introduction to Classical Athens*. London and New York: Routledge.

Roochnik, David. 1985. "*Apology* 40c4–41e7: Is Death Really a Gain?" *Classical Journal* 80, 212–20.

Rosen, F. 1968. "Piety and Justice: Plato's *Euthyphro*." *Philosophy* 43, 105–16.

Rudebusch, George. 1999. *Socrates, Pleasure, and Value*. New York: Oxford University Press.

Santas, Gerasimos Xenophon. 1979. *Socrates: Philosophy in Plato's Early Dialogues*. Boston and London: Routledge & Kegan Paul.

Santilli, Paul C. 1990. "Socrates and Asclepius: The Final Words." *Studi Internazionale di Filosofia* 22, 29–39.

Sealey, R. 1983. "The Athenian Courts for Homicide." *Classical Philology* 78, 275–96.

Seeskin, Kenneth. 1987. *Dialogue and Discovery: A Study in Socratic Method*. Albany, NY: State University of New York Press.

Smith, Nicholas D. and Woodruff, Paul B., eds. 2000. *Reason and Religion in Socratic Philosophy*. New York: Oxford University Press.

Spitzer, Adele. 1976. "Immortality and Virtue in the *Phaedo*: A Non-Ascetic Interpretation." *The Personalist* 57, 113–25.

Stewart, Douglas J. 1972. "Socrates' Last Bath." *Journal of the History of Philosophy* 10, 253–59.

de Stryker, Emile and S. R. Slings 1994. *Plato's Apology of Socrates: A Literary and Philosophical Study with a Running Commentary*. Leiden, New York, and Köln: E. J. Brill.

Tate, J. 1933A. "Reply to Professor A. E. Taylor." *Classical Quarterly* 27, 159–61.

———.1933B. "Socrates and the Myths." *Classical Quarterly* 27, 74–80.

———.1936. "Plato, Socrates, and the Myths." *Classical Quarterly* 30, 142–45.

Taylor, A. E. 1952. *Plato: The Man and His Work* (sixth edition). Reprint. New York: Meridian Books, 1956.

Taylor, C. C. W. 1998. *Socrates: A Very Short Introduction*. Oxford: Oxford University Press.

Trotignon, Pierre. 1976. "Sur le Mort de Socrate." *Revue de Métaphysique et de Morale* 81, 1–10.

Tulin, Alexander. 1996. *Dike Phonou: The Right of Prosecution and Attic Homicide Procedure*. Stuttgart and Leipzig: B. G. Teubner.

Versenyi, Lazlo.1982. *Holiness and Justice: An Interpretation of Plato's Euthyphro*. Lanham, MD: University Press of America.

Vlastos, Gregory, ed. 1971. *The Philosophy of Socrates*. Garden City, NY: Anchor Books.

_____.1981. *Platonic Studies* (second edition). Princeton, NJ: Princeton University Press.

_____.1991. *Socrates: Ironist and Moral Philosopher*. Cambridge: Cambridge University Press and Ithaca, NY: Cornell University Press.

Weiss, Roslyn. 1998. *Socrates Dissatisfied*. New York: Oxford University Press.

West, T. G. 1979. *Plato's Apology of Socrates*. Ithaca, NY: Cornell University Press.

White, David A. 1989. *Myth and Metaphysics in Plato's 'Phaedo.'* London and Toronto: Associated University Presses.

White, Stephen A. 2000. "Socrates at Colonus: A Hero for the Academy." In Smith and Woodruff 2000, 151–75.

Woodruff, Paul B. 1976. "Socrates on the Parts of Virtue." *Canadian Journal of Philosophy* 2 (supplement) 101–16.

_____, ed. 2000. "Socrates and His *Daimonion*: A Correspondence among Gregory Vlastos, Thomas C. Brickhouse, Mark L. McPherran, and Nicholas D. Smith." In Smith and Woodruff 2000, 176–204.

Woozley, A. D. 1979. *Law and Obedience: The Arguments of Plato's Crito*. Chapel Hill, NC: The University of North Carolina Press.

Zimmerman, J. E. 1971. *Dictionary of Classical Mythology*. New York: Bantam Books.

INDEX OF PASSAGES

GENERAL INDEX

Socrates: attitude towards death
156, 166, 171–81, 189–90n67,
190n73, 244–5; as gadfly 138–9,
185; as a sophist 49–50, 89–90,
97–9, 152; commitment to
philosophy 130–2, 203, 231–5,
243; historical 3–6; ignorance
65, 99; irony 54; method of
inquiry 204–5; military service
95, 122, 227–33, 247–8; mission
98–105, 107, 122–3, 129, 132–4,
138, 144, 147, 161, 166, 187n40,
242; and the myths 20–5;
poverty 164, 167; principles
210–11; wisdom 65, 97–105,
187n37; see also knowledge
Sokratikoi logoi 3–4
Sophists 88–90, 92, 107, 111, 139,
187n46
Soul: care of 183–4; damage to 21,
182–4; migration of 177–8,198,
253; perfection of 103,132–8;
value of 208–10
Smith, N. 68n28, 143, 186n21,
n26, 187n38, 189n63, n64,
190n69, n79, n81, 191n85, n90,
n94, n96, 192n97, n107, 250n9,
251n23, n24
Spitzer, A. 272n18
Stambaugh, J. 192n101
Stewart, D.J. 272n19
strict compliance theory of law,
220–30
de Stryker, E. 185n3, 186n22, n23
stylometry 4
sunêgoroi (supporters) 74, 77

Tate, J. 7n18
Taylor, A.E. 67n16, 187n42,
187n44, 191n93

Taylor, C.C.W. 191n95
technê (craft) 200–1;
see also craft
Theophrastus 262
theory of Forms 36–8, 253–4
Theseus 197
Thirty Tyrants 78, 93, 150–4,
191n86
Thrasybulus 152
Thrasyllus 2
Thrasymachus 186n27
Thucydides 186n20
Tulin, A. 66n4, n6, n11, 67n12, n13

Versenyi, L. 67n15
virtue 62, 87–8, 92, 125, 127, 128,
133, 137, 139, 146, 156, 166,
183, 188n56, 192n106, 242;
see also aretê
virtue as powers 58–62; sufficiency
thesis of 181; whole/part
relation 55–62, 192n106
Vlastos, G. vii, 58, 67n18, 68n21,
n22, n26, 143–4, 186n20,
188n51, 190n69, n76, n77, n78,
n82, 192n105, n107

water-clock 75
Weiss, R. 190n68, 249n2, 250n11,
n13, 251n26, n28, n29
West, T. 187n44, 191n93,
"What is F-ness?" question 19–20
White, D. 272n18
White, S. 272n18
wisdom 58, 64, 90, 97–105, 123,
127, 129, 132–34, 137, 138, 142,
147, 156, 179, 181, 184, 189n56,
192n106, 200; human 97–8,
101–2, 129–30; see also
knowledge